A HISTORY OF THE MODERN BATTLESHIP

DREADNOUGHT

By Richard Hough

Introduction by C. S. Forester

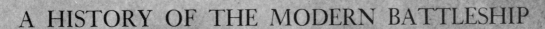

BONANZA BOOKS · NEW YORK

ALSO BY RICHARD HOUGH

The Fleet That Had to Die

Admirals in Collision

The Potemkin Mutiny

Fighting Ships

Captain Bligh and Mr. Christian

Copyright © MCMLXIV, MCMLXXV by Richard Hough
All rights reserved.
This edition is published by Bonanza Books,
a division of Crown Publishers Inc.,
by arrangement with Macmillan Publishing Co., Inc.
a b c d e f g h
BONANZA 1979 EDITION
Manufactured in the United States of America

Library of Congress Cataloging in Publication Data
Hough, Richard Alexander, 1922-
Dreadnought: a history of the modern battleship
Includes bibliographical references and index.
1. Battleships—History.   2. Dreadnought (Battleship)
I. Title.
V765.H58 1979   359.8'3   79-9170
ISBN 0-517-29367-6

To the late Dr. Oscar Parkes

O.B.E., Ass. I.N.A.

who should have written this book

Acknowledgments

This book owes much to the courtesy, encouragement, and practical assistance given by the officers and staff of the Historical Departments of the British Admiralty and United States Department of the Navy. Information was also supplied by many other sources, in particular the Naval Attachés of the London Embassies of all the naval powers.

The main sources of reference are given in the footnotes. But special reference must be made to *British Battleships* by Oscar Parkes, and to all the issues of that great annual, *Jane's Fighting Ships*, its editors, and to the publishers, Messrs. Sampson, Low, Marston and Co., Ltd.; who also most generously gave permission for the reproduction of the beam diagrams in the Specifications at the end of the book.

My thanks are also due to the Executors of the late Admiral Sir Reginald Bacon, to Doubleday & Co., and to Hodder and Stoughton Limited for permission to quote from *The Life of Lord Fisher of Kilverstone* by Admiral Sir Reginald Bacon; and to Hodder and Stoughton Limited for permission to quote from *Memories* by Admiral of the Fleet Lord Fisher.

Finally, I should like to offer a word of thanks to the Photographic Officers at the Imperial War Museum in London and the Historical Department of the United States Navy in Washington, to Richard Perkins, Esq., that superb photographer, and to the staffs of a number of photographic agencies who were so helpful and patient during my searches.

Acknowledgments are due to the following for permission to quote copyright material: Messrs. Jonathan Cape, Ltd. (*Fear God and Dread Nought: The Correspondence of Lord Fisher of Kilverstone*, Vol. 1, edited by Arthur J. Marder; Messrs. Hodder and Stoughton, Ltd., and Doubleday and Company (*The Life of Lord Fisher of Kilverstone*, by Admiral Sir Reginald Bacon, and *Memories*, by Lord Fisher of Kilverstone); The Hutchinson Group (*My Memoirs*, by Grand Admiral Alfred von Tirpitz); Messrs. Victor Gollancz, Ltd. (*The Navy from Within*, by Vice-Admiral K. G. B. Dewar); Messrs. Cassell and Co., Ltd. (*With the Battle Cruisers*, by Filson Young); Messrs. Sampson, Low, Marston and Co., Ltd. (*Battleships in Action* by H. W. Wilson); Messrs. Putnam and Co., Ltd. (*Early Bird*, by W. Geoffrey Moore).

Contents

The numerals thus (37) in the captions to the illustrations refer the reader to the appropriate statistical data on the ship represented, found under Dreadnought Specifications at the back of the book.

Introduction

The writer of this introduction can remember visiting Bonifacio in Corsica in early 1930 and entering into conversation with an old gentleman sitting in the winter sunshine, looking down at the strait with Sardinia sharply visible beyond. The old gentleman told me that years ago, many years ago, he had watched a big English ship of war turning circles in the strait, circling round and round for no apparent reason, and missing all the navigational hazards by mere hairbreadths. He could not understand why she was doing this; he watched her straighten herself up and steam out of the strait, and he still was unable to offer any explanation for why she had indulged in those curious and dangerous maneuvers. My suggestion that he had been witnessing some incident in the submarine campaign of 1917 was turned aside; this had happened many, many years before 1917, in peacetime, and she was a great big ship full of big guns. I was inclined to discount the tale, thinking of how it could have been distorted in an old man's memory during twenty-five years. Only much later did I hear that H.M.S. *Dreadnought*, during her shakedown cruise after commissioning, had experienced steering trouble in the Strait of Bonifacio, and the old gentleman, watching her "turning like a saucer," as Mr. Hough quotes in this book, had witnessed an incident that with a slightly different ending might have changed history.

For in a sense the eyes of the world were on H.M.S. *Dreadnought* even though the old gentleman was the only person to witness these freakish maneuvers. The announcement of the details of her design had caused a great sensation in the admiralties of the world. In England the political repercussions had been very marked; the new Liberal administration, dedicated to peace, retrenchment, and reform, found itself responsible for—one might almost say "saddled with"—the most deadly fighting machine ever launched in the history of the world. There was a considerable disturbance of naval sensibilities as well. Conservative minds in the Royal Navy—and they were many—withheld approval of the innovations embodied in the *Dreadnought;* they were doubtful about the abandonment of the secondary armament, about the adoption of turbines, and most decidedly they did not approve of the innovation of berthing the officers forward—officers had berthed aft in every navy as far back as the Battle of Salamis. Nor did they approve of Admiral Sir John Fisher, who was responsible not merely for the *Dreadnought* but for a series of sweeping reforms in the Royal Navy along every line. Fisher had a great many enemies; the *Dreadnought* had many critics.

If in the course of her gyrations in the Strait of Bonifacio—which were due to errors of design in her novel double rudders which could be, and were, largely remedied—she had touched on a rock, many people would have been delighted. If she had run hopelessly aground, wrecked herself completely, the consequences might have been incalculable. Public opinion in England, in the reaction from the high hopes built up around the ship by Fisher's adroit handling of the press, would not have stopped to consider that the disaster was the result merely of a badly designed pair of rudders. The all-big-gun armament, the turbine engines, the increased displacement, all would have been condemned in a single convulsion of disappointment. Fisher would have been forced to resign, and all his followers would have found themselves powerless to influence policy. The Liberal Government might have found itself in difficulties.

England would have reverted as a result (at least temporarily) to the building of battleships with four big guns and a varied secondary armament. It is just conceivable that the German Government (faced otherwise with the necessity for rebuilding the Kiel Canal) might have gladly followed the British example. The intensity of Anglo-German naval competition might not have reached the same pitch, for comparison of the number of Dreadnoughts was so simple a calculation that the popular press in both countries could use it to exacerbate public opinion, and England's vast pre-Dreadnought fleet would have made German competition far less effective.

But that is a wild flight of fancy; Jutland would still have been fought, even if with fleets not generically different from those that fought at Tsushima. In any case, the *Dreadnought* type, as Mr. Hough points out, was taking shape in many minds besides Fisher's. If England—and Fisher—had not built the first Dreadnought, someone else would have done so soon enough. Such a ship—invincible, practically omnipotent—had been discussed in many conferences of naval designers but had been dismissed as wildly impracticable because she would cost quite a million pounds and would have to displace at least twenty thousand tons, and no nation would venture on such folly—naval designers, despite their peculiar opportunities for learning, had a higher opinion of national wisdom than events were to justify.

It should be remembered as well that the development of the *Dreadnought* —like that of the submarine and the torpedo—progressed with the advances in scientific and technological research. To fire an instantaneous salvo of four twelve-inch guns called for the employment of electrical equipment of considerable complexity even before director firing was devised; to estimate the range at which to fire needed optical instruments of the utmost refinement, and to make the necessary deductions from the successive falls of shot called for calculating machines of an efficiency hitherto undreamed of. Military requirements stimulated scientific research—but it was at least equally true that technical and scientific invention stimulated the evolution of new military concepts. In our own day the guided-missile cruiser has been made possible only by the perfection of the process of electronic miniaturization.

The most extraordinary thing Fisher did was not to plan the *Dreadnought*, but to build her—to gain the consent of the government, to gain the cooperation (however grudging) of his service, and to carry the construction through with a rapidity and a secrecy that astonished the world; the dismay and irritation felt by foreign powers was, in his opinion, not the least of his rewards. We have seen the American public similarly dismayed in our own lifetime when it was first informed that the Soviet Government had perfected an atomic weapon.

Fisher was a man of such remarkable ability, of actual genius, that it is with acute disappointment that we encounter his limitations. He could see no virtue in moderation; on the contrary, he looked upon moderation as a vice symptomatic of weakness. In the material field this meant that his creations were developed beyond the limits of practicability, specialized (like the dinosaurs with which they were often compared) until they could not face more restrained rivals. If speed were desirable, more speed was more desirable still; if big guns conferred an advantage, still bigger guns conferred greater advantages. The law of diminishing returns was forgotten, and the eventual result was the construction of huge light cruisers like *Courageous*, which, as battle was to prove, combined the minimum of value with the maximum of cost. Fisher's advocacy of ships in which overmuch was sacrificed in exchange for gunpower and speed had been evinced from the start, in the first battle cruisers and in the early Dreadnoughts. He was deficient in what may be called critical imagination. The plans he conceived he executed superbly, but he was incapable of examining those plans from the opposite point of view. He could not admit the possibility of the existence of flaws in those plans, so that there was no chance of his doing anything to eliminate them. He would not consider the chance, in the misty North Sea and the confusion of a battle, of an ordinary light cruiser slipping in under the guard of the big guns of *Courageous* and finding before her a target ideal for the employment of her six-inch guns. He could advocate a plan to "Copenhagen" the German Navy while losing sight altogether of the irreparable damage any such attempt would inflict upon England. He could contemplate landing an army on Germany's Baltic coast without regard for the difficulties of taking it there, and forgetful of the German statesman's reply to a question as to what he would do if a British army landed on the German coast. He would send the police to arrest them, he said—and the reply was hardly more grotesque than the original plan.

Fisher was confirmed in much of his self-confidence by what can only be termed British complacency. Few people in England—for that matter few people in Germany—had any doubt that the Royal Navy was the best in the world qualitatively as well as quantitatively. The matter had never been put to the test at all since the coming of steel, but it was taken for granted that because a ship or a captain or a plan was British it was the best that could possibly be, and greatly better than the next best. The standard of comparison arbitrarily decided upon—not only by the British public but by British naval authority—by which the relative value of fleets was to be compared was the weight of broadside. It was something easily calculable, even though it made no allowance for such closely related factors as gunnery and quality of fuses. The British weight of broadside was so overwhelmingly greater than the German that the result of any battle could not be in doubt.

When Jellicoe assumed command of the Grand Fleet, he began to question the validity of this deduction. He pointed out with reason that the correct standard of comparison was displacement; every ton devoted to armament necessarily meant a ton diverted from some other—possibly more vital—purpose. He even went so far as to suggest that German designers in the last decade might have been as good as British designers; the suggestion naturally was derided as un-English and defeatist. Jellicoe's writings made it clear that (as soon as he became responsible for the fleet in battle) he had formed a strong suspicion that the German designers had actually done better work than the British designers inspired by Fisher. Jellicoe, measuring with an anxious mental eye the height of British armor plating above the waterline, and thinking about such hidden details as compartmentation, did not have such high hopes of British success in battle as had the government that directed him. He had to remember—what many people forgot—that the British ships had necessarily been built to be habitable for long periods in any part of the world, while the German ships had been built to house their crews during only the briefest excursions into the North Sea. It cannot be said that he distrusted the instrument he had to wield, but all his actions showed that he did not share the prevailing optimism regarding its superlative merits; it may perhaps have been as well—that is a question that is still being debated.

But, irrelevant as it may be, there is a tribute that must be accorded here to Jellicoe and the British Navy. Jellicoe commanded an enormous fleet, the largest ever assembled under a single command, and he had to handle it in some of the stormiest and most treacherous waters in the world. Yet the losses from the hazards of the sea were minute, fantastically small when it is remembered how frequently and rapidly the Grand Fleet left and entered Scapa Flow in the most dreadful weather. Jellicoe's force was always ready for action, it was always efficient, it was always in the best of health and spirits. There was never any question regarding British seamanship or British morale, and there can be no question regarding the efficiency of the staff work which on the one hand kept the ships ready for action and on the other supplied the enormously complex (and unprecedented) routine departure orders—the "sortie plans" in American phraseology—and the further formation orders which carried the Grand Fleet punctually and without confusion from harbor to battle. It was all so well done that few people pause to think how easily it could have been done badly, and the credit must be given to the commander in chief and to the discipline and order for which he was ultimately responsible.

So there was justification for some of the complacence, and the complacence was fortified by the ineptitude of the German high command as displayed—to give a single example—at Heligoland. Neither were there at first any rude shocks to disturb the complacence. The defeat at Coronel could be discounted as resulting from the weakness of the ships of the pre-Dreadnought era; the victory at the Falklands was confirmation of the effectiveness of the battle-cruiser type. The Dogger Bank had the effect of increasing the complacence. By this time the press had the bit between its teeth. Everything the Royal Navy did was above criticism. In public no voice was raised—and hardly one in private—asking by what defect in leadership or doctrine or gunnery three German battle cruisers were allowed to escape from five British who had the much vaunted superiority of speed to enable them to keep their targets within range. The sinking of the hybrid and nearly valueless *Blücher* was accepted as proof of a resounding victory, especially as there was published a spectacular photograph of the unfortunate vessel capsized and sinking. To hint that Beatty's battle-cruiser force should have done better would have been defeatism close to treason, and it seems that even in the Navy itself criticism was mostly silent.

So the losses at Jutland came as an unpleasant surprise. The first British communiqué to appear after the battle was not issued until several hours later than the German one, because of the need to bring the ships home before publication. It was an honest attempt to give the known facts, a remarkably close estimate of the losses on both sides, a paragon among communiqués, and it was received first with horror and then with an outburst of furious unbelief. So outraged was the public that a fresh communiqué was hastily issued, and the estimate of German losses now included all the possibles and the doubtfuls, listed as probables. With the estimated German losses now exceeding by a shade the admitted British losses, the British public could sit back satisfied; they had won a paper victory by forcing their government to publish knowingly the suggestion of a falsehood—something rare enough in modern British history to call for special note.

The passage of time, even of a few weeks, eased the situation considerably. It became apparent that whatever else might be said about it, Jutland was obviously not a decisive German victory. The command of the sea had not changed hands; British ships were as free to sail as ever; Germany was as securely blockaded, and the German fleet was displaying no desire at all to fight another battle to alter this state of affairs. It was slowly realized that a considerable portion of the appalling loss of British life was due to the destruction of the old armored cruisers which had no business at Jutland and which achieved nothing except to swell the casualty lists, and which could be counted on in future never to try to interfere with their betters. The loss of the battle cruisers could be attributed, with considerable show of truth, to a series of unfortunate coincidences by no means the fault of the British command. Complacence returned, except among the committees which were feverishly at work studying the lessons of the battle and recommending the rapid building of extra protection into the finished ships and the redesign of those new ones far enough from completion for this to be possible.

More than a hundred years earlier the British public had suffered a similar shock, when in a series of minor actions the American Navy had won a succession of minor victories. The pinpricks so inflicted were excessively painful, because for the last twenty years the British Navy had enjoyed an almost unbroken period of triumph. Many of the battles, both major and minor, had been won against considerable odds; so consistent was the record that it seemed that the assumption was quite justified that there was something intrinsically superior about the Englishman at sea. Now here was an indication that another nation could evolve a navy which ton for ton and (much more mortifying) man for man could be considered to be at least the equal of the British. There had been the same search for excuses, and there had been the same determination to find a remedy. British frigates were forbidden to plunge lightheartedly into battle against odds, and the shipyards were set to work to razee ships of the line so as to provide fitting antagonists to meet the improved American frigates. The capture of the *Chesapeake* and of the *President* came in time to soothe ruffled feelings and even to lessen the shock of the loss of the *Cyane* and the *Levant*.

The second half of the Great War provided no such spectacular victories to compensate for the destruction of the battle cruisers; the surrender of the German fleet, however significant and however thoroughly exploited by the press, was in the mind of the public a poor substitute for a victory gained in a pitched battle. And with the publication of documents and the letting loose of controversy, a clearer picture could be formed of what had happened and of what might have happened. There could be no denying the fact, for instance, that at the commencement of the battle-cruiser action the German *Von der Tann* had fought an unimpeded ship-to-ship duel with the British *Indefatigable*. In fourteen minutes' firing with her eleven-inch guns the *Von der Tann* had sunk the *Indefatigable* without receiving a single hit from the *Indefatigable*'s twelve-inch. There was something in the thought to chill the blood; back in 1914, during the opening days of the war, Milne, commanding in the Mediterranean with the *Inflexible* and this same *Indefatigable*, had been straining every nerve to catch the German battle cruiser *Goeben* and light cruiser *Breslau* which had evaded action and had escaped to the shelter of the Dardanelles. Their escape had been a bitter disappointment to the British authorities, and the political results of their arrival in Turkish waters had been profound. Now in the 1920's there was time to think about the other possibility, to wonder about what would have happened if Milne had intercepted the *Goeben* and *Breslau*. In 1914 it had been taken for granted (even by the German admiral) that in the event of such an encounter the two British battle cruisers would destroy the *Goeben*. But the German battle cruiser displaced two thousand more tons than the *Von der Tann* and she mounted two more eleven-inch guns. If, in company with the *Breslau*, she had encountered *Inflexible* and *Indefatigable* there would have arisen a very similar tactical situation as when, in the next war, *Hood* and *Prince of Wales* had encountered *Bismarck* and *Prince Eugen*. It would not have been at all unlikely that the result would have been just as similar. One or both of the British battle cruisers could have been destroyed; the German Navy could have won a stunning victory, in the very first week of the war, in the Mediterranean, which had so long been looked upon as the undisputed preserve of the British and French navies.

What the consequence would have been defies calculation—necessarily much greater than actually resulted from the tame extrance of the German ships into the Dardanelles and their pretended sale to the Turkish Government. Certainly there would have been the most profound political convulsion and a hasty realignment of neutral sympathy. The history of the world might well have taken a totally different turn. The Committee on Designs sitting in the spring of 1905 told themselves with truth that they were making history, but it is hard to believe that they realized on how great a scale. The crude figures before them, awaiting refinement, of armor plate and turrets, horsepower and subdivision, could influence the lives of generations not yet born. There are committees sitting today making similar technical decisions on an even grander scale, determining—or perhaps it would be better to say changing—the destiny of humanity.

When the Washington Treaty cruisers came to be built, there was conveyed something of a feeling of relief in the absence of claims put forward for them, and in the frank admission implied in the description of them as "eggshells armed with hammers." No one would ever be disappointed or particularly cast down if a Treaty cruiser met with a sudden end. In consequence the Battle of the River Plate in 1939 had a special significance. Here the German pocket battleship *Graf Spee* was thoroughly beaten. She, too, had been built under a ten-thousand-ton limitation, which was part of the peace terms imposed on Germany and not because of the Washington Treaty. But there had been no limitation on cost, and the German designers had in consequence had a free hand to use every material and every method of construction that would save weight and would add to her fighting efficiency; nor (as might have been expected) had they been overcareful to observe the limitations of weight. So that into her final twelve thousand tons was packed everything to make her a formidable warship.

What the German Government revealed about their first pocket battleship sent a wave of apprehension through the nations which had ocean-borne commerce exposed to destruction. Here was the ship that embodied all the dreams the designers had dreamed for generations—the ship that could fight anything that could catch her and could escape from anything that could fight her, with a vast radius of action and a destructive capacity almost unlimited. No one could doubt that the painstaking German staff had worked out exactly the most profitable employment for the three pocket battleships that were built, and no one could doubt that they would be manned by picked crews drawn from the large available German naval forces. And successive German governments, seeking respect and confusing it with fear, played upon the apprehensions of other countries (and bolstered their own people's confidence) by making claims for their ships in a style closely resembling Fisher's inspiration of the press regarding the *Dreadnought*.

Yet the war was only three months old when the civilized world heard with delight that one of these monsters had been intercepted, beaten into impotence, and driven to take refuge in neutral waters by a handful of cheap British cruisers. Within a period measured in hours after that she was to blow herself up, with all the world looking on, sooner than submit to internment or—more important—risk a second battle.

The real cause for rejoicing was not so much that a pocket battleship had been destroyed as the facts regarding her destruction. The German staff might have planned carefully, but the British staff had penetrated the German strategy. And the battle had shown that the Royal Navy could both fight and think. There had been no disorderly attack, no Light Brigade charge, nothing heroic or harebrained. There had been a carefully thought-out plan of battle making the utmost use of the available force, and when the plan was put neatly into execution it was British gunnery that ensured its success. The *Graf Spee* had been both outfought and out-thought. With this convincing proof that the Royal Navy could profit from the lessons of the past, England could face the dark future with more confidence.

That confidence was to receive some staggering blows. All the circumstances regarding the loss of the *Hood* were deplorable, even though the destruction of the *Bismarck* more than compensated for the loss. The sinking of the *Prince of Wales* and the *Repulse* was a decided proof that the day of the battleship was passing, but the interception and destruction of the *Scharnhorst* was a late and brilliant example of what the British battleship could do, while in a score of actions in the Mediterranean the Royal Navy covered itself with glory and at the same time earned the respect—the admiration—of the world through the long and toilsome campaigns in which those actions were only incidents, and in which both skill and courage were needed to win victory against crushing odds.

The day of the Dreadnought was passing, but the evening of that day was long drawn out. Through the endless Pacific campaigns the Dreadnought learned to subordinate her role to the carrier's. The Dreadnought was no longer the queen of the seas, but proved to be a worthy helpmate to the new queen. It would be hard to say that the battleship proved herself indispensable; it is possible to argue that with the development of carrier fleets other types of supporting vessels might have been more efficient, so that the battleship was employed only as an available second best. The discussion of such technical points could be endless, and probably without profit. But was it significant or merely symbolic—or was it pure accident—that the peace terms with Japan were signed on the deck of U.S.S. *Missouri*?

C. S. Forester

DREADNOUGHT

CHAPTER 1

"An Enormous
Ship"

"I christen you *Dreadnought!*"

The bottle of Australian wine failed to break against the battleship's mighty stem—that in later years was to slice in two one of Germany's most destructive U-boats—and King Edward VII had to swing the bottle with its garland of flowers a second time. The glass scattered, the wine streamed down the steel plates, and the King, in bicorne hat and full-dress uniform of Admiral of the Fleet, took up the chisel and mallet made from a fragment of timber from Nelson's *Victory*, and severed the last securing cord with one strike. The dogshores were released, and at once, with mighty and steadily increasing momentum, the battleship slipped toward the water that was to embrace its hull for the next sixteen years.

Among the distinguished gathering in the enclosed red-and-white-draped platform was Rear-Admiral Carl Coerper, representing the King's nephew, Kaiser Wilhelm II of Germany. Details of this epochal and revolutionary vessel were already known to his Admiralty, and work on existing German battleships had been halted as a result. The vast crowds outside the Royal Box, who had streamed in from Portsmouth or had arrived from London that morning in special trains, witnessed the event from the dockyard quays and from a multitude of vessels offshore. There was everywhere a consciousness of the importance of the occasion, which had in no way been diminished by Court mourning for the late King of Denmark, which forbade the use of all but the most important flags and bunting and restricted the ceremonials; nor by the overcast, dour weather that hung like some chill threat over the sky all day.

H.M.S. *Dreadnought* afloat, after being launched and named by King Edward VII, and after only one hundred days on the stocks (1). *Imperial War Museum*

The *Dreadnought*'s period of freedom was brief. One moment she lay helpless in Portsmouth harbor waters, a 520-foot empty hulk of steel with her cradleways like scattered afterbirth about her; the next she was being hustled by little paddle tugs toward her fitting-out basin, accompanied by packed light craft of all kinds carrying casual sightseers—"a vast multitude of onlookers," *The Times* described them—and many parties of schoolboys, dispatched on a Saturday afternoon to witness this new evidence of their nation's might. Among them from Osborne was young Stephen King-Hall, who was to become a notable naval officer and popular commentator on current events. The next day he wrote home:

DEAR MAMA AND PAPA,

Yesterday we had a fine time. We were given a whole holiday and we went over to Portsmouth in two gunboats to see the *Dreadnought* launched. She went in without a hitch. She is an enormous ship. Coming back it was very rough and a lot of chaps were seasick though I was not. . . .

The *Dreadnought*'s launching was unquestionably the most important naval event leading up to the First World War. The effects on naval opinion and architecture everywhere of this ship's appearance were incalculable but fundamental. Never before or since has the construction of one man-of-war had such an effect on service opinion, domestic politics, and international relations. H.M.S. *Dreadnought*, at her time the largest, fastest, and most powerful battleship, by a wide margin, provided not only the generic name for all her imitators, from Japan to Brazil, from the Austro-Hungarian Empire to the United States of America, but also presaged a new era in capital-ship design, and naval strategy and tactics. She was the initiator of an age of fearful naval competition. But her influence went far beyond the narrow boundaries of naval architecture and maritime theory and conflict. The *Dreadnought* was the manifestation in Krupp steel armor plate and Parsons' turbines and twelve-inch ordnance of the nations' need to vaunt their power, and their riches, and to instill fear in those who might seek to intimidate, deprive, or deter. She and her successors that sped down the slipways of the world's shipyards at an ever-increasing tempo from 1907 were the massive representatives of the struggle between the old colonial powers, intent on holding what they had, and the new colonial powers, equally determined to grasp their share of new lands and new markets. She was the first of the jargon-weighted weapons, the Edwardian ultimate deterrent, created in a simpler age and in a form that allowed arithmetical competition denied to a later era of bacteriology and nuclear fission. Dreadnoughts could be counted, watched, and photographed, and the arms races that culminated in the half-time respite agreed on in Washington in 1921 were spectacles the whole world could observe and argue over.

We are not concerned with the morality of the *Dreadnought*. Her purpose was always ugly and wicked, and she was, like any weapon of violence, a symptom of man's baser characteristics. But no one can deny the imposing grandeur of the ironclad battleship, which achieved a new scale of grace and splendor with H.M.S. *Dreadnought* and reached its ultimate, and appropriate, zenith and finale in the *Missouri*, *Vanguard*, *Tirpitz*, and *Yamato* thirty-five years later. Throughout its brief life the Dreadnought has had more zealous enthusiasts and devotees than any other single weapon. Its detractors were often almost as numerous and were highly vocal. The Dreadnoughts' theoretical contests were as frequent as their own combats were brief and rare.

The Dreadnought capital ship (a term that embraces both battleships and their swifter cousins the battle cruisers) first fired her guns in anger in 1914, and for the last time off Korea in 1953. The first of her kind was commissioned in December, 1906; fifty-eight years later, as this is written, the future of the surviving United States and French battleships still remains unsolved. The intervening years have been filled with controversy and rancor, praise and condemnation, all of which have played their part in influencing the shape of the vessel. Keen visionaries saw the *Dreadnought* herself as obsolete before that chill winter day in 1906. Pacifists, and then air and torpedo advocates, endeavored to prune back her growth and numbers. After engaging with her own kind for a mere hour or two, and doing negligible damage with her mighty guns in the First World War, she again became the subject for hot debate and exhaustive test; was intermittently internationally banned or restricted in size and gunpower; rose again in general esteem when war again became inevitable; and remained a proud and expensive symbol, with more of her kind still being built, even after fleets of Dreadnoughts had been crippled by new carriers of explosive destruction.

That she has survived in the world's armories for so long is evidence of the Dreadnought's power to inflame men's imaginations, and to overwhelm by her ever-increasing size and ever more massive guns any suggestion that her supremacy has expired.

H.M.S. *Dreadnought* herself, the vessel that set the pattern for all her 177 successors, was the inevitable product of the period in which she was designed and built. She came into existence by a combination of circumstances. For some twenty-five years, since sail had finally been discarded by naval architects, the chief principles governing battleship design had remained unaltered. A main armament of two or four heavily protected big guns, supported by a mixed battery of guns of a smaller caliber, was mounted in a hull carrying great sheets of protective hardened steel, and driven through the water by reciprocating steam engines at speeds from about 12 to 18 knots. The displacement of these battleships—the earlier term "ironclad" was being discarded—was from 10,000 to 17,000 tons. There were wide variations in the arrangements of the guns, which in many cases remained muzzle-loaders;

in the siting, thickness, and quality of armor plate; and in the operating range and seagoing qualities. But by the turn of the century the general principles of design of the world's battleships had set into a tradition of conservatism in marked contrast with the rapid progress in many other fields of design and engineering. One reason for this was the long peace. Almost a hundred years had passed since there had been a major naval war. There had been no fleet actions to arouse speculations and controversies and disturb the nations' admiralties and navy departments. Radical theories were nowhere encouraged during the second half of the nineteenth century. In addition, naval opinion by tradition is cautious and suspicious of innovation; and governments that were prepared to invest a few thousands in, say, a Maxim gun were not disposed in the comparatively tranquil international scene to upset the *status quo* and risk hundreds of thousands on a revolutionary battleship. (If a failure, heads would roll; if a success, all existing battle fleets would be rendered useless.)

Long before the first blueprints of H.M.S. *Dreadnought* were drawn up, the more perceptive naval architects recognized that the ships being laid down to their designs were inefficient and likely soon to be made obsolete in any case. A step toward the next stage of development must eventually have been taken; and it was certain to include fundamental changes. It was taken in the early years of the new century because the temper of the times was conditioning the nations once again toward the likelihood of giant conflicts. For years the seeds of the Dreadnought had remained dormant; they began to flourish and grow roots in the hothouse of international anxiety.

The clearest practical expression of the Dreadnought principle emanated from the Italian engineer Vittorio Cuniberti, who was born in Turin in 1854 and died, before the first Dreadnought combat, at Rome on December 19, 1913. With his master Benedetto Brin, whose great work was done in the 1870's, Cuniberti was in the line of masterly Italian naval architects that continued down to Umberto Pugliese, designer of the last class of Italian battleships. Ever since the Renaissance, the Italian engineering mind has always had a special capacity for viewing a project with a fresh and practical artistry. The Italian talent for stripping down to bare essentials the elements of compromise, which is the heart of all creative design, has never been surpassed; and it was desperately needed to break clear from the archaic form of warship architecture that had lingered on for a quarter of a century. At the age of twenty-three, Cuniberti was a fully qualified civil engineer in the Italian Navy's Engineer Corps. His first work was in the field of propulsion, and he became one of the earliest pioneers of the oil-burning marine engine and the naphthalene-propelled torpedo. His work on the automobile torpedo, itself an Austrian invention, made him more aware than most of his contemporaries of the new underwater threat, and in the early 1890's he carried out much close study on the underwater protection of warships.

During these years in the corps of engineers, the concept of new designs of all classes of fighting ships had much exercised his mind, and he had developed strong views on their requirements. His opportunity came at last when he was entrusted with the overall design of a new class of Italian battleship.

The pure Cuniberti principle was manifested for the first time in the *Vittorio Emanuele* class of four light battleships, the first of which was laid down in 1901, and which became the most praised and most controversial warships of their time. Their two 40-caliber 12-inch guns were supported on either beam by no fewer than twelve 8-inch weapons, all on a displacement of under 13,000 tons. By the use of electric power for the guns and their ammunition hoists, by a special girder construction of the hull with ultra-light scantlings, by the use of asbestos in place of much of the traditional woodwork (which was also a great fire risk), and by numerous other innovations, Cuniberti kept the weight down to a minimum without a reduction in strength or rigidity, gave his ships a speed, at 21 knots, at least 4 knots better than foreign battleships. The *Vittorio Emanuele* influence was widespread. "There can be no question," wrote Fred T. Jane, "but that for a power unable to maintain a large fleet, ships of the *Vittorio Emanuele* type represent the best possible value for the money to be expended."

The same 1903 issue of *Fighting Ships* contained more portentous information than this: and the author was Cuniberti himself. The article was called "An Ideal Battleship for the British Fleet"; and it was to have a momentous effect on the shape of the world's navies. This was not the first time Cuniberti had expressed his views on the evolution of the battleship. As long before as May–June, 1900, in an article in *Marine Rundschau*, entitled "The New Type of Armoured Ship," he called for a moderate-sized, swift vessel with "the greatest possible armament" and protected with a minimum of six inches of armor plate. On this occasion, Cuniberti laid special emphasis on the importance of speed. It appears likely that at this time his ideas had not sufficiently crystallized to allow him to be more specific; it also seems likely, according to Jane himself,* that he reached his final conclusions only after exhaustive discussion with a British engineer and friend resident in Italy, Charles de Grave Sells.

The next clear indication of the direction in which his mind was working appeared in a series of articles Cuniberti contributed, now as Chief Constructor of the Italian Navy, to the *Rivista Maritima*, the official organ of the Ministry of Marine, during 1902. He was manifestly wrong when he spoke of "the propelling power" of the warship probably being "more nearly at the apex of the curve of progress than the artillery"; the reverse turned out to be the case. He showed a great deal more percipience in his belief that the 12-inch gun "is now the least caliber of big guns"; and reached the very

---

* *Your Navy as a Fighting Machine*, by Fred T. Jane (1914).

5

The shape of the pre-Dreadnought battleship: Sir
William White's *King Edward VII*, carrying a mixed
battery of four 12-inch (fore and after in twin turrets),
four 9.2-inch in single-beam turrets, and ten 6-inch in
main-deck casemates. The scattered twenty-eight
quick-firing 12-pounders and 3-pounders, the booms and
rolled net all reveal the attention paid to torpedo defense.
Imperial War Museum

heart of the matter when for the first time he came out with the startling
prophecy that in future the artillery of the battleship "will consist of from
12 to 16 guns of this same size, bringing with it the well understood advantages of one size of ammunition, which is absolutely necessary. . . ."
Again Cuniberti returned to the paramount importance of speed, referring
to Sir William White's latest *King Edward VII* class of battleship as "those
monsters with short legs. . . . It cannot be too much insisted upon," he
concluded, "that fast ships are an absolute necessity of the day, and slow
ships, however powerful they may be, have everything to lose in the future
development of strategic warfare due to the employment of scouts and
wireless telegraphy, for, like Offenbach's gens-d'armes, *Ils arriveront toujours
trop tard!*"

Cuniberti offered the fruit of his years of study to his own government some time after these articles were published, but they were refused. "This design," according to Jane,* "was altogether too ambitious for the Italian Navy; but permission was given for him to publish the general idea, subject to official revision." It was therefore offered to the editor of *Fighting Ships* for the 1903 edition by Charles de Grave Sells, who was also a friend of Jane.

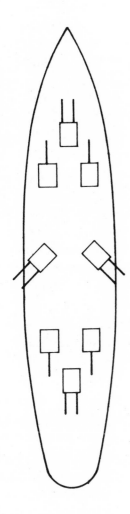

Cuniberti disposition for 12 x 12-inch

Stripped down to its fundamentals—and omitting some romantic analogies with personal close combat to which this great designer was prone—Cuniberti's "ideal battleship" was to possess numerous 12-inch guns "so as to be able to get in at least one fatal shot on the enemy's [armor] belt at the water-line before she has a chance of getting a similar fortunate stroke at us from one of the four large pieces now usually carried as the main armament." Its protective armor was also to be twelve inches thick, in order to resist all but the heaviest of the enemy's high-explosive shells. An abundant supply of ammunition was called for; but, above all, Cuniberti laid stress on the need for

a very high speed—superior to that of any existing battleship afloat.

We thus have outlined for us the main features of our absolutely supreme vessel—with medium calibres abolished—so effectually protected as to be able to disregard entirely all the subsidiary armament of an enemy, and armed only with twelve pieces of 12-inch. . . . Without wasting ammunition, secure in her exuberant protection, with her twelve guns ready, she would swiftly descend on her adversary and pour in a terrible converging fire at the belt. Having disposed of her first antagonist, she would at once proceed to attack another, and, almost untouched, to despatch yet another. . . .

The appearance of this article in the famous annual had a profound effect on naval thinking everywhere. A number of the most influential men connected with the British Admiralty, to whom it had of course been specifically directed, treated it with skepticism or derision. Almost every officer over the age of forty-five had served under masts and yards in the junior ranks. To them, the elimination of all secondary armament smacked of profanity. Sir William White, the ex-Director of Naval Construction (D.N.C.), was outraged. Jane himself considered it a Wellsian fantasy. Little interest was attached to it by the French Ministry of Marine. But among the younger, more intelligent, and more farsighted officers, both in Britain and abroad, the impact of Cuniberti's theories was immense. It was not, after all, as if he were a fanciful theorist or romanticist. He was a Chief Constructor with a number of notable designs behind him.

The Navy Departments in Washington and Tokyo responded most favorably to Cuniberti's conception. This was not surprising, for the American and Japanese navies had less to lose by the premature obsolescence of their battleships than those navies possessing large fleets, and a spirit of

* *The British Battle Fleet,* by Fred T. Jane (1915).

eagerness to embrace new ideas was more prevalent there than anywhere else. An "ideal battleship" for the Royal Navy could also well be the most suitable type both for the United States and Japanese fleets, fresh from their glories in the Spanish and Chinese wars; and conscious of new threats from Europe and the Far East.

The vagaries of chance, the pressures of conservative and radical opinion, the ebb and flow of the tides of militancy, the actuality of war, and above all the influence of one provocative and domineering personality, all played their part in the design and building of the first all-big-gun battleship, and in the revolution in naval philosophy and the massive arms race this brought about. These factors also combined to decide that the first of these vessels to be commissioned should be British, a nation that, it could be argued (and was, hotly), had most to lose and least to gain by the building of a superbattleship.

It now appears clear that Cuniberti's early Italian articles had little general influence, but caused a number of radical naval minds to break into new lines of thought on the shape of the battleship of the future. Cuniberti confirmed doubts and stimulated controversy. Not until his processes of thought had become more closely defined and more widely disseminated in the 1903 edition of *Fighting Ships* could theoretical hostilities begin on a serious scale. A few months later the Russo-Japanese War broke out, and theories were at last put to the test of combat in the waters of the Far East. Japanese torpedo boats attacked the Russian fleet outside Port Arthur on the night of February 8, 1904, and other units covered the first army landings on Korean soil. At first neither side showed great enthusiasm for committing its battle fleet to combat, but on August 10, 1904, an action took place that to acute observers appeared to bear out Cuniberti's theories, made known to the world less than a year earlier. The general belief at the time was that combat between opposing battle fleets would open at ranges of about 5,000 yards, and practice firing was normally carried out at ranges of around 3,000 yards. To the astonishment of a British naval observer in one of the Japanese battleships, the *Tsarevitch* and *Retvizan* opened fire with their 40-caliber 12-inch guns at a range of little less than 19,000 yards, and at once caused near misses on the *Mikasa* and *Asashi*. With the closing of the range to 13,000 yards, Togo's flagship was struck forward close to the waterline by a 12-inch shell, causing damage that could have been crippling or even fatal if the seas had been rougher. Later in the course of this leisurely and intermittent engagement, and still at long range, the Russian flagship *Tsarevitch* was in its turn struck twice in quick succession by Japanese heavy shells. These two hits decided the battle in a dramatic and decisive manner. The first killed the Russian commander in chief, Admiral Witthoft, and his fleet navigator, and severely wounded his chief of staff and flag captain.

The second exploded against the conning tower and killed and wounded everyone inside, including the steersman, whose corpse fell over the wheel and jammed the rudder hard to starboard, bringing total confusion to the Russian line.

The importance of the lessons of this first exchange of fire between modern battleships was recognized at once by the two belligerents, and there is evidence that both Russian and Japanese naval architects had decided before the end of 1904 that the 12-inch gun was the only weapon likely to prove decisive in future fleet actions, that the intermediate calibers uselessly absorbed space, weight, and personnel that could be better used for more big guns, and that the "splash" from the smaller shells only served to blanket the target and confuse spotting. There is no record that Russia went so far at this stage as to prepare plans for all-big-gun battleships, although later the Admiralty invited Cuniberti to design their first Dreadnought. But before the end of 1904, Japanese plans were complete for their own first all-big-gun ships, and it was later discovered, with considerable astonishment, that the first of these was actually laid down at the navy yard at Kure in March, 1905, some three months before Tsushima was fought, and long before the keel plate of the *Dreadnought* herself was laid at Portsmouth. Until 1905, only light craft had been built by the Japanese themselves, all their battleships having been constructed in foreign yards. The gunpower of this revolutionary battleship was even more remarkable. It followed almost exactly, in numbers and arrangement, the Cuniberti design, with 12-inch guns, in four pairs arranged in four double and four single turrets: with a total big-gun armament three times heavier than that of any existing battleship, and with a broadside 50 percent more powerful. Her speed of 20 knots was also at least two knots higher than that of the fastest battleship afloat. Only in her armor belt, of nine inches, did she fail to match up to Cuniberti's ideal.

In fact the Japanese *Aki* was beset with all manner of constructional difficulties and hindrances, and was not completed until 1911, when the Dreadnought had become a commonplace among the great naval powers. Nor was she, finally, a pure Dreadnought type. Within three months of her being laid down, Japan was victorious, and close to bankruptcy. There was delay in delivery of her machinery from America, and only four 12-inch guns could finally be found for her. In place of the eight 12-inch in her beam turrets, the Japanese therefore substituted twelve 10-inch guns; giving the *Aki* a most formidable total armament, while lacking the fundamental ordnance uniformity which was the main strength and whole *raison d'être* of the Dreadnought type. With her half-sister *Satsuma*, she was officially listed as an anomalistic first-class battleship and semi-Dreadnought, and survived until after the First World War. But a year after her completion she was joined by the *Kawachi* carrying the full quota of twelve 12-inch guns and with

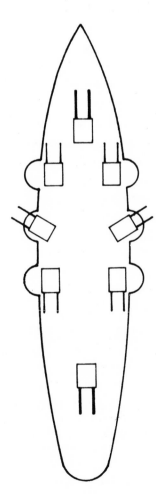

Japanese *Aki:*
4 x 12-inch,
12 x 10-inch

9

Kawachi's sister ship, *Settsu*, second Japanese
Dreadnought, on her trials. Fourteen-pounders
were later added to turret crowns. End turrets mounted
50-caliber 12-inch, wing turrets 45-caliber 12-inch,
a unique arrangement (49).

the 12-inch armored belt as specified by Cuniberti, which confirmed the
quality of the home-manufactured product and demonstrated Japan's am-
bition to become a first-class naval power.

Cuniberti wrote in 1902:

Looking to America, one realises that chaos reigns in the designing department
of the United States Navy, and hardly a month seems to pass without a new
type being brought out, more and more loaded with guns; and if the *Vermont*
is really to have the announced armament *—four pieces of 12-inch, eight of
8-inch, and twelve of 7-inch—one naturally wonders what special advantages
they expect to gain by adopting the two different sizes of 8-inch and 7-inch; for
from the point of view of general efficiency and rapid delivery of ammunition,
it would appear much more advantageous to put them both into a crucible and
draw forth twenty pieces all alike of 7½-inches.†

* She and her three sister ships did.
† *Fighting Ships*, 1902.

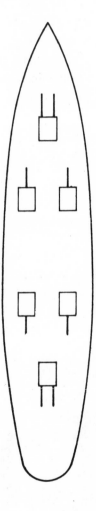

First *Michigan* design:
4 x 12-inch,
4 x 10-inch

Cuniberti's strictures were rather severe. The position in Washington was not nearly as bad as this. Since the Civil War the responsibility for the design and construction of American warships had been the joint responsibility of three bureaus, the Bureau of Construction and Repair, the Bureau of Steam Engineering, and the Bureau of Equipment. This was not a happy working arrangement, and not until 1940, when the responsibility was unified under the Bureau of Ships, was satisfactory coordination achieved. In spite of this, from about 1885, when the United States Navy ceased to be a fundamentally coast-defense force equipped with ships appropriate to this function, many remarkably advanced features were built into American battleships, and during the Anglo-German Dreadnought race, they at least matched, and in many cases excelled, their European rivals. The renaissance in American naval philosophy occurred simultaneously with the British. Here there was no roaring evangelist to cut a way through the political and defense jungles. Nor could there be the same fiery sense of urgency caused by the threatened imminence of war. A new spirit of enterprise became evident in the United States Navy soon after the reelection of Theodore Roosevelt as President in 1901. Roosevelt was a real "navy" man, and under his influence the radical elements received warm encouragement. Lieutenant Commander William Sowden Sims brought about a complete revolution in United States naval gunnery, and from the outset was a powerful advocate of the all-big-gun battleship, with its advantage of uniform shell splash for long-range salvo spotting. He, and others with the same strong beliefs, warmly welcomed the exciting new plans for heavy ship construction that were rumored to be under consideration in Washington in 1904. During the previous year the complement of naval constructors and assistant naval constructors was raised to seventy-five. The quality of personnel was also high. For some time their training had included courses in Europe, at Greenwich and at the Ecole d'Application du Génie Maritime in Paris. In the same year a man of brilliant skill and foresight, Washington L. Capps, was appointed Chief Constructor.

The same sharply accelerating curve of progress in battleship design occurred in Washington and Tokyo simultaneously. Cuniberti provided the spark of inspiration, the battle of August 10th between the Japanese and Russian fleets provided the charge: an exchange of shots causing negligible damage to either combatant sounded the death knell of the slow, mixed-battery gun platform and heralded the glorious and last era of the ship of the line. Like the Japanese *Aki*, the United States Navy's *South Carolina* and *Michigan* were projected at least six months before the first formal discussions were opened in London to decide on the design of the *Dreadnought*. The two *Michigans* began modestly enough. A mixed 12-inch and 10-inch battery was first considered, with twin turrets fore and aft and four single turrets arranged two on either beam. Then it was decided that all should be 12-inch, and for this reason she was technically a Dreadnought type.

Final *Michigan* design:
8 x 12-inch

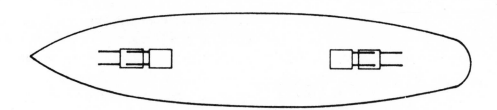

But the weight of her broadside was still no greater than that of numerous mixed-battery battleships in the world's fleets, and was less than that of the preceding *Kansas* class. But this was soon rectified, and her final design showed the eight heavy guns arranged in four twin turrets, all on the center line and with one pair superfiring over the other both fore and aft.

The plans for the two *Michigan*s went before Congress and were approved early in 1905: they must therefore be regarded as the first all-big-gun Dreadnought-type battleships to be projected and approved, and later completed as planned. What is more, as we shall see, they were quite as controversial vessels as the *Dreadnought* herself, and in the arrangement of their main armament were far in advance of the British vessels whose generic name they were to carry through their life.

America's first, and first non-British, Dreadnought to be completed, in August, 1909. The highly advanced U.S.S. *Michigan* at sea (23). *U.S. Navy*

CHAPTER 2

Dreadnought Origins

The clear, analytical, ingenious mind of General Vittorio M. Cuniberti provided the spark of architectural inspiration for the first all-big-gun battleship; the resolution and drive of a British admiral translated his revolutionary theories into 18,000 tons of steel and the most formidable fighting vessel in the world's navies. The achievement could not have been accomplished if circumstances—and his nation's wealth, maritime traditions, and prevailing anxiety—had not supported him. Equally, the Royal Navy could not have obtained a lead of three years over its rivals but for the qualities of Admiral Sir John Fisher. Fisher was volatile, egocentric, overbearing, belligerent, and bellicose. He was also passionately patriotic, brilliantly intelligent, and possessed of prophetic powers that were almost uncanny in their accuracy. Even his contemporary enemies, of whom there were many, had to acknowledge that he had been responsible for almost every important innovation incorporated in the battle fleet in 1914; and all but a handful of the capital ships that fought at Jutland had been built or conceived during his unusually long term in office as First Sea Lord, from 1904 until 1910. The Grand Fleet, the most powerful single fighting force the world had ever known, was Jackie Fisher's, in numbers, size, material, and fighting quality. Arthur J. Marder has written:

Without money or influence, with few friends, with nothing but sheer ability, indomitable willpower, love of his country and the Navy . . . and an idea that dominated his whole career—the efficiency of the Navy—he emerged from obscurity to climb to the top of his profession. Once there, he swept the Augean stables as they had never been swept before. He found a Navy paralysed by dead formulae; his electrifying ardour for efficiency and reform left it vibrating with a new and intense life.*

Fisher claimed that "the first thought of the *Dreadnought* came into my brain . . . so long ago as 1900." † He was at this time serving as Commander in Chief of the Mediterranean Fleet. He gave full credit to William H. Gard, Chief Constructor of Malta Dockyard, whom he was later to promote to Assistant Director of Naval Construction; and acknowledged that "the vision of the *Dreadnought*" was discussed with him at this time. It is his first reference to the all-big-gun conception. Sir Philip Watts later claimed in a paper read before the Institution of Naval Architects on April 9, 1919, that Fisher and he had together drawn up plans for a battleship mounting eight 16-inch guns, arranged thus,

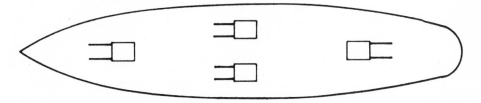

* *Fear God and Dread Nought: The Correspondence of Admiral of the Fleet Lord Fisher of Kilverstone*, Vol. 1, selected and edited by Arthur J. Marder (1951).
† *Memories* by Admiral of the Fleet Lord Fisher (1919).

as long ago as 1882, just after Fisher's *Inflexible* had performed so well at the bombardment of Alexandria. There is no reason to disbelieve this, but Fisher made no recorded reference to the event later; nor in his references to the 1900 Gard designs did he make any acknowledgment to Italian thinking on the subject, to Cuniberti, or to this designer's important articles in *Marine Rundschau* published in the same year. All that is recorded in his published correspondence during this period is that he was far from satisfied that, with the vessels then under his command, he could be confident of victory over the French, with whom his country had had uneasy relations at that time. In January of 1901, the year following these "discussions" with Gard, he limited the definition of his requirements in a letter to the Earl of Selborne, the First Lord of the Admiralty (1900–1905), thus: "It is clearly necessary to have superiority of speed in order to compel your opponent to accept battle, or to enable you to avoid battle and lead him away from his goal till it suits you to fight him."

Another four years passed before the Fisher-Gard plans were significantly advanced, and began to take shape on paper. On his return from the Mediterranean, Fisher had been appointed Second Sea Lord, and in the latter part of 1903 took over the Portsmouth command, with Gard as Chief Constructor. Among the mountains of work, and multitudes of reforms, with which Fisher at once became involved, he and Gard found time over the following months to draw up plans for a mythical H.M.S. *Untakeable*, a swift all-big-gun ship very closely following the lines of Cuniberti's "ideal" recently published in *Fighting Ships*. There were two alternative designs, "A" and "B," the first mounting no less than sixteen 10-inch guns thus,

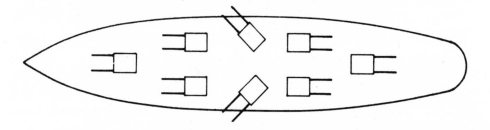

and the second eight 12-inch guns arranged as in the 1882 design.

Fisher had been persuaded into offering a 10-inch-gunned vessel by Sir Andrew Noble, a distinguished ballistics authority with the armament firm of Armstrongs, and by the evident success of this caliber in the recent light battleships *Swiftsure* and *Triumph*. At the same time he made clear his preference for the smaller number of larger-caliber guns in spite of their slower rate of fire: "Suppose a 12-inch gun to fire one aimed round each minute. Six guns [on the broadside] would allow a deliberately aimed shell with a huge bursting charge every ten seconds. Fifty per cent of these would be hits at 6,000 yards. Three 12-inch shells bursting on board every minute would be HELL!"

The paper was detailed and in parts highly technical. But its essence can be summed up thus:

1. Eight 12-inch guns, with a fire of six guns forward and to the rear, and on any bearing from 60 degrees before to 60 degrees abaft the beam. No other guns except light quick-firers to deal with close attack by torpedo boats.
2. High speed so that "she can choose the range at which she will fight. This will naturally be a long range, so that gunnery skill can be used to the best advantage," and because of "the dread of the torpedo." Speed will demand high power, length, light draft and adequate height forward.
3. Unsinkability; with the emphasis, again, on the threat of the underwater weapon. Revolutionary compartmentation, each compartment self-contained between two transverse bulkheads, and *unpierced*. Twelve-inch armor plate on the turret redoubts, and on the main belt against heavy shellfire.

The detailed specification was shown in confidence to Lord Selborne at Portsmouth on July 23, 1904, and, according to Fisher, "commended itself" to the First Lord. During the succeeding two months these were elaborated and privately printed and circulated, still in confidence, to the most intelligent and farsighted of his friends for their consideration. These were Captains Henry B. Jackson, R. H. S. Bacon, John R. Jellicoe, Charles E. Madden, Commander Wilfrid Henderson, Mr. William H. Gard, and Mr. Alexander Gracie of the shipbuilding firm of Fairfield.

The sequence of events, which can only be considered as breathtakingly swift in view of the conservatism of the service, the huge number of other reforms with which Fisher was concerned, the sweeping nature of the proposals, and the freedom from major wars which the country had enjoyed for almost a century, can be dealt with quickly. On August 10, 1904, the Japanese and Russian battle fleets demonstrated the hitting power and accuracy of the big gun at unprecedented ranges. On October 21st (Trafalgar Day, at his request) Fisher took office as First Sea Lord. On December 22nd a Committee on Designs, incorporating Fisher's seven "best brains" and nine others, including the Director of Naval Intelligence (D.N.I.) Rear Admiral Prince Louis of Battenberg, and the D.N.C., Sir Philip Watts, was appointed to consider the basic features of the new battleship. Fisher acted as chairman.

This Committee on Designs, later to be known as the "*Dreadnought* Committee," first met thirteen days later, and its existence, and terms of reference, were made known to the public thus: "to review the principles on which the different classes of modern warships are constructed and the features embodied in them." "The public await with great interest the publication of the instructions actually given," commented *The Times*' Naval Correspondent, and quoted Lord Selborne's Memorandum: "a new and definite stage in that evolution of the modern steam navy which has been going on for the last thirty years." It was by then clearly evident to keen naval students that something big was in the wind: only a privileged few in several foreign admiralties, where blueprints for all-big-gun battleships had been completed for some time, recognized that the greatest naval power in the world, with unparalleled ship-building and naval ordnance resources, was about to embark on a battleship design at least as revolutionary as their own.

The disposition of Cuniberti's basic "twelve 12-inch guns" dominated the prolonged discussions in which the Committee indulged over the next weeks. Various arrangements of wing turrets, superimposed and even super-super-imposed turrets in pairs, were all considered, and at one stage, inevitably, even a reversion to mixed 12-inch and 9.2-inch batteries was suggested by the D.N.C.* Objections were made to all these permutations, and the final compromise, as under, was reached because no design satisfactory to all members of the Committee could be agreed upon within the displacement restriction of 18,000 tons.

Dreadnought disposition

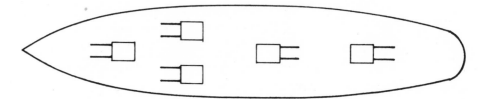

In this way Fisher obtained the end-on fire which, as an aggressive enthusiast for pursuit action rather than tamer broadside action—by his calculation the enemy would always be "flying"—he had always hankered after. And *Dreadnought*, in spite of a total of only ten heavy guns, still offered a broadside of 12-inch projectiles 100 percent greater than any existing battleship. The thickness of the armor belt at 11 inches was only just short of Cuniberti's ideal; and the inner compartmentation was to be as elaborate, secure, and radical as he had originally proposed, with solid unpierced bulkheads, first tried out some years earlier by the Russians and French. The scantlings possessed exceptional strength, too, in order to resist the shock of a full broadside of eight guns, and her exceptionally high forecastle distinguished her outwardly from her predecessors. But it was in her machinery that *Dreadnought* was to reveal her most transilient and startling feature, ensuring her acceptance for all time as a product of great daring and genius.

The steam-driven reciprocating engine had developed at a comparatively slow rate, ever since the days of Watt and the elder Stephenson: by its fundamental nature, it is not, as a translator of heat to power, capable of a high degree of sophistication, as was already being achieved at that time with the internal-combustion engine. Marine reciprocating engines at best were unreliable and incapable of full power for any length of time. They were clumsy, heavy, inefficient, and demanded great space for power produced. They were also messy. "When steaming at full speed in a man-of-war fitted with recipro-

* All these designs are illustrated and described in detail by the late Dr. Oscar Parkes in his *British Battleships* (1957).

The apotheosis of the early twentieth century battleship.
H.M.S. *Dreadnought*, the cynosure of the naval world
and the most feared maritime weapon, puts to sea in
1906 (1). *Imperial War Museum*

cating engines, the engine room was always a glorified snipe marsh; water lay
on the floor plates and was splashed about everywhere; the officers often were
clad in oilskins to avoid being wetted to the skin. The water was necessary to
keep the bearings cool. Further, the noise was deafening; so much so that
telephones were useless and even voice-pipes of doubtful value." Thus wrote
Bacon, in later years, in his biography of Fisher.*

* *Life of Lord Fisher of Kilverstone* by Admiral Sir R. A. Bacon (1929).

In 1894 a company had been formed called the Marine Steam Turbine Company, Ltd., the object of which was to investigate whether the condensing turbine as applied to driving dynamos "had excelled that of the compound reciprocating engine for the same purpose." The development and practical application of the rotary steam engine, later described by Lord Kelvin as "the greatest advance made in steam since the days of James Watt," had been in the hands of the Honorable Charles A. Parsons, the youngest son of the third Earl of Rosse, himself a prominent man of science. Parsons later told how this new company set about its experiments: "From the first it was obvious that the turbine was suitable to fast rather than to slow vessels, and, consequently, it was decided to commence by building an experimental vessel of the smallest size consistent with the possibility of attaining exceptional speed. The vessel, the *Turbinia*, of 42 tons displacement, after many alterations to her machinery, developed 2,400 h.p. on trials.*"

The performance of this vessel was highly successful, its publicity exploits quite out of character with the modest, self-effacing man who had conceived her power plant. At the 1897 Queen Victoria Diamond Jubilee Naval Review, the little *Turbinia* broke all regulations and upset the solemn protocol of the occasion by racing up and down the lines of anchored men-of-war, and darting in and out of them in an astonishing display of maneuverability and speed, defying the efforts of the patrol boats which attempted to cut her off. In improved form the *Turbinia* revealed a maximum speed of 34 knots, and after further development of the marine turbine even the pre-Fisher Board of Admiralty was obliged to give serious attention to this new form of propulsion.

But in 1905 only two turbine-powered torpedo-boat destroyers, the *Viper* and *Cobra*, had been completed, their best speed of 36.5 knots being far ahead of any of their contemporaries. To agree to turbine machinery for "H.M.S. *Untakeable*" was therefore a decision of almost reckless daring, reached by a group of men inspired by a persuasive prophet and caught up in the momentum of their own enthusiasm. It was also a decision blessed with success from the start, which brought fame and fortune to Parsons, and caused a revolution in marine propulsion almost as dramatic as the change from sail to steam. In stark statistical terms, the *Dreadnought*'s predecessors of the *King Edward VII* class with a standard displacement of 16,350 tons could steam at 18.5 knots with 18,000 h.p. from their reciprocating engines; *Dreadnought*, of 17,900 tons, steamed 21.6 knots on her trials from 23,000 h.p. But that was only the beginning of the story. She could sustain high revolutions reliably and with far less vibration and noise. On her trials she steamed, with no evident strain, 7,000 miles at an average of 17½ knots, a figure far beyond the capacity of any warship afloat. To have reached the same *maximum* speed would have required an additional 1,000 tons in weight and £100,000 in cost. Finally, the

---

* *The Marine Steam Turbine from 1894 to 1910* by the Hon. Sir Charles A. Parsons, read at the Institution of Naval Architects, July 5, 1911.

The *Dreadnought* in detail. Note here forward "A" turret, with exposed 12-pounders atop; bridges and fore funnel; forward funnel and tripod mast; barrels of starboard beam 12-inch guns; rolled net and booms— later removed (1). *Richard Perkins*

conditions in the engine room at high speed were transformed from a sodden cacophonous hell to a paradise of quiet orderliness. "In the *Dreadnought* when steaming at full speed," Bacon wrote, "it was only possible to tell that the engines were working, and not stopped, by looking at certain gauges. The whole engine-room was as clean and dry as if the ship was lying at anchor, and not the faintest hum could be heard." *

* *Fisher* by Bacon.

The design of the *Dreadnought* featured a multitude of epochal innovations which, one by one, were to be imitated by every naval architect in the world. It was therefore in accord with the spirit of the men who conceived her that her construction and presentation to the world should be as dramatic and well managed as a great theatrical production. To achieve maximum security and moral effect, urgency governed the decisions and actions from the moment her general shape was agreed upon. While J. H. Narbeth, her constructor, worked on the drawings, arrangements were put in hand to ensure rapid construction. Materials of all kinds were stacked at Portsmouth long before her keel plate was laid. Plates were ready-cut to standard sizes; her guns were purloined ruthlessly from those already being manufactured for two battleships that would not be completed until long after "*Untakeable*," and would carry the doubtful distinction of being the last pre-Dreadnoughts in the post-Dreadnought Royal Navy.

The *Dreadnought* was laid down on October 2, 1905, just under a year after Fisher took office as First Sea Lord, was ready for launching four months later, and was complete and ready for her trials one year and one day after work began on her. It was calculated that this achievement would astonish the world, and prove to her rivals not only that Britannia was prepared to derate the whole of her battle fleet and start afresh with new superbattleships but also that she had the wealth and means to do so while her rivals were still recovering from the shock of *Dreadnought*'s appearance. It was a gesture of splendid and characteristic arrogance and contempt for the lesser imperialists of the world. And it was to bring in its train dismay and wonder, and a political furor.

The might of the German High Seas Fleet of 1914, like that of Admiral Sir John Jellicoe's Grand Fleet, had its origins in the influence, power, and abiding determination of one man. Alfred von Tirpitz possessed much in common with John Fisher. Both men reached positions of high responsibility when their service and their country most needed them, fought their way through apathy, the opposition of pacifists, liberals, reactionaries, and counterclaimants to defense appropriations, to create the two most formidable fighting fleets in the world. Both men were in turn given the highest honors, discarded and discredited. Tirpitz and Fisher: their names, little known today, represented for more than a decade, and for two nations, the fearful suspicions, the defiance, and the very stuff of predatory jingoism that smoldered at ever-rising temperatures—and burst into flames in August, 1914. Who can judge now the degree of blame they must carry for the crises and militant state of mind that overshadowed Anglo-German relations from 1900 to 1914? It can be argued that, like the Dreadnought fleets they created, they were only the products of an era increasingly and inevitably conditioned to conflict. It can also be argued that each man, by the influence he acquired and wielded, aggravated every acrimony and suffocated every breath of a rapprochement.

Eight years before the launching of the *Dreadnought*, the German Navy was still little more than a token coast-defense force, and the nation's maritime interests were limited to home waters. Since the Franco-Prussian War, the state of the navy in relation to the army had not improved, and by the standards of the time was quite out of proportion to Germany's ever-growing trade and overseas commitments. The German military command seemed content with this situation, and the people reconciled to the inferiority of their navy compared with the immense fleets of Britain and France. All this was changed by the appointment of Tirpitz to the post of Secretary of State for Naval Affairs in January, 1897. Tirpitz began at once to attempt a conversion of public opinion toward the idea of Germany becoming a great naval power. He established a Navy League based on the British model, a Press Bureau, encouraged naval correspondents on newspapers, and worked at all political levels to bring about a change of heart. Within twelve months Tirpitz had been so successful in his campaigning that he had succeeded in getting through the Reichstag a first Navy Act which provided for an increase in the size of the fleet by more than 100 percent.

The opening of the Boer War gave an immense new impetus to his cause. The German people regarded Britain as a predatory aggressor determined at all costs to exclude further German colonies and trade in the African continent. When German vessels were seized off the African coast, and the navy was helpless to intervene, German anger was vehement. The time was ripe for Tirpitz's next step. By a second Navy Act, of June 2, 1900, the battle fleet was to be increased to no less than thirty-eight battleships, including reserves, with supporting cruisers and small craft in proportion. Such a fleet would make the German Navy the second most powerful in the world and totally upset what Britain considered to be the traditional maritime balance, namely, that the Royal Navy should exceed the strength of the combined navies of France and Russia. In case the statistics were not clear to the chancelleries of Europe, and to the British Admiralty in particular, the Prefatory Memorandum to the Act specified in the clearest and most intimidating terms Germany's intentions. "Germany," it said, "must have a battle fleet so strong that, even for the adversary with the greatest seapower, a war against it would involve such dangers as to imperil his position in the world." Intentions could not have been more plainly stated.

The immense peacetime strength of the Royal Navy was justified by the worldwide extent of imperial responsibilities, extending from Hong Kong and Australasia and every continent, as well as home waters. The small, rich industrial island relied for her security and very existence on her trading "lifelines." So fearful was this new German threat—underlined when seven first-class battleships were laid down between 1900 and 1903—that Britain was forced to bestir herself from her state of aloof independence and seek reliable friends. An alliance was sought, and signed in 1902, with Japan, the new naval power in the Far East, and steps were taken to mend relations nearer home, with friendly approaches to Russia. The Entente Cordiale with France was signed, and "at last, after decades of isolation, we had transformed a dangerous rival into a powerful friend." *

The launch of the *Dreadnought*, then, marked a historical realignment of the great powers and a new era in international relations. The *Dreadnought*'s revolutionary specification was also the most clear and provocative confirmation to Tirpitz in particular, and the world at large, that Britain was determined to destroy any delusions of maritime grandeur that might be gaining ground across the North Sea, and pursue even more assiduously her policy of encirclement and the "hammering" of "hatred . . . so blatantly and so unpleasantly into the people." † To Tirpitz the event was one of a "chain of political and naval threats, accompanied by wild agitation of public opinion. . . . On the one hand England's naval measure contained the admission that our fleet-building was being taken seriously. On the other hand the demand for our political humiliation, which had been going on for almost a decade, was now known, and the status of our fleet at that time was too small to explain such measures as the concentration of British squadrons in the North Sea. At the bottom of it all there was the clear intention of making us afraid, and if possible of nipping in the bud our impulse towards international independence." Tirpitz saw another sinister intention behind the *Dreadnought*'s launching: that it was "on the assumption that the German Navy would not be able to get ships of similar dimensions through the locks of the Kiel Canal."

The Kiel Canal was immensely important to the German Navy. It had been built, from 1886, as a sixty-one-mile-long safe strategical shortcut between the Baltic and the North Sea. Its completion eliminated the long and hazardous journey round Denmark and all need for a separate Baltic Fleet in defense against Russia's powerful force in this sea. It had been built when the biggest battleships in the world were under 12,000 tons and when there was still no hint of the imminent increase in battleship displacement, or of the dramatic increase in status of the German fleet. Tirpitz's last class of pre-Dreadnought battleships, of 13,200 tons, were the largest size that could be accommodated in the Kiel locks; anything larger would require immensely long and costly widening.

Fisher knew this; the information was widely known. His decision to press for an even larger superbattleship was therefore widely regarded in Germany as a challenge of the most provoking nature. The German Navy must either retire from the competition or spend many years and many millions on this vast civil-engineering project. Fisher's supporters stoutly deny that he gave any thought to the dilemma into which he was throwing Tirpitz, and there is no evidence in his published correspondence that this

* *Before the War*, by G. P. Gooch (1939).
† *My Memoirs*, by Grand Admiral von Tirpitz, Vol I (1919).

fundamental factor influenced his decisions. It is, however, difficult to believe that it did not influence arguments pursued by the Committee on Designs in January and February, 1905. "A new Kiel Canal, at the cost of many, many millions," Fisher wrote in his memoirs,* "had been rendered necessary by the advent of the *Dreadnought* . . . worse still . . ." he went on, "it was necessary for them to spend further vast millions in deepening not only the approaches to the German harbours, but the harbours themselves, to allow the German Dreadnoughts, when built, to be able to float." The note of satisfaction cannot be denied.

The provocative element in the construction of the *Dreadnought* was to be debated hotly and to form the basis for political controversy for years to come in Britain. But for Tirpitz and his powerful supporters, to whom surrender was unthinkable, the only possible response to this superbattleship was to imitate, and then excel. And this is just what happened.

German thought had not lagged behind on the need for a fundamental reappraisal of battleship design. How far this had progressed at the time of the *Dreadnought*'s launch it is impossible to judge accurately. One of the arguments later used to justify her design was the fear that the German Navy was about to steal a march on Britain. One authority claims that "when the German naval attaché in London produced plans of 12-inch guns made by Vickers early in December, 1904, the Emperor said that 'this is the gun of the future.' " † There is other evidence that Tirpitz had committed the battle fleet to all-big-gun ships of a size that would have demanded the widening of the Kiel Canal long before the launching, and possibly even before the laying down of the *Dreadnought*.

In July, 1906, while the *Dreadnought* was still fitting out, under the conditions of extreme secrecy that characterized all German warship construction, a battleship of great size was laid down at Wilhelmshaven. She was credited, according to Brassey,‡ with an armament of eight 11-inch guns, carried in pairs fore and aft, and on each beam (like the Fisher-Watts 1882 arrangement), and this was later supported by Jane. As more than five months elapsed between the acceptance of the broad design of the *Dreadnought* and the day when her keel was laid, and everyone concerned was working at extreme pressure, it is reasonable to presume that German design teams, less experienced and less accustomed to rapid draftsmanship and shipbuilding, spent considerably longer on their first all-big-gun battleship.

The plans of S.M.S. *Nassau*, Germany's first Dreadnought, were therefore almost certainly completed before those for *Dreadnought* herself, and at about the same time as the American *South Carolina* and Japanese *Satsuma*. But progress on her construction was halted as soon as the details of the

* *Memories*, by Lord Fisher (1919).
† *The Navy from Within*, by K. G. B. Dewar (1939).
‡ *Brassey's Naval Annual* (1910).

S.M.S. *Nassau*, first German Dreadnought, completed
two months after the American *Michigan* and three years
after the *Dreadnought* herself. Note her wide beam and
hint of sturdiness (37). *Imperial War Museum*

British ship were made known and it was realized that she was going to be
outgunned. For the next three years the details of the *Nassau* and her sisters
Westfalen, Posen, and *Rheinland* were the subject of the wildest surmise
and anxious speculation, especially in London. German security arrangements
were in marked contrast with the careless manner in which details of
warships under construction were bandied about in Britain. "A detachment
of soldiers with responsible officers is told off to watch the shops in Krupps,
where . . . intruders are rigorously excluded. The shipyards are even more
carefully protected, and cases are known where for months it was kept secret
whether a ship being constructed was a war or mercantile vessel. . . ." *
The success of the German security arrangements can be judged by the
inaccuracy of the forecasts published annually in *Fighting Ships*, which
credited them in turn with fourteen 11-inch, ten or twelve and even fourteen
and sixteen 11-inch, and then ten or twelve again in the 1909 issue. (This

* Quoted in the House of Commons debate on the Navy Estimates, July 26, 1909.

British tendency to overestimate the power of German capital ships under construction before the First World War—with profound effects on morale and ship design—was exceeded only by a similar British underestimation of the power of the Second World War battleships in the 1930's.)

Shortly before the *Posen* was launched at Kiel in December, 1908, Captain Reginald Hall, later to become the greatest of all D.N.I., planned a ruse of some daring in an effort to acquire the sorely needed information for the Admiralty. With two other officers, dressed as engine-room artificers, Hall took the Duke of Westminster's large, fast private motor launch, specially borrowed for the occasion, to Germany and sailed it into Kiel Fjord. Then at 40 knots they raced up the harbor to Krupps' dockyard, where they came to a halt with simulated engine failure, and took rapid photographs of the ship through the launch's conning tower.* On August 8th of the same year the *Scientific American* came out emphatically in favor of the correct final armament of twelve 11-inch. But the disposition was misrepresented, and the guns were described as 50-caliber, which were introduced only when the *Moltke* was completed in October, 1911.

* Recounted in *The Eyes of the Navy* by Admiral Sir William M. James (1955).

The German High Seas Fleet: Units of the First Squadron, with *Westfalen* (37), nearest camera, exercising in Heligoland Bight. *Imperial War Museum*

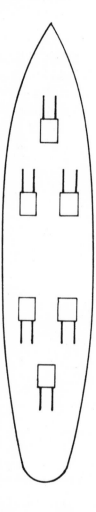

Nassau disposition

Not until the following year did the British Admiralty acquire the confirmatory evidence they had sought for so long. This was provided by the naval historian and student, Oscar Parkes, who photographed them fitting out. It was seen then that, after all, Tirpitz had settled for a conservative disposition of the main armament, merely adding two more wing turrets to give a broadside and end-on fire the same as the *Dreadnought*'s. With their "retrograde" 5.9-inch secondary armament disposed along the main deck (*Dreadnought* eschewed all but a scattering of 12-pounders), their old-fashioned reciprocating engines, and their lumpy pre-Dreadnought appearance, the *Nassau*s seemed very inferior articles, and it is easy to understand why Fisher was so cock-a-hoop, with seven Dreadnoughts completed before the first of Tirpitz's had joined the fleet, and with the first super-Dreadnoughts * carrying ten 13.5-inch guns on the center line already on the way.

It was not until they were tested under the rigors of war that the true virtues of the *Nassau*s could be appreciated. Certainly they were overgunned for their displacement, and the main armament disposition was greatly inferior to that of the *Michigan* and *South Carolina*, and even to that of the *Dreadnought*. The retention of reciprocating engines, with all their handicaps, also hinted at a timorous spirit, and provided a speed nearly two knots inferior to the *Dreadnought*'s. The accommodation of the crew was cramped and deplorable by British standards. But at this time the power of the German 11-inch gun, with its very high muzzle velocity and flat trajectory fire, and the ease with which its shell could pierce British armor at extreme range, had still to be publicly proved. The German *Nassau*s were horribly uncomfortable, their nominal radius far less than the *Dreadnought*'s; but they were intended for operation in home waters for brief spells at a time, with the crew living ashore in barracks in between, whereas British capital ships had to be prepared for permanent occupation, for operation in tropical waters and long voyages between coaling stations to all parts of the world.

The *Nassau*s were certainly slower than their British contemporaries, but they were very steady gun platforms at all speeds. Their real merit, however, lay in their protection. German armor plate tended to be only slightly thicker and to cover a modestly wider area, and its quality was in no way superior to its British counterpart. But these four vessels possessed the internal protective provisions that caused all German capital ships up to the justly named *Tirpitz* herself to be more nearly unsinkable than those of any other nation. Tirpitz worked in the belief that, however shattered a battleship may be, so long as she remains afloat she can be refitted in a fraction of the time and at a fraction of the cost of replacing her. The state of many units of the High Seas Fleet—and of the battle cruisers in particular—after Jutland, and the rapidity with which they were made ready for sea again, exactly bore out his theory. Time and again in both world wars

* This term was first applied to capital ships carrying as main armament guns over 12 inches in caliber.

the damage that German capital ships were able to endure never failed to surprise their adversaries. "In contrast to the British ships, ours were well-nigh indestructible," Tirpitz observed immodestly but accurately. British battleships were able to prove that they could take a hammering, notably the *Warspite* at Jutland, which received between thirteen and twenty-two (reports conflicted) direct hits from heavy shells without suffering serious damage. But some conception of the care and thoroughness that was taken at the behest of Tirpitz can be judged from the following résumé from his *Memoirs*:

The deadly injury of that part of a ship below the waterline is the ultimate aim of the weapon of attack, and the increase of buoyancy the main object of protective measures. Until 1906 our ships were but little protected against attack below the waterline, while the English ships were badly protected even as late as this [1914–18] war. With the *older ships*, a hit by a torpedo generally resulted in the sinking of the ship. . . . As soon as the Navy bill was settled I caused this question of buoyancy to be taken up with great thoroughness. We soon found that we had to experiment with actual explosions in order to gain sufficient experience. As we could not sacrifice modern ships, and could not learn enough from the older ones, we built a section of a modern ship by itself and carried out experimental explosions on it with torpedo heads, carefully studying the result every time. We tested the possibility of weakening the force of the explosion by letting the explosive gases burst in empty compartments without resistance. We ascertained the most suitable kind of steel for the different structural parts, and found further that the effect of the explosion was nullified if we compelled it to pulverize coal in any considerable quantity. This resulted in a special arrangement of a portion of the coal bunkers. We were then able to meet the force of the explosion, which had been modified in this way, by a strong, carefully constructed, steel wall which finally secured the safety of the interior of the ship. The "torpedo bulkhead" was carried without interruption the whole length of the vital parts of the ship. These experiments, which were continued through many years, and on which we did not hesitate to expend millions, yielded, moreover, information concerning the most suitable use of material and the construction of the adjoining parts of the ship. In addition to this the whole part of the ship below the waterline was designed to provide for failure to localize the effects of the explosion or for several hits being made, and so forth; endless labor was expended upon details such as the pumping system or the possibility of speedily counteracting a list by flooding corresponding compartments.

The photographs and published statistics of Germany's first Dreadnoughts were not impressive. On paper they appeared to be no more than enlarged pre-Dreadnought *Deutschland*s, with four wing turrets carrying "outmoded" and relatively puny 11-inch guns in place of the fourteen 6.7-inch of the earlier ships, and with the secondary battery of unnecessarily large secondary guns disposed too close to the water to be worked (according to experience at Tsushima) in any but the calmest seas. Not only had *Dreadnought* herself stolen all the thunder, but owing to the slow building of the German ships, Britain had an enormous lead, and her designers were, arithmetically, already two steps ahead in the battleship race.

But much had happened both in the field of naval shipbuilding and in international rivalry since the *Dreadnought* had been sent down her slip by the King of England on that cold day in February, 1906. Already by 1909 the battle cruiser (of which more later) had appeared, to embellish the aspect of grandeur and intimidation of the superbattleship, and three improved Dreadnoughts had already joined the British fleet. Everywhere, technical developments were going on apace. In Germany, six improved *Nassau*s were on the stocks, two of them with 12-inch 50-caliber guns, and three battle cruisers of formidable dimensions and power had also been laid down. In Europe a Dreadnought fever was in the air. France, suddenly conscious of her deficiencies, was completing plans for her first four. Italy had laid down her first Dreadnought, the *Dante Alighieri*, designed by Cuniberti, of course; and this same prophet's plans had won the Russian competition for the best battleship, four ships incorporating many new features being already on the slips. In Japan, the semi-Dreadnoughts *Aki* and *Satsuma* were not yet complete, but two "pure" Dreadnoughts were on the stocks, and both were

Pure Cuniberti: *Dante Alighieri*, Italy's first Dreadnought, almost exactly filled Cuniberti's original specification for the all-big-gun battleship. Her triple 12-inch-gun turrets, first fitted in any Dreadnought, were of British design and manufacture (59). *U.S. Navy*

quite as advanced and powerful as anything building in Europe. In America the position was even more interesting, and must be considered in greater detail before a final summary of the world's battle fleets at the end of 1912 can be considered.

CHAPTER 3

First Generation Dreadnought Controversy and Competition (1906–1912)

"I thoroughly believe in developing and building an adequate number of submarines," wrote President Theodore Roosevelt.* "I believe in building torpedo-boat destroyers; there must be a few fast scouts, and, of course, various auxiliary vessels of different kinds. But the strength of the navy rests primarily upon its battleships, and in building these battleships it is imperatively necessary, from the standpoint alike of efficiency and economy, that they should be the very best of their kind." These words were written at the height of the Dreadnought controversy in America, the heat and extent of which was exceeded only in Britain.

There is a curious similarity between the theoretical arguments on the battleship that occurred in Britain and the United States between 1906 and 1909. In both countries the terms of the debates were conditioned by an awareness of dangers and new responsibilities, and the precariousness of isolation. The importance of naval strength in a world of threatened, and shrinking, frontiers was becoming increasingly recognized; and only the most daring and radical thinkers were at this time forecasting the end of the battleship as the first instrument of naval power.

The controversial aspects of the battleship were its size, cost, speed, protection, and above all its armament. At this distance of time, it seems curious that this highly specialized field of architecture should have been debated so widely, popularly, and hotly. Great numbers of people who could scarcely distinguish a battleship from an armored cruiser took up one side or the other in the great Dreadnought debate. An even more striking and curious point is that both in Britain and America the argument was about a *fait accompli*. In Britain, under Fisher's impetus, the first all-big-gun ship was on her trials before the real implications of her characteristics were properly understood and before the forces of opposition were mobilized. Everyone knew that there could be no turning back: there she was, in all her magnificence and terrible beauty, at a cost of £1,797,497—almost $9,000,-000—an increase of 20 percent over the last pre-Dreadnoughts. In America, the *South Carolina* and *Michigan*, although delayed for nearly two years after they were authorized by Congress, were on the stocks before the first blow fell.

The attack was opened by the distinguished naval historian Captain Alfred Thayer Mahan, a tall, scholarly, peppery former officer in the United States Navy. His background was Irish, his education private until he went to Columbia University and then to the Naval Academy. He was little known in his own country, and quite unrecognized in Britain, before 1886. In that year he delivered a painstakingly prepared series of lectures at the War College at Newport. They formed the basis for one of the most influential books of naval history, *The Influence of Sea Power upon History, 1660–1783*. This was followed six years later by *The Influence of Sea Power upon the French*

* Letter to the Chairman of the Naval Committee of the House of Representatives dated January 11, 1907.

Revolution and Empire, 1793–1812. The second confirmed the authority and breadth of vision of the first, and in Britain especially he acquired the distinction of recognition as the most profound naval thinker of his day. On contemporary naval problems, however, he was to prove surprisingly retrogressive. While he was campaigning for a higher status for the American Navy, his theories on strategy and ship design were a good deal less sound. There were few people who could quarrel with his analysis of Nelson and the Battle of Trafalgar; his conclusions on Togo and Tsushima were a good deal more controversial.

Shortly after the *Dreadnought* had been completed, Mahan delivered a lecture on the lessons to be learned from that battle. This amounted to a massive broadside against the Dreadnought principle. Because the Russians suffered great casualties and damage to their upper works from Togo's 6-inch and 8-inch shells, and because Rozhestvensky's survivors described in graphic terms the terror and bewilderment of "the rain of fire," Mahan drew the conclusion that the smaller calibers had played a vital part in the battle, and would be an important influence in future naval battles. This was false on several counts. First, Mahan disregarded the decisive effect of long-range 12-inch fire at the Battle of Tsushima; and, second, he failed to take into account the special circumstances at the battle where the outmaneuvered, outpaced, and thoroughly demoralized Russian fleet had been engaged at the later stages at the closest range by a confident and disdainful enemy. Tsushima was an annihilation, not a combat between foes of comparable power and skill, and the range was closed not by mutual consent but for the kill. For this reason, Mahan deplored the Dreadnought-inspired tendency to discard the second battery. "It has long been my opinion that [it] is really entitled to the name primary, because its effect is exerted mainly on the personnel, rather than the material of a vessel."

Alas for Mahan, during the "long" period he had held this opinion, the world's navies had suffered a revolution in ordnance and gunnery. The modern 12-inch shell could fire, and hit and sink, at more than ten miles; and with the rapid improvement in power and range of the torpedo, battleships were mutually happier to remain as far from each other as possible. Science was on the march forward; Mahan and his many disciples on both sides of the Atlantic were busily engaged in walking backward in blinkers.

On almost every count, Mahan's theories were in direct contradiction to Cuniberti's. "Speed at its best is a less valuable factor in a battleship than fighting power," ran Mahan's thesis. "To obtain increase of speed by increasing the size, whether the proportion of gun power be maintained or not—though especially if not—is also a mistake. . . ." At a time when Fisher was already advocating oil-firing to replace coal, and telescopic funnels, Mahan was preaching: "The loss of a modern funnel will be like the loss of a former-day lower mast. . . . The funnels are open to serious injury by guns of that secondary battery. . . ." Mahan wanted no increase in the size of battleships, when history had already shown that this was inevitable, and was later to show that in the eighty-five-year life of the armored steam ship of the line only international compromise reached by fear of cost, size, and numbers could halt its growth from less than 10,000 tons to nearly 70,000 tons. He wanted no sacrifice of protection or gunfire for speed, even at the expense of size. He wanted a larger number of medium-sized and less costly battleships. In these views he had many renowned and wise supporters, for special qualities—not often possessed by historians—were needed to appreciate that the pace of technology was so rapidly increasing.

The opinions of the powerful Mahan school could not be disregarded, and Roosevelt recognized the need for satisfying the American electorate before construction on the *South Carolina* and *Michigan* was further advanced and before their successors were laid down. He therefore demanded a full report, and appointed Lieutenant Commander William Sowden Sims to draw it up. Sims was the one great figure thrown up by the American Navy during its vital years of development, and represented in that service many of the qualities of both Jellicoe, the thinker, stategist, the leader in war, and of Percy Scott, the gunnery specialist and innovator, in the Royal Navy. Sims revolutionized American gunnery in the early years of the century, was Mahan's leading contestant in the Dreadnought controversy, and commanded the United States Naval Forces in European waters in the First World War. Sims's reasoned, sagacious, and totally crushing attack on the Mahan school decided American battleship construction policy in the vital years leading to 1912. Sims made America a major maritime power.

In his report to Roosevelt, Sims was obliged to go back again to the lessons of Tsushima. Mahan had contended that few hits were made at the longest ranges at Tsushima because the distance between the lines was constantly changing and that, by this reasoning, battle fleets would in future close in so that the greatest concentration of fire from all calibers could damage the enemy structurally as well as piercing funnels, destroying the upper works, and killing the exposed members of the crew. Sims refuted Mahan's conclusions, and insisted that the initiative and choice of range were with the Japanese throughout, underlining again the paramount importance of speed, which can only be obtained by an increase in displacement; and that the main reason why Togo closed Rozhestvensky's fleet was that at above 5,000 yards his gunlayers were finding it impossible to follow the flight of their 12-inch shells visually and the splashes on which they had to rely to adjust their aim were confused by the splashes of the more frequent smaller shells exploding in the water. He also claimed a point that had not previously been considered: that the distortion to the Japanese range finders caused by the rising heated powder gas from the numerous smaller guns frequently upset the shooting of the big guns.

Sims dealt next with Mahan's belief that large all-big-gun ships were a "growing wanton evil" that caused "the wilful premature antiquating of good vessels." Sims wrote: "It seems to me that the mere fact of there being a common demand for such vessels is conclusive evidence that there must be a common cause that is believed to justify the demand." This "common demand" was based on sound technical and tactical considerations:

I will assume [wrote Sims] a fleet of ten 20-knot battleships, of about 20,000 tons displacement, each having a main battery of five 12-in. double gun turrets, or a broadside fire of eight 12-in. guns disposed as in the Dreadnought type. Assuming the cost of these ships to be ten million dollars each, or 100 millions for the fleet, and assume that the same sum of money will build twenty battleships (though the number in reality would be considerably less) of the smaller type of, say, 13,000 tons and 16 knots speed, each ship armed with two 12-in. double gun turrets or a broadside fire of four 12-in. guns, and as many of the smaller guns recommended by Captain Mahan as can be mounted upon this displacement. It is further assumed that as all the gun crews of the fleet are behind heavy armour in the 12-in. turrets of new design, neither the crew nor guns can be materially injured by the intermediate guns of the fleet of small vessels; whereas, on the contrary, the majority of the men composing the gun crews of the small vessels . . . are behind the [thin] armour of the intermediate guns . . . and these guns and their crews must be disabled or destroyed early in the action.

Not only would the effective broadside weight of shell be greater with the ten larger ships, continued Sims's thesis; they would also provide a greater concentration of fire owing to the shorter length of their line. Thus, the total weight of their gunpower could be brought to bear on half the line of smaller, more numerous ships, utterly overwhelming them; while the larger vessels would themselves be within the range of fire of only half the smaller vessels. Sims made numerous further, and all deadly, strikes against Mahan's arguments. He cited simplification of fire control, economy (those twenty smaller battleships would actually cost 120 to 130 millions) in initial outlay and maintenance, as well as in the total personnel: it would require fewer men to serve the *Dreadnought*'s ten heavy guns than the battleship *Missouri*'s twenty mixed 12-inch and 6-inch.

The summing up was annihilating:

The final conclusion is, that for the sum that it would cost to maintain the twenty small battleships we could maintain a fleet of ten large ones, that would be greatly superior in tactical qualities, in effective hitting capacity, speed, protection, and inherent ability to concentrate its gunfire, and have a sufficient sum left over to build one 20,000-ton battleship each year, not to mention needing fewer officers and men to handle the more efficient fleet.

The President accepted these arguments as overwhelming; and they cast aside all technical doubts—except among the most diehard reactionaries—in the Department of the Navy. Political doubts endured for much longer, however, and appropriations for the Navy were debated warmly, if only because the one unquestioned feature of the Dreadnought-type battleship was its higher cost. In the discussion on the 1908 program, for example, Representative James A. Tawney, of Minnesota, Chairman of the Appropriations Committee, claimed that the Dreadnought policy "implies a total disregard of necessity or expense and requires that, like children competing for the most expensive and glittering toys, we must compete with the nations of the world in the construction of the largest and most expensive battleships in order to satisfy our national pride and vanity." John S. Williams, of Mississippi, deploring the laying down of the *Michigan*, considered that it should at least be given a more resounding name to match up to its claimed omnipotence. The motion he put forward ran, "That whereas the battleship sea monster we are imitating has been named the *Dreadnought*—an archaic name—this man o'war is hereby named the *Skeered o' Nothin'* as an expression of our true American spirit: *provided further*, that it is hereby made the duty of the first captain who shall command her to challenge in the nation's name the so-called *Dreadnought* to a *duel à l'outrance*, to take place upon the sea somewhere in sight of Long Island, and that upon the occasion of the combat the President and his Cabinet . . . shall be entertained on the quarter deck as guests of the ship and the nation." (John S. Williams's argument, in spite of his facetious tone, had some validity. The French in the eighteenth century had understood the importance of minatory nomenclature; in the twentieth century only the British seemed able to break away from states and cities and accord to battleships suitable names like *Swiftsure* and *Indomitable*, *Colossus*, *Thunderer*, and *Indefatigable*.)

Construction of the *South Carolina* and *Michigan* was proceeded with apace, however, and when the latter was completed in August, 1909, as the

U.S.S. *South Carolina:* Lattice masts, superimposed turrets, the heavy piled effect amidships, and secondary armament mounted in casemates distinguish this highly economical American Dreadnought from its British counterparts (23). *U.S. Navy*

first non-British Dreadnought, and several months ahead of the German *Nassau*, her qualities were at once recognized. On a displacement of only 16,000 tons, 2,000 tons less than the *Dreadnought*, she offered with her twin turrets all on the center line an equal broadside and end-on fire. This economical disposition, by means of superimposed turrets, was at first viewed with some doubt in Europe and America. The blast effects of the upper guns on the gun crews in the lower turrets was considered by most authorities to make this arrangement impractical. In the *Indiana* class, completed in 1895–1896, the blast from the high-wing 8-inch turrets was said to make the working of the lower 13-inch guns impossible, and the freak double 13-inch and 8-inch turrets of the *Kearsarge* and *Kentucky* had been notorious failures. But in the *Michigan*, "by virtue of the improved sighting ports and the closely-fitting port shields employed, and other arrangements, it will be possible, in an emergency, to fire any of these 12-inch guns in any position of training without serious interference with the work of the other gun crews," reported the *Scientific American;* with the added comment: "If this should prove to be the case, our Navy Department will be the subject of congratulation on having produced, in proportion to their displacement, by far the most powerful fighting ships built or building in the world today."

This favorable comment was confirmed by one of the most prominent naval students of the day, Commander William Hovgaard of the Massachusetts School of Naval Architecture, whose influential essays were a feature of many issues of *Fighting Ships* during this period. In 1910 he wrote of the American superimposition arrangement, which was to be imitated by naval constructors everywhere:

The ideal arrangement of the *heavy gun turrets* seems to be the American . . . where two turrets are placed at each end of the ship in the centre-line, the guns nearest amidships firing over those nearest the ends. By this disposition the guns obtain the maximum arc of fire, the position of the upper turrets is commanding and dry, the arrangement of ammunition rooms is simple and ample room is left amidships for an efficient and well protected secondary and anti-torpedo boat battery.

Hovgaard also approved of the lattice, or cage, mast, another American innovation, which served its purpose (of insulating the fire control from the shock of heavy gunfire and the vibration of stressed machinery) until one was destroyed in a storm. Hovgaard described it as "ingenious," "ideal in point of construction," and "probably very resistive to gunfire."

When the *Michigan* and *South Carolina* had been on the stocks for only a year, the United States Navy laid down two further First Generation Dreadnoughts, to be named *Delaware* and *North Dakota*. The size of these battleships, at 20,000 tons, represented the biggest leap in displacement since the recent renaissance of the American Navy. This was mainly accounted for by the additional overall length demanded by a further pair of 12-inch guns disposed aft, and provided a broadside 25 percent heavier than that of any

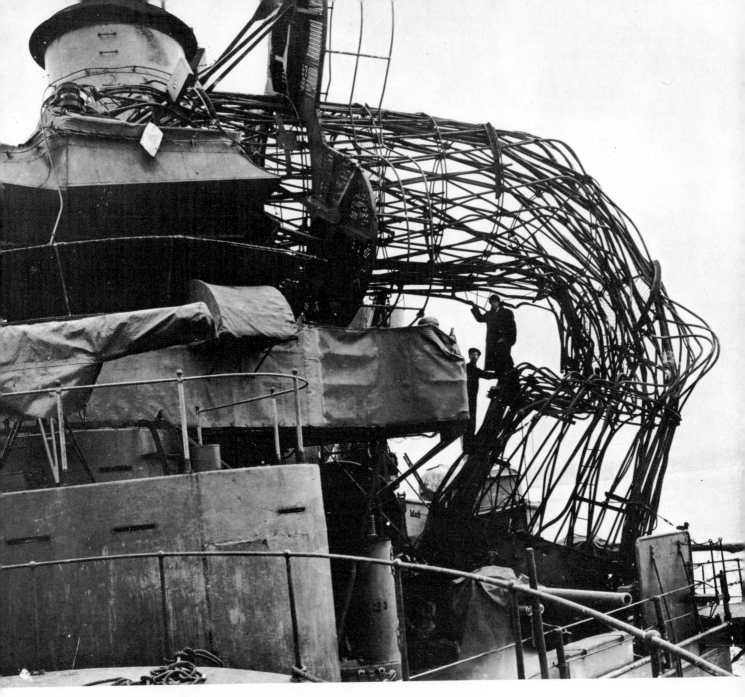

A storm in 1918 proves too much for *Michigan*'s light
cage mast. *U.S. Navy*

existing battleship; and by the increase in the weight of armor, and of
machinery to provide the same speed as in the earlier ships. In the *North
Dakota* turbines were resorted to for the first time, and with complete
success.

Mahan's fears were being realized in full. The *Utah* and *Florida*, with
many features in common with the *North Dakota*s and launched in 1909
and 1910, showed an increase in displacement of less than 2,000 tons. But
the *Arkansas* and *Wyoming*, both completed in 1912, made another notable
increase in size and armament. A new mark of 12-inch gun was introduced

39

Another 60 feet in length and 4,000 tons in displacement permit a fifth turret in the second group of American Dreadnoughts. The secondary battery is now 5-inch caliber, and because of its extra weight has to be carried lower on the main deck, with severe interference in a seaway. This is the *Delaware* (24). *U.S. Navy*

The *Delaware* at Rosyth while serving with the British Grand Fleet in 1918. The year she was laid down, *Fighting Ships* wrote: "Both in ships with high-powered guns or impervious to vital injury at long range the U.S. Fleet is superior to any other navy in the world" (24). *Imperial War Museum*

The *Florida* slips under Brooklyn Bridge. Note
searchlights, carried in great numbers in American
battleships at this time. This class was distinguishable
from *Delaware* and *North Dakota* by having mainmast
abaft the second funnel (25). *U.S. Navy*

Another 45 feet in length, another 4,000 tons, and the
Wyoming packs in another pair of guns. Only the
monstrous H.M.S. *Agincourt* carried more center-line
turrets. Even in this calm sea the secondary battery is
almost unworkable at speed (26). *U.S. Navy*

in these ships, the 50-caliber, with considerably higher muzzle velocity and
penetrating power than the earlier 45-caliber. Moreover, there were now no
fewer than twelve guns all on the center line. This number was never reached
by any capital ship *designed and completed* for the Royal Navy, and never
exceeded by the Germans. The *Arkansas*'s firepower set new standards
at a time when the development in ordnance, size, protection, and displacement among the world's capital ships had reached a frenzied pace.

At the end of 1912, then, the United States Navy had in commission six
First Generation Dreadnoughts. In all of them, the wing turret was eschewed
in favor of center-line disposition; the turbine had arrived; armor plate and
internal subdivision were equal to all but the German Dreadnoughts; the
average speed was rather below those of its rivals, the gunpower rather above;
in size, the latest pair exceeded that of any other capital ship in the world
except the latest British battle cruiser. There was nothing graceful or
balanced in their appearance, but with the concentration of their lattice masts,
control platforms, derricks and funnels into a small area rather forward of
amidships, and the domination of the rest of the ship by the three raised and
three lower turrets, they gave a sense of purposefulness and fitness to their
role of destruction.

Apart from her battle cruisers, which must be considered separately, Britain in the closing months of 1912 had already commissioned fourteen all-big-gun battleships and her yards were packed with new and even more formidable contenders in the battleship race with Germany. The *Dreadnought* herself, splendid in her arrogance and grandeur, secure for all time as the progenitor of a new race of battleships—". . . the first that ever burst into that silent sea"—still basked in the acclaim that met her wherever she sailed. She was a confirmed success, but among those who proudly served in her, the drawbacks in some of her features had rapidly become evident. As with all wing, or lateral, turrets, the blast and flame damage to the ship's upper works when these were fired fore and aft had been experienced; proving once again the wisdom of the American choice of superimposition.

One officer who joined her in 1910 expressed the views of many who had

Arkansas in her early days before either of her major refits. Unshielded 5-inch on fore superstructure foreshadow American acceptance of unprotected secondary armament (26). *Imperial War Museum*

suffered from the odd placing of the tripod mast and fire-control top abaft the fore funnel. Up here, "the view of the range-takers and control officers was frequently obscured by smoke. Shortly after I joined, we purposely carried out target practice in an unfavorable wind. The centralised control completely broke down and decentralised control was impracticable because the turrets were not supplied with range-finders . . . and the officers could not identify the fall of their own shot. Thus our most powerful battleship might have been placed at the mercy of a ship half her size." * The same officer also criticized the location of the conning tower, which was "surrounded by a mass of shell-bursting structure which so obscured the view that the C.-in-C. could not use it."

Like any good thoroughbred, the *Dreadnought* was not an easy ship to handle. "She would not steer at any speed under ten knots," wrote one of her captains, "at lower speeds if the helm was put over, nothing would stop her from turning like a saucer, although at higher speeds she steered beautifully. I was so impressed by this that when by ourselves in foggy weather I took the risk of steaming at 10 knots so that the ship would be thoroughly under control in any emergency. It was almost impossible to turn her at rest, and her astern power was very small . . . [it was] startling to find that I must stop the engines at least half a mile before letting go an anchor." † Especially compared with the first German Dreadnoughts, the living accommodation was lavish and spacious. The officers' cabins were large, and the men fared better than in any ship in service. Because of her great length, and the distance from the bridge and conning tower to the normal position of the admiral's and captain's quarters right aft, the traditional arrangement was reversed, and the men found themselves with all the advantages of a sheltered quarterdeck, while the officers had to fabricate for themselves a simulated quarterdeck forward, and suffer the chills and wetness of their situation.

From April, 1907, until May, 1912, the *Dreadnought* served as flagship of the Home Fleet. But by the end of that year she was moved to the Home Fleet's First Division, a demotion that signified her coming obsolescence: for the pace of development was still accelerating, and she would have been as rapidly annihilated by the latest super-Dreadnoughts as she would earlier have destroyed her predecessors.

Fisher's intention had been to follow the swift construction of the *Dreadnought*, if she proved successful, with as rapid as possible a buildup of a Dreadnought fleet in order to wring every possible advantage from his superiority over Tirpitz in shipbuilding facilities. Before that became possible, however, he had to contend with an avalanche of criticism at home, not only of the principle of the vessel and her characteristics but also, and contradictorily, of the huge expenditure made necessary by the fact that she

---

* *The Navy from Within*, by Dewar.
† *My Naval Career*, by Admiral Sir Robert Fremantle (1949).

outclassed every other battleship in the world. Sir William White took the part Captain Mahan played so dramatically in America; and his qualifications were as renowned. White had been D.N.C. (Director of Naval Construction) prior to Sir Philip Watts and the Fisher era. During his term of office he had been responsible for many fine ships from the *Royal Sovereign*s, completed in the early 1890's, to the immediate pre-Dreadnoughts of the *King Edward VII* class. His poor health during his last years of office no doubt contributed to the bitterness and resentment he felt over the *Dreadnought*, with all her attendant publicity and claims of superiority over her predecessors. His attack on "the cult of the monster warship," as he described it, had strong and prompt support, especially from many of the senior officers in the service, whom Fisher, with his verbal violence and uncompromising attitudes, had estranged. Fisher's old foe, Lord Charles Beresford, at once took up arms in the Parliament. Admirals Sir William Custance and Sir Gerard Noel were among White's staunchest allies, and they received the highly influential support of Lord Brassey, who edited the *Naval Annual*. Many of Mahan's arguments were used on the other side of the Altantic. With more medium-size ships, it was contended, the loss of one from the line represented a less serious proportional reduction in fighting strength. Also, with her vast resources, and the assurance that she could always catch up, Britain would have done better to follow her traditional practice of letting others do the experimenting instead of wiping out her superiority at one blow. The additional burden of expense aroused criticism from the Treasury, many politicians and many taxpayers. On the technical level the absence of any substantial secondary armament was condemned. Not only was the deadly "rain of fire" from the smaller calibers cited, but the poor visibility in the North Sea—the inevitable arena if Germany were Britain's enemy—was said to make long-range gun duels unlikely.

For some months Fisher fought back with two hands tied behind his back; for the tactical justification for the *Dreadnought*, in confirmation of Cuniberti's purely theoretical arguments, had been calculated in battle practice, and the results assessed in secret, before the final design was approved. The Board of Admiralty could not keep the existence of the ship confidential, but it was not in the interests of the nation to divulge all the reasons for her construction. Fisher was saved by Sims's letter to President Roosevelt, which included almost every argument that had persuaded the Board of the vital importance of making this leap forward. This letter put an end to the need for discretion.

The Dreadnought controversy on the technical level muttered on for some time. On the political plane the echoes reverberated at an undiminished volume for three years. For the first time, naval construction took a leading part in British domestic politics as the expenditure, and international tension, both increased. It was a misfortune for Fisher that a month before the *Dreadnought*'s launching, there occurred in May, 1906, the Liberal victory at the General Election, which further jeopardized his carefully planned program. To the sniping, on technical and tactical grounds, of the all-big-gun principle itself was now added a general and political attack on the policy of massive naval rearmament. The Liberal Party's platform was based primarily on social reform and a reduction of international tension. Whether the *Dreadnought* matched up to Fisher's expectation, or was a proved fiasco, defense expenditure was certain to come under the closest scrutiny. The rancorous controversy continued unremittingly, from club level, through the technical and popular press, to the annual debates on the Naval Estimates. Those from 1907 to 1909 were the most important; the tone of the speeches varied from out-and-out jingoistic to the balanced wisdom of Sir Edward Grey, British Foreign Secretary from 1905 to 1916, who summed up the deep anxieties of many of his wisest contemporaries thus:

There are those who like and those who dislike naval and military expenditure. There are those who like the martial spirit and those who dislike it. . . . That the nation should take pride in its power to resist force by force is a natural and wholesome thing. It is a source of perfectly healthy pride to have soundness of wind and limb and physical strength . . . but I would ask the people to consider to what consequences the growth of armaments has led. The great countries of Europe are raising enormous revenues and something like one half of them is being spent on naval and military preparations . . . [or] what are, after all, preparations to kill each other. Surely the extent to which this expenditure has grown really becomes a satire and a reflection upon civilization.*

A few days earlier a more humble member of Parliament had expressed an even more heartfelt plea, and anxious forebodings:

When two great civilized nations in their Assemblies begin measuring against each other their military and naval strength there ought to be in the heart of every man who has any regard for the general progress of mankind and the peace of Christendom the utmost sense of responsibility. The character of the debate [on the Estimates] from beginning to end is a menace to Germany. Complaints have been made that the German people were making naval preparations only as a menace to this country, and an Hon. member speaking from the Labour benches compared the preparations of the German people with those of a burglar. That is the seed of war. . . . Have the Germans no cause for complaint? Have Ministers and ex-Ministers read the foul and disgusting language of menace which has disgraced the pages of some of the leading magazines and newspapers of this country for the last three or four years? †

This was a just accusation. Throughout the period of Anglo-German rearmament the most extreme sentiments of warlike patriotism in the German press could not begin to match the provocative tone of the ultramilitant editorials in the *Daily Mail, Daily Telegraph*, and many of the more outspoken weeklies. It was difficult for Tirpitz's more moderate advisers to

* *Hansard*, March 30, 1909.
† Mr. Dillon, the Member for East Mayo, *Hansard*, March 18, 1908.

persuade him that the policy of, say, *Vanity Fair* was not that of an influential section of the Government. As long before as 1904, there were hints of a preventive war by Britain against the new Germany before she became too strong. One *Vanity Fair* editorial stated:

The real enemy is Germany. . . . There are men at the British Admiralty today who understand that naval victory against an efficient enemy depends largely on the success of the first blow. There is no room for illusion in naval affairs.

> Thrice armed is he who has his quarrel just,
> But four times he who gets his blow in fust.

Germany is the enemy. The German Fleet is built and maintained for no other purpose than to profit by English disaster. . . . Do not let us be under any illusion as to the reality of German enmity to this country.*

On several occasions *Vanity Fair* pleaded for a surprise "preventive" war, and for "Copenhagening" the German Fleet before it grew too large. "Day and night Germany is preparing for war with England. She will strike only when she is ready to strike. . . . If the German Fleet were destroyed the peace of Europe would last for two generations. . . ." Expressions like these, and those of a similar nature in the *Daily Mail*, naturally caused extreme resentment in Germany, and provided Tirpitz, the German Navy League, and all their militaristic supporters with the ammunition for which they craved. Nor was Tirpitz unreasonable in claiming that these sentiments were not limited to the more militant press and Members of Parliament. Fisher himself on several occasions recommended a surprise "preventive" attack, and although once he was rebuked by King Edward, to whom he made the suggestion, these threats certainly filtered back to Tirpitz.

In Britain and Germany during these crucial years the influences on public opinion varied from the most ferocious and extreme militancy, through simple appeal for "economy," to humane pacifism. In the end arithmetic and fear won the day. Figures, as always, could be twisted and misinterpreted. They were, on both sides. In 1909, for example, the cry for capital ships was "We want eight, and we won't wait!" The Germans, it was said, would equal our battle fleet in numbers by 1912. The controversy over this proposed record increase in the strength of the battle fleet raged for weeks. Even Fisher had not asked for as many. "In the end a curious and characteristic solution was reached," wrote Churchill. "The Admiralty had demanded six ships, the economists offered four; and we finally compromised on eight." †

Three years earlier, Fisher's enemies at home were more firmly entrenched, and it was for a time touch-and-go whether he got his new battle fleet at all. It says much for his powers (and to all those in his perjoratively

* *Vanity Fair*, Nov. 3, 1904.
† *The World Crisis*, by Winston S. Churchill, Vol. I (1927).

The rising tempo of the battleship race: The launch of
the *Ajax* on the Clyde, in 1912, a year when fifteen
Dreadnoughts took to the water (7). *Richard Perkins*

named "fishpond") that not only did the Dreadnought principle survive but
also that the 1906 program, representing the *Dreadnought*'s first reinforcements, was whittled down so modestly by the new Liberal First Lord of
the Admiralty, Lord Tweedmouth, from four to three battleships. We shall
now glance briefly at these ships, and their successors completed up to the
end of 1912, which joined the fleet in growing numbers as replacements for
Sir William White's now antiquated mixed-battery vessels.

The First Generation *Bellerophon*, *Téméraire*, and *Superb* closely followed the general outlines of the *Dreadnought*'s design, which was evidence
of the satisfaction felt at the outcome of the earlier ship's extensive trials.
The same arrangement of the main battery was followed, and there was only
a small increase in the size and disposition of the torpedo-defense battery.
For the first time antitorpedo bulkheads were fitted, a recognition of the
increasing power and range of that weapon, and this additional protection,
offset by a slight reduction in the thickness of the main armor belt, was largely

Bellerophon, the Royal Navy's second Dreadnought, with gunnery target. Two big tripod masts add strength to her appearance. Secondary armament is new quick-firing 4-inch, eight now in casemates; those on turret crowns were later removed to the superstructure (2).
Richard Perkins

responsible for the increase in displacement by 700 tons. The *Dreadnought*'s puny and inadequate tripod mainmast was replaced by a full-sized tripod, and the earlier awkward fore "reversed" tripod abaft the fore funnel was positioned where it should always have been. The effect was neat and satisfactory, and when they joined the Home Fleet in the early part of 1909, the *Bellerophon*s were greatly admired.

The continuation once again of the original single-caliber formula in 1907–1908 was caused in part by expedience and in part by a resurgence of conservatism encouraged by the flattery accorded to the *Dreadnought*. The creation of an entirely fresh design would have absorbed time and skill it was calculated could better be employed in refining a proved success. This was a mistaken and shortsighted policy. There were minor modifications

49

The *Téméraire* in 1919: note double-decked 4-inch and
absence of net defense (2). *Richard Perkins*

to the main armor belt; there was further rearrangement of the secondary battery, but the only prominent distinguishing marks from the *Bellerophon*s were the narrower fore funnel and the longer gun barrels. Like the improved German 11-inch and American 12-inch weapons, the increase to 50-calibers provided the shells of the *St. Vincent*, *Collingwood*, and *Vanguard* with greater penetrating power (a further half-inch of steel could be pierced at 3,000 yards) and higher muzzle velocity.

Within two years of the *Dreadnought*'s completion it was becoming clear that a broadside of eight heavy guns would soon be inadequate and that if, ship for ship, the Royal Navy was not to lose its lead, a heavier main armament or a new disposition of the main armament had become urgently necessary. The American *Delaware* and *North Dakota*, already in an advanced state of construction, were to have a broadside weight 25 percent greater than any British battleship so far planned; twelve 12-inch weapons, all on the center line, had already been decided on for Cuniberti's *Dante Alighieri*; and, above all, the lack of certainty about Germany's new battleships (with rumors of up to sixteen big guns still rife) caused great anxiety.

The *Neptune*, laid down in the first weeks of 1909, and intended to offset any gunpower disparity, was the unadventurous product of Sir Philip Watts and his fellow designers, whose decisions in turn were governed by a still ultraconservative Board. It was by then common knowledge that the American Department of the Navy had overcome the concussive effects associated with superfiring. In spite of this the Admiralty remained opposed to it, and merely rearranged the five twin turrets so that the two lateral turrets amidships were sited *en échelon*, giving them an arc of cross bearing, and compensating for the extra length this demanded by raising the fourth turret above the fifth aft. This offered a nominal broadside of all heavy guns on either beam but carried with it many objections. The arc of cross-bearing fire of the midships turrets was very small, and when they were so fired there was considerable strain on the structure of the ship, which later had

St. Vincent, first Dreadnought to mount the new 50-caliber 12-inch gun. Here she is in her early guise. Some 4-inch were later removed, to provide defense for merchantmen against U-boats (3). *Richard Perkins*

Neptune—the new shape: superimposed turrets aft;
staggered beam turrets to provide a narrow arc
of cross-deck fire; double flying boat decks—the forward
one being removed in the war, with the after control
top. Later the forward funnel was raised and fitted with
a clinker screen, and the secondary armament in the
three superstructures were fitted with screens (4).
Imperial War Museum

to be reinforced. Nor was fore-and-aft fire possible for these guns because of damage from blast to the bridgework. Finally, the superimposed guns aft were not permitted to fire over the lower turret, again because of blast risk, and could be trained only on the beam. *Neptune* was no faster than *Dreadnought*, no better protected, and her appearance with two flying boat decks, between her funnels and forward of the second mast, was not so imposing.

In spite of her handicaps, evident to anyone with superficial knowledge of warship design, the *Neptune*'s retrogressive features were repeated in two almost identical ships, *Colossus* and *Hercules*, laid down later in the same year. These were further handicapped by a return to the foremast abaft the fore tunnel: just as if her designers had never heard of the drawbacks to

Neptune at Portsmouth in 1911 (4). *Richard Perkins*

Hercules under way in Portsmouth Harbor, 1911. She and *Colossus* were distinguishable from *Neptune* by absence of main tripod mast, and by reversal, and placing abaft the fore funnel, of forward tripod: a reversion to *Dreadnought* practice (5). *Richard Perkins*

this location in the *Dreadnought*. As a reversion to pre-Dreadnought practice, the officers' and men's quarters were resited in the traditional manner; as a hint of more serious preoccupations in the future, it was thought necessary to give *Neptune* armor protection to her upper deck and magazines "against aero-craft." This was surprisingly farsighted, and very curious, considering their Lordships' disdain for the flying machine for another eight years.

After a brief period of omnipotence, then, British Dreadnought design had entered a period of statistical deceit that was to be exposed only under the demands of combat. All the battle cruisers designed up to 1914, and the battleships from the *Neptune* to the *Iron Dukes*, suffered under this disability. It was not that British Dreadnoughts were fundamentally unsound. But their actual fighting value was disguised under arithmetical falsehood. For practical purposes, the *Neptunes* did not really have a broadside of ten 12-inch guns. The maximum thickness of their armor belt was less than that of the *Dreadnought;* this fact was naturally not advertised, but the protection of the battle cruisers, as we shall see later, was deliberately and grossly exaggerated. The superimposition of guns offered no benefits except in a reduction of overall length. But far more serious than all this was the failure to explore more fully the dangers of underwater explosion, from mine and torpedo. While the Germans carried out exhaustive tests and applied the results to all their capital ships, little research was conducted in Britain. The more important thing was to have the ships, quickly. Numbers—arithmetic—won the day every time. "We want eight . . ." and so long as the ships and their guns were big and numerous, only a small, specialized minority cried out for material that was superior in fighting power as well as in numbers.

The 1909 class of battleship, *Orion, Conqueror, Monarch,* and *Thunderer* forming the backbone of the "eight" that were "wanted," typified this policy. Arithmetically they were splendid. There were now, at last, ten guns all on the center line, two superimposed fore and aft, to give a true useful broadside of ten big guns. Fore-and-aft fire now appeared to be four guns; but again the retention of old-fashioned sighting hoods, with all the concussive effects on the men within when the raised guns were fired close to them, effectively prohibited axial fire. None of the positive benefits of superimposition was therefore manifested; but one of the drawbacks was

H.M.S. *Colossus,* 1911: The sense of threatening power inspired by her name was reinforced by her rig and flying decks (5). *Richard Perkins*

The super-Dreadnoughts *Orion, Conqueror, Thunderer,*
and *Monarch* on a North Sea sweep in 1918. A kite
balloon offers greater vision. Units of the United States
Navy—left background—offer support (6). *Imperial
War Museum*

that the increased height of the center of gravity caused the class to be wicked
rollers in a heavy sea, and more elaborate bilge keels had later to be fitted.

Any protests about these demerits were, however, drowned by the
thunder of her new guns. While Krupps continued to develop and improve
their powerful and highly efficient 11-inch gun, fitting it in a 50-caliber form
to ships laid down as late as 1911, British ordnance factories were encouraged
to go one step further to 13.5-inch from 12-inch. The 50-caliber 12-inch
had not been an unqualified success; the 13.5-inch was a successful gun from
the start. Its only crime was to blind the public, and many experts, to the
deficiencies in the ships that acted as its platform. Fisher's efficient propaganda
machine stupefied even the best brains on the Board of Admiralty. The
13.5 hurled a shell almost 50 percent heavier than the 12-inch over a greater
range and with more accuracy. "The whole naval outlook has been changed
by the dramatic appearance of the new 13.5-inch gun, of unparalleled

The "fearful 13.5." Aft turrets of H.M.S. *Audacious*,
first Dreadnought casualty in the First World War (7).
Imperial War Museum

power," wrote the *Daily Telegraph*'s naval correspondent,* ". . . and now Germany's plans have again been disorganized." All that remained was to ensure that Britain should not lose a lead that would retard German plans by a year. "We have got the start," ran a leader in the *Daily Mail* at this time,† "and we must see to it that we are not overtaken. We cannot afford to abate our efforts even for a moment. . . . We have to face the certainty that neither in size of ships nor in weight of armament have we approached the limits of competition."

Under the pressure of opinion of this weight, applied without letup during the crucial years of the Fisher-Tirpitz battleship race, it is understandable that arithmetic won the day in Britain, and sight was sometimes lost of the less exciting factors that contributed vitally to a battle fleet's efficiency and fighting power. The famous "eight" were all completed and with the fleet

* October 27, 1910.
† August 22, 1910.

by the end of 1912: two 12-inch-gun battleships, four of the new super-Dreadnoughts mounting 13.5's, and two 22-knot battle cruisers. Britannia, it appeared to Britons and to most of the world that was interested, still ruled the waves—at least on the sacrosanct arithmetical 2:1 ratio basis.

Germany, and Tirpitz, had their troubles, too, as the pace of the deadly race intensified. On the one hand, of course, naval architecture and marine engineering were not steeped in the conservatism and complacency that Britain suffered as the result of years of class-dominated maritime supremacy and peace. But they had much to learn on the specialized techniques associated with heavy-warship construction. German pre-Dreadnoughts were not very good ships, not so sound as Sir William White's or as exciting as the Italian and American battleships. Tirpitz complained that "the administrative officials at the Admiralty had been given too much power over the technical side of the navy," that "our shipbuilding accommodation was particularly inadequate," that "we were immediately faced with a labyrinth of technical and organizing problems and differences of opinion," and that "private enterprise enticed many good engineers away from us," * because the Admiralty could not or would not pay them adequately. Money, as always, loomed as the most pressing problem. But under Tirpitz's leadership, higher appropriations and higher skills were both channeled into the effort toward making Germany the second naval power in the world. The High Seas Fleet was built up relentlessly and still under a cloak of design secrecy. Tirpitz deliberately refrained from the chauvinistic outbursts so freely indulged in across the North Sea, nor did he play the arithmetical game of comparing caliber for caliber, broadside for broadside, speed for speed, and tonnage for tonnage.

Later on, when comparative statistics were indulged in by his enemies at home, this got him into trouble. When it came to numbers, in ships, guns, weight of shell, speed, the German Dreadnoughts came off worse. As a consequence, the High Seas Fleet was assessed everywhere below its real power in 1914, even by its own officers and men; and this sense of inferiority had a profound effect on strategy until the Battle of Jutland proved otherwise. Tirpitz was close to the truth when he wrote:

We had secured the superiority in quality of our fleet over the English for the decisive years in Germany's development and thereby acquired an important counterpoise for our inferiority in numbers. Naturally few people in Germany knew anything definite about this superiority; many, but not all, trusted the creators of the fleet. A ship afloat in time of peace did not exhibit its solid qualities and fighting value; it was a matter of indifference whether its armour plating was thick or thin. On the other hand an opportunity was afforded, and eagerly grasped by fault-finders in Germany, when it was a question of our heavy guns being of a smaller calibre than the English; it was *not* seen that, apart from our

* *My Memoirs*, by Tirpitz.

58

S.M.S. *Oldenburg:* Second class of German Dreadnought, the first to fit 12-inch main armament, though this still disposed two-thirds in wing turrets (38). *Imperial War Museum*

Simplicity of German superstructure design is emphasized by temporary removal of *Helgoland*'s (38) searchlights. *Imperial War Museum*

more effective projectiles, we obtained in practice the same results in the matter of armour-piercing with our smaller calibre as the English with their greater, and besides, obtained other very important advantages.*

The Navy Act of 1908 authorized the laying down of four German Dreadnoughts annually for the next four years; and was incidentally the chief cause of the alarm in Britain and the further intensification of the

* *Ibid.*

Surrendered *Ostfriesland*, handed over to the United
States Navy, completes her Atlantic crossing—to be
destroyed by General "Billy" Mitchell's bombs. Her wide
beam, ten feet more than contemporary British ships
(restricted by size of existing dockyards), allows wing
turrets to be placed well inboard, with greater protection
to magazines (38). *U.S. Navy*

race. Three of these were of the *Helgoland* class, and a fourth unit of the same
class, *Oldenburg*, was added in 1909. When the *Helgoland*, *Ostfriesland*, and
Thüringen were made public in the summer of 1911, they were received
with the same sense of anticlimax. It was thought that at least a more up-to-
date and economical disposition of the main turrets would be achieved.
Instead they turned out to be merely enlarged *Nassaus*, distinguishable from
these earlier ships by their three funnels, and with 12-inch replacing 11-inch
as the main battery. They had a chunky, curiously pre-Dreadnought appearance. They were all to prove tough adversaries, and, as a surrendered
target ship, the *Ostfriesland* tested all Billy Mitchell's resources in the 1921
bombing trials.

The same apparent absence of any great innovations was evident in the

S.M.S. *Grosser Kurfürst*, First German Dreadnought to be completed with all-center-line main armament: a starkly simple layout governs the overall design, which was the most satisfactory of all the First Generation ships (40). *Imperial War Museum*

succeeding First Generation class, *Kaiser, Kaiserin, Prinzregent Luitpold, König Albert,* and *Friedrich der Grosse,* Scheer's flagship at Jutland. The same disposition and number of big guns—still 12-inch—were followed as in the British *Neptune,* and the midships lateral turrets had the same drawbacks and limitations; corrected in the all-center-line *König, Markgraf, Kronprinz,* and *Grosser Kurfürst* of the 1911–1912 programs. *Kaiser* steamed nearly 24 knots on her trials; but, conservative as ever, the German Admiralty gave her speed officially as 20 knots. The real strength of the *Kaiser*s and *König*s, and of every German capital ship that succeeded them, was in the remarkable thickness of the armor plate, no less than 14 inches on the main belt and 12 inches on her turrets, representing an advantage over her British contemporaries of between 20 percent and 30 percent. The underwater protection was in keeping, and exceeded in complexity and thoroughness even that of the *Helgoland*s, with double solid longitudinal bulkheads and minute subdivision throughout. It is extremely doubtful if any of this class would have succumbed to British shellfire alone at Jutland if they had been exposed to it; all five went to the bottom of Scapa Flow in 1919. Their appearance, with tall twin funnels hugging the masts, and a long sweeping forecastle extending back to the aft superimposed turret, was a great deal more dignified than that of earlier German Dreadnoughts.

Of the other great powers, Japan had completed in only three years her own first "pure" Dreadnoughts, the swift *Kawachi* and *Settsu*. The Italians,

König, showing damage to upper works after Jutland battle. "Q" 12-inch turret between funnels, 5.9-inch in upper-deck casemates, 24-pounder behind shield on fore superstructure. German Navy retained net defense long after it was discarded by British (40). *Imperial War Museum*

Dieses ist ein geheimer Gegenstand im Sinne des § 1 des Gesetzes gegen den Verrat militärischer Geheimnisse vom 3ten Juni 1914, M. V. Bl. 1914, Seite 205.

Admiral Scheer's flagship, S.M.S. *Friedrich der Grosse*,
unkempt at Scapa after surrender. Light catches the
beveled top of very deep 14-inch main armor belt (39).
Imperial War Museum

Giulio Cesare at Taranto in 1917, a year after her sister
ship *Leonardo da Vinci* was blown up there. Her main
artillery arrangement was unique. Identifiable from
Conte di Cavour by higher fore funnel. Tripod foremast
later placed forward of first funnel (60). *Imperial
War Museum*

Andrea Doria before complete rebuild (61). *Imperial War Museum*

too, always preferred fast ships, at the expense of a certain amount of armor protection. Their first class of Dreadnoughts, following the more or less experimental *Dante Alighieri*, was also in the best Cuniberti tradition. Every effort to save unnecessary weight by the use of light metals, and an ingenious disposition of the main armament, resulted in the design in 1909 of the *Conte di Cavour, Giulio Cesare,* and *Leonardo da Vinci* with a broadside of thirteen 12-inch guns, one more than Cuniberti's "ideal" and greatly superior to that of any British ship then building. Triple turrets were placed fore and aft with superimposed twin turrets, and a third triple amidships between the two tall funnels, so arranged as to give a 130-degree arc of fire on each beam. Maximum speed was close to 23 knots, armor protection rather weaker than that of the *Dreadnought*'s. After completion, the tripod mainmast abaft the fore funnel was moved forward as in some British ships. *Caio Duilio* and *Andrea Doria,* laid down two years later, differed from the earlier ships to only a minor degree and in the substitution of 6-inch for 4.7-inch secondary armament.

French development was staid and orthodox compared with her exciting and bizarre designs of the pre-Dreadnought era, and, like Italy and Russia, produced no Second Generation ships. The *France, Courbet, Jean Bart,* and *Paris* of 1910 were followed two years later by the *Bretagne* class of three ships (*Bretagne, Lorraine,* and *Provence*), very expensive, rather slow,

Courbet in 1913, the year she was completed. First two funnels were later trunked. She ended her life on D-Day as a breakwater at Arromanches (55). *Imperial War Museum*

France leaving Toulon, 1916. She ran aground and subsequently sank in Quiberon Bay in 1922. All this class were completed with pole mast abaft second funnel (55). *Imperial War Museum*

Jean Bart, in 1928, as rebuilt with two funnels and tripod foremast. She survived two torpedo hits from an Austro-Hungarian submarine in First World War (55). *Richard Perkins*

Lorraine, in 1928. Completed in 1916, she was last of France's First Generation Dreadnoughts. Tripod foremast was fitted later. A year after this photograph was taken, she was converted to oil-fired boilers and modified again (56). *Richard Perkins*

Bretagne in 1928, after pole foremast was replaced by tripod. As with so many Dreadnoughts of her period, forward main-deck secondary-gun casemates have been plated over (56). *Richard Perkins*

smaller and less well-protected versions of the dozen 13.5-inch-gunned British super-Dreadnoughts of this period. The same main-armament disposition was followed. They were quite undistinguished, and took nearly four years to build. It is as if the French, after joyously challenging British maritime supremacy almost to the moment of signing the Entente Cordiale, were at this stage in history content to sit back and observe the rising tempo of Anglo-German competition, secure in the knowledge of their military might. "It must be admitted," Charles Farrère has written, "that in spite of the efforts of certain ministers . . . the French Fleet in 1914 was a poor fleet, and only the English alliance saved her." *

Evidence of how widespread the Dreadnought fever had become was to

* *Histoire de la Marine Française* (1956).

The second of the Austro-Hungarian Dreadnoughts to be completed, the 20,000-ton *Tegetthof*. Their unexpected construction upset the *status quo* in the Mediterranean (65). *Imperial War Museum*

be found at Trieste and Fiume, where that slightly improbable service, the Austro-Hungarian Navy, was fitting out four up-to-the-minute Dreadnoughts, quite as formidable as any in the world. News that these ships were under construction had been received at the French and British admiralties with considerable alarm, three years earlier, for they threatened to upset the balance of power in the Mediterranean. The Austro-Hungarian *Viribus Unitis*, *Tegetthof*, *Prinz Eugen*, and *Szent Istvan* were neat, powerful, and wholly satisfactory vessels of 20,000 tons, with a speed of 21 knots and mounting a dozen 12-inch guns carried in four triple turrets, superimposed fore and aft. Besides the Italian-designed Russian Dreadnoughts under desultory construction in the Baltic, only Cuniberti's own ships had so far utilized the triple gun turret. Like superfiring guns, the British were to have nothing to do with this sensible and economical arrangement for a long time. The Americans were thinking about triple turrets. The French jumped this stage and went straight on to quadruples.

Then there were the Russians. They neither built distinguished ships nor used them in a very distinguished manner. Cuniberti's design for the *Gangut* class of 1911 was considerably modified by the Russian Admiralty, and by the time they were completed some five years later were completely outclassed on every count. Their war was generally fruitless, and eventful mainly in terms of mutiny and humiliation. It was also obscure. All that is clear is

There were few moments of drama in the
Austro-Hungarian Navy. One occurred on June 10,
1918, when an Italian motor launch put two torpedoes
into the *Szent Istvan* and sent her to the bottom (65).
U.S. Navy

Russian *Marat*, completed before the First World War
and mildly rejuvenated between the wars. The design
was Cuniberti's (63). *Richard Perkins*

An exceedingly rare shot of the Russian *Oktyaberskaia
Revolutia* (formerly, and later again, *Gangut*) taken in
the Baltic, probably in the mid thirties. Amphibian plane
on "X" turret; light antiaircraft guns on "Y" turret (63).
U.S. Navy

that they sailed under various flags and ended up with the appropriately
Marxist names of *Oktyaberskaia Revolutia* (ex-*Gangut*), *Mikhail Frunze* (ex-
Poltava), *Marat* (ex-*Petropavlovsk*) and *Parizkaia Kommuna* (ex-*Sevastopol*), although they were finally given back their original names. They were
mildly refurbished between the wars, and served with equal lack of distinction
in the Second. A trio of similar ships, the *Imperatritsa Maria*, *Imperator Aleksandr III*, and *Imperatritsa Yekaterina II*, completing in the Black Sea at the
beginning of the war (a fourth was never completed), was also caught up in
the bizarre tides of fortune that engulfed so much of Imperial Russia's battle
fleet, from the Turkish war of 1877–1878 through the Russo-Japanese de-
bacles to the Communist Revolution. The *Imperatritsa Maria* was the first to
be completed, and actually exchanged fire with the *Yavuz* (ex-*Goeben*) and
forced her to flee: in itself a notable achievement for a Russian battleship. In
November, 1916, she was mysteriously sunk as a result of internal explosions,
was raised for long enough in 1919 to be renamed *Demokratiya*, and broken
up as being beyond repair. *Yekaterina II* had perhaps the briefest and most
uneventful career of any Dreadnought, and certainly retained her original

Imperial Russia's Black-Sea–built Dreadnoughts led brief,
obscure, and mainly inactive careers, lighted by bizarre
violent moments. This one, completed in time for the
revolution, served under the Tsar, revolutionary groups,
the Royal Navy, and the Bolsheviks. She was named, in
this order, *Imperator Aleksandr III*, *Volia*, and *General
Alexeieff*. Design was based on Baltic Fleet's *Ganguts*
(64). *Imperial War Museum*

name for a shorter period than any other. She had a few weeks' existence as
the *Svobodnaya Rossia* before loyal imperial sailors acquired her and destroyed her to prevent her falling into insurrectionist hands. The *Aleksandr
III* flew the imperial flag momentarily, then sailed under Communist colors,
was captured by the Germans, and finally by the British—by then she was
named the *Volia*. She escaped from the Black Sea in late 1920, and was
eventually scrapped at Bizerta just before World War II. Her heavy guns
were used by the Germans in shore batteries on Guernsey, Channel Islands.

The middle period of the Dreadnought was also enlivened by a naval
competition in South America that was a satirical reflection in miniature of
the hysteria-ridden Anglo-German race. Ironclad status was not a new
thing to the South American republics. Peru, Chile, Argentina, and Brazil
had for many years purchased new armored fighting ships from European

yards or had taken over the castoffs of the major naval powers for purposes of local prestige, intimidation, and even frontier war. Many at some time in their careers became the first target of rebel leaders, the possession of "the fleet" being tantamount to control of the country. Brazil was the most bellicose of these minor naval powers, and when news reached the country of the *Dreadnought* she determined to be first with an all-big-gun ship, which would wipe out at one blow Argentina's superiority in coastal-defense battleships and armored cruisers. Negotiations were therefore opened with the British firm of Vickers—one of several European companies that thrived on South American warship orders—which produced a number of alternative plans. The result was that this large, thinly populated, and near-bankrupt nation had a pair of Dreadnoughts on the stocks at the same time as Germany and the United States and had them ready while her competitors were still wondering how she was going to pay for them and how they were going to contrive to pay for their own. The *Minas Gerais* and *São Paulo* were modern to the minute. Vickers gave them superfiring turrets fore and aft while the British Admiralty was still arguing about the dangers from blast, and two more wing turrets gave them a total broadside 25 percent heavier than the *Dreadnought*. In 1910 there were no more powerful battleships in the world.

In the same year Argentina entered the lists. She had long ago recognized the dangers of the situation and had been sending naval missions on prospective shopping trips to Italy, Germany, Britain, France, and the United States for the last year. She eventually got in America what she thought was the best bargain, a sorry blow to British shipbuilders, who had been taking the lion's share of warship orders (including almost the entire Japanese Navy until she started building herself). The *Rivadavia* and *Moreno* were laid down by the Fore River Company and the New York Shipbuilding Company at about the time when the two Vickers ships were crossing the ocean to Brazil. They were, inevitably, nearly half as large again as the Brazilian Dreadnoughts, carried more armor, and were faster. They also filled their part and purpose by looking a great deal more powerful; although, without resorting to cross-deck fire, their broadside was no heavier. In addition, mostly because the Ministry of Marine was so vacillating in its requirements while they were building, they were not ready until 1915. Brazil, it would seem, had got the better bargain.

But the Brazilian authorities were not to rest on their laurels. Their ambitions were now without limit. They were determined to be possessed of the most powerful battleship in the world—no less. And they very nearly got her. This is what happened. Various designs, including one for a super-super-Dreadnought of over 31,000 tons and armed with ten 15-inch guns, were discussed with European shipbuilders before a contract was signed with Armstrongs for an even larger ship carrying twelve 14-inch. Before this could be implemented, there was a change of government who viewed the project with slightly more caution. The new Minister of Marine, in the

Brazilian battleship: Brazil was easily first off the mark in
the minor Dreadnought race. This is the *São Paulo*,
completed in 1910, an admirably balanced ship designed
and constructed in Britain (67). *Richard Perkins*

course of a trip to Germany, was also advised by Kaiser Wilhelm, a great naval theorist, of the advantages of an armament uniform with that of the earlier ships. A revised contract was therefore signed with Armstrongs for a 27,500-ton battleship armed with no less than fourteen 12-inch weapons, all on the center line. The *Rio de Janeiro*, then, would not therefore be the world's biggest Dreadnought; but she would certainly carry the largest number of heavy guns, would be the longest, and in appearance would be the most formidable in the world. In these three qualities she remained unique throughout her life of eight years. If ever there was a bristling gun platform, with the evident sacrifice of everything to artillery, then she was the *Rio de Janeiro;* a ship to strike terror in the heart of any South American republic having aggressive designs on Brazil. But soon after she was launched in 1913 the Brazilian government began to have doubts about paying for her. In her unfinished state, she was therefore put up for auction, and Turkey, who already had a super-Dreadnought building in Britain, bought her for £2,725,000 ($13,625,000) and renamed her *Sultan Osman I*. Her departure for the Mediterranean was deliberately delayed by the British Government during the last weeks of peace in 1914, although her Turkish crew were ready to man her, and she was compulsorily acquired and handed over to the Royal Navy against strong Turkish protests, and renamed, once again, *Agincourt*. She served throughout the war with the Grand Fleet, and was in the line at Jutland. "She was the last in line and during the short time she came into action seized the opportunity to fire full fourteen-gun salvoes. The sheet of flame was big enough to create the impression that a battle cruiser had blown up; it was awe-inspiring." *

Nor could Chile afford to remain outside the race for prestige and power in South America. Armstrongs' yard on the Tyne got this order, too, and late in 1911 the first of two 28,000-ton fast battleships was ordered, each of which could have outpaced if not outgunned the *Rio de Janeiro*. As it turned out, Chile had to wait for nine years for one, and never got the second. The *Almirante Latorre* was a larger version of the 13.5-inch-gunned British super-Dreadnoughts, armed with 14-inch guns and with a speed of 23 knots. On her completion in 1915, she was taken over by the Royal Navy as the *Canada*, and, like the *Agincourt*, spent most of the rest of the war in Scapa Flow. The Chilean Navy eventually got her in 1920. Her sister ship, the *Almirante Cochrane*, was converted into a British aircraft carrier, and renamed *Eagle*.

Three further minor powers caught up in the Dreadnought fever in the years preceding the First World War were Spain, Turkey, and Greece. The Spanish Ministry of Marine built three sensible little Dreadnoughts. The *España*, *Alfonso XIII*, and *Jaime Primero* were really coast-defense vessels, and apart from the later German pocket battleships were the smallest Dread-

* See *The Marine Engineer*, May, 1919, from which much of this information has been drawn.

Only American-built foreign Dreadnoughts were
Argentina's *Rivadavia* (seen here) and *Moreno*, laid down
in answer to the Brazilian British-built ships (68).
Imperial War Museum

Fourteen big guns, the heaviest main and secondary
battery, the longest ship of her time, the greatest number
of heavy gun turrets of any Dreadnought. Brazilian
dreams of grandeur resulted in H.M.S. *Agincourt*, here
seen in the North Sea with *Erin*, which was also
commandeered, from the Turks in 1914 (9). *Imperial
War Museum*

Chile's only battleship had much in common with British
super-Dreadnoughts, and served in the Grand Fleet as
Canada before being delivered as *Almirante Latorre*.
Here she is in 1919, under British colors (69).
Richard Perkins

The basic and eminently sensible local-built *España*, Spain's
first Dreadnought (66). *Imperial War Museum*

Erin as Nore Flagship, 1919. The Turkish Navy, for which she was built, never got her (8). *Richard Perkins*

noughts ever built, displacing some 15,000 tons, and armed with eight 12-inch arranged in twin turrets fore and aft and in echelon amidships. British yards scooped the Turkish Dreadnought program, and again the advantage was not only financial. The *Reshad V* and *Reshad-i-Hamiss* were laid down in 1911 as super-Dreadnoughts carrying ten 13.5's disposed as in the contemporary British ships. After the Balkan Wars, the Ottoman government canceled the order for the second (although compensating for this loss later by buying the Brazilian ship), and renamed the first *Reshadieh*. But she suffered the same fate as the *Sultan Osman I*, being complete just as war broke out, and the Royal Navy took her over as the *Erin*. The forced acquisition of these two powerful ships caused vast resentment in Turkey, where the money for one had been subscribed, it was said, by the common peasantry. The Grand Fleet sorely needed them at the time, but it was certainly a contributory cause of the Turkish entry into the war on the German side. So was the escape of the *Goeben*, and Germany's shrewd gesture of presenting her to the

Turkish Navy. Greece's contribution was to have been a battle cruiser. A German yard began to build her in 1913, but her 14-inch American guns could not be got through the British blockade after the war began. The ship was never finished—and the Royal Navy got the gun᷈ instead, using them in monitors.

The immense importance attached to the possession of the all-big-gun battleship can be seen from this list of the Dreadnought stakes at the end of 1912:

	Built	*Building*
ARGENTINA		2
AUSTRALIA	1	
AUSTRIA-HUNGARY	1	3
BRAZIL	2	1
CHILE		2
FRANCE		7
GERMANY	13	10
GREAT BRITAIN	19	12
ITALY	1	5
JAPAN	1	5
NEW ZEALAND	1	
RUSSIA		8
SPAIN		3
TURKEY		1
UNITED STATES	8	4
	47	63

CHAPTER 4

The Battle Cruisers: The "New Testament" Ships

Tortoises were apportioned to *catch hares*.
Millions of tortoises can't catch a hare.
The Almighty arranged the greyhound to catch the hare—
the greyhound so largely bigger than the hare as to annihilate it. . . .

—ADMIRAL OF THE FLEET LORD FISHER OF KILVERSTONE *

The battle cruiser was the product of one of the doctrines of Vittorio Cuniberti, which always laid strong emphasis on speed. Fisher embraced with special warmth this aspect of the Italian general's beliefs and saw to it that the *Dreadnought* outpaced every other battleship in the world. She also carried a healthy margin of protection. The British Dreadnought battle cruiser, however, for all its life remained a vulnerable and dangerous anomaly, its role confused and doubtful; yet paradoxically in war worked harder, fired its guns more often than all the many more numerous battleships, and sank more ships. Its combination of great size and high speed also made the battle cruiser the most intimidating, awe-inspiring, and magnificently romantic class of warship ever conceived.

The battle cruiser, then, should never have happened. Why was it conceived at all? Its origins are also paradoxical, and date back to an earlier naval rivalry: the Anglo-French competition of the 1880's and 1890's. The French Admiralty, recognizing that they could never hope to outpace Britain in battleships, sensibly laid down a number of powerful, lightly armored, swift commerce raiders. In war, these would have been spread out over Britain's worldwide trade routes, starving her of supplies and forcing the dispatch of hunting forces. These would necessarily be numerous, thus whittling down the strength of the battle fleet in European waters to bring about a state of parity, or near parity. In answer to this policy Britain built armored crisuers with greater gunpower and higher speed specifically designed to hunt them down. This class of ship reached its ultimate limit of power and size in the *Minotaur* class, which carried an armament of four 9.2-inch and ten 7.5-inch guns, and a main armor belt of six inches on a displacement of 14,600 tons. Speed was 23 knots.

In 1902, at a time when Fisher was beginning to contemplate the Cuniberti-inspired *"Untakeable,"* he also gave much thought to an equally innovatory next stage in armored-cruiser design. Again with Gard as draftsman and fellow theorist, the main features of a mythical "H.M.S. *Unapproachable"* were drawn up. Emphasis was of course laid on speed, obtained with oil-firing and turbines that would allow for telescopic funnels, because a low silhouette and small target area were important requirements. He also wanted the boiler and engine rooms right aft, well out of the way of the guns, their mountings

* *The Times,* London, September 9, 1919.

and ammunition rooms: in this he was about half a century ahead of his time. The guns were to be of mixed calibers, the largest of smaller caliber than that of a battleship's heaviest armament. However, when it became known that both Cuniberti's *Vittorio Emanuele* hybrid fast battleship-armored cruisers and the latest Japanese 20-knot armored cruisers were to carry 12-inch guns, Fisher recognized that his theoretical ship might still be unapproachable but would certainly be takable, and that a much more radical step forward was called for if Britain was to retain the lead in this class of vessel.

All this was exercising Fisher's mind during his months as Second Sea Lord and as Commander in Chief, Portsmouth. With his appointment as First Sea Lord in 1904, the main features of what was to become known as the "Gard-Fisher Design A" had been worked out. With eight 12-inch guns (and no secondary armament beyond 4-inch to deal with torpedo craft) they were to have near equal artillery status with the projected Dreadnought battleship—and double the primary armament of existing battleships. Her speed was to be not less than 25 knots; her armor plate on a par with her cruiser predecessors. Such a man-of-war, he envisaged, must at once antiquate every armored cruiser in the world as the Dreadnought-to-be must make obsolete every navy's battle fleet.

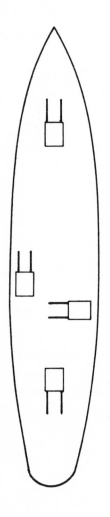

Invincible disposition

Between January and March, 1905, the Committee on Designs considered various alternatives for this superarmored cruiser at the same time they were thrashing out the new battleship designs, and a decision was reached simultaneously on both vessels. However, in contrast with the jubilant publicity accorded to the forthcoming battleship, the only reference to the "*Unapproachable*" was an announcement that three of the four armored cruisers in the 1905 program were to be completed in the unusually short period of thirty months. Details remained secret, but some hint of the armament, it was suggested at the time, reached German naval authorities, because they countered with their own superarmored cruiser, the *Blücher*, mounting a main armament of twelve 8.2-inch guns, which would have had a marked superiority over the supposed all-big-gun arrangement of eight 9.2's on the British ships. But poor *Blücher* turned out to be a superhybrid, and quickly succumbed to the bigger guns of her contemporaries at the Dogger Bank engagement.

The first of these battle cruisers (the term did not come into accepted use for another five or six years) was laid down five days before the *Dreadnought* was launched. All three were ready for sea in the late summer of 1908, and before Germany had put down the keel plate of her first battle cruiser. In their armament, speed, and appearance the *Invincible, Inflexible,* and *Indomitable* came fully up to expectation, and confirmed all the impressions of arrogant superiority engendered by the *Dreadnought*. Their eight 12-inch weapons, disposed fore and aft and in lateral echelon amidships, offered a broadside of six big guns: or a weight of metal of 5,100 pounds against the latest German armored cruisers' broadside of 1,722 pounds. This, and the

Inflexible, one of the first battle cruisers, as great a
sensation in her day as the *Dreadnought*, presaging a
new era in cruiser design (16). *Imperial War Museum*

superiority in their guns' range, were demonstrated when these two German
ships were shattered by the *Invincible* and *Inflexible* at the Battle of the
Falkland Islands. The wing turrets were arranged to give a narrow arc of
cross-deck fire, but owing to blast effects they could be fired only when
the other turret had been put out of action. Fore-and-aft fire was also
restricted by blast considerations, and in practice was limited to four guns.

The protection of these first First Generation battle cruisers was officially
given as seven inches on the main belt, with a maximum of ten inches on

the turrets. These figures were false: their belt was only six inches, and it was very narrow, and tapered to four inches at the bows and nothing at all abaft the aft turret, and the maximum armor thickness on the turrets was only seven inches. This deceived the future enemy and the British taxpayer; the price was paid at Jutland.

But it was the speed of the new ships that caught the imagination. Their 41,000 h.p. turbines were the most powerful in the world, and their official speed of 25 knots was as underrated as their protection was exaggerated. All were capable of 28 knots—at which speed their appearance was impressive beyond words—and the *Indomitable* crossed the Atlantic from Quebec at 24.8 knots, steaming 25.13 knots for three consecutive days. Of this performance, the *Scientific American* said that she "was certain to have a powerful influence upon the design of future warships," for "the presence of the *Indomitable* on the high seas has upset all existing calculations as to the value of the armoured cruiser."

As "ocean greyhounds" they had exceeded the highest expectations. The trouble was that the new combat calculations that they demanded were diffuse and conflicting in their definition. The confusion about the role of the battle cruiser stemmed from Fisher's arithmetical fixations. He has had no parallel in modern naval history as an administrator and wielder of influence. But he had grave faults as a strategist, and his understanding of

Indomitable and *Inflexible* on North Sea war service in 1918. Their sister ship *Invincible* had blown up at Jutland, and as a result these light, thinly plated battle cruisers had received additional protection to turrets and magazines. Note plane on starboard wing turret (16).
Imperial War Museum

Inflexible from the forecastle: 4-inch quick-firers on the
12-inch turret crown were removed and the bridgework
was elaborated during the First World War (16).
Imperial War Museum

tactics was elementary. He was a victim of his own jargon. "Speed equals
protection," he constantly reiterated; for "repetition is the soul of journalism,"
as he was still repeating within weeks of his death. He visualized the battle
cruiser in terms of spectacle, and of the "fixed picture": the swift wing of
the battle fleet racing in pursuit of a fleeing enemy, or sweeping in close to
the enemy coastline to shatter coastal defenses during his favorite "Pomeranian
landing" project that was planned to break the deadlock in trench warfare.
He failed to recognize that if a cruiser was to be given the armament of a
battleship, the qualities of aggression which he so warmly extolled in a
naval leader must result in their engaging in a line of battle with their own
kind. In fact, the 12-inch gun which, with their high speed, was their *raison*

d'être proved also their undoing. The battle cruiser was like a heavyweight boxer with an eggshell skull; alone in the ring the master of any challenger until the arrival of another heavyweight with equal agility and punch. While her speed was greater than that of any equally powerful foe, it was not an adequate substitute for protection. In short, the battle cruiser was fine so long as the enemy did not have any.

The role of the armored cruisers had been clear-cut, but the arrival of the fast Dreadnought battleships made them as obsolete as the pre-Dreadnought battleships. They were intended to scout, or support scouting light cruisers; to round up enemy commerce raiders; to pursue a defeated enemy and pick off crippled stragglers; and in a fleet action to initiate enveloping movements round an enemy. Armored cruiser operations with a fleet of Dreadnoughts (though Jellicoe misguidedly thought otherwise and lost three at Jutland) were now ruled out owing to their near equality in speed. The battle cruisers could have filled these fleet duties if they had not possessed an armament that was bound to tempt a commander in chief to place them in line for the sake of their big guns, risking a hit on their vulnerable vital areas. What, then, was the role accorded to them by the Board? It was never formally announced. However, their numerous critics decided roles for them, and at once knocked them down again like gunnery targets. "Vessels of this enormous size and cost are unsuitable for many of the duties of cruisers," stated Lord Brassey in his *Naval Annual.* "The three or four knots extra speed which she has must involve a large sacrifice of fighting power," stated *Blackwood's* naval correspondent. "The details published are insufficient to determine its extent. The want of information is not material, because the omission of such ships from the new programme is an eloquent indication that such ships are dead, and that no more will be built. By argument they have been killed, and it only remains to inter them decently away from the public gaze." *

Alas! the program for the following year revealed three more. Before he was replaced at the Admiralty, Fisher had finished or completed arrangements for nine battle cruisers, and still their functions in time of war remained undefined. The position remained unchanged when war came, and Vice-Admiral Sir David Beatty—as swashbuckling and romantic as the great swift ships he led—found "his task at that time was rendered easier (for an unacademic sailor like him) in that the duties of a battle cruiser squadron at sea had in no wise been laid down either by the Admiralty or the Commander-in-Chief. . . ." † So wrote Filson Young, who served under Beatty at this time, and was an old friend. "It was thus left to its commander to invent duties for it, as well as train and exercise it in the performance of them. . . ."

The splendor and power of the battle cruiser were not to be denied,

---

* October, 1906.
† *With the Battle Cruisers,* by Filson Young (1921).

however, and the Germans were forced to reply if they were not to deprive their new Dreadnought battle fleet of its scouting wing. When they did so, the results showed superiorities over their British opposite numbers as great as their battleships possessed over the First Generation Royal Navy Dreadnoughts. The *von der Tann* was the first, a fine-looking twin-funneled vessel having main armament disposed like that of the *Invincible*, the disadvantage of the smaller caliber (11-inch against 12-inch) being offset by her practical broadside of all eight guns through quite a wide arc. Her displacement was 2,000 tons greater, and this was mainly absorbed in a much more comprehensive and tougher protection, her main belt being deeper, thicker by 3¾ inches, and extending for almost the full length of her hull—though Brassey reassured his readers that it was no more formidable than the *Invincible*'s. In addition she was equipped with a double torpedo bulkhead and intricately elaborate inner compartmentation. Her theoretical speed was less than that of the *Invincible*s, but in practice there was a margin of scarcely a knot. She was completed in less than two years, the shortest time of any German capital ship, which reflects the sense of urgency and anxiety felt by the German Admiralty at this time.

By the time the *von der Tann* had joined the fleet, two more of an enlarged and improved class were on the slips, and the Royal Navy had five more battle cruisers under construction. The battle-cruiser competition was becoming as intense as the Dreadnought race of which it was an integral part. The belief was growing that one could not live without the other, and as the money and shipbuilding facilities were limited in Britain as well as in Germany, each battle cruiser represented the loss of a battleship. Indeed, they were soon costing more and absorbing more labor and materials than their contemporary Dreadnoughts.

Britain's second batch of three battle cruisers (still called armored cruisers) was laid down from February, 1909, to June, 1910. They were as disappointing and conservative as the *Colossus* and *Orion* classes of battleship, and can be regarded as the worst ships built for the Royal Navy during the Fisher era. The only excuse that can be made for the *Indefatigable, Australia*, and *New Zealand* is that the naval situation at the time of their designing was the politicians' whipping boy. In fact, the navy got two of them only by a circuitous "arrangement" with two of the Dominion governments whereby it appeared that they were paying for them. This was good for imperial solidarity, shipbuilding shareholders and shipyard workers, and apparently good for the British taxpayer. The vessels themselves were none the better for it, however. By stretching out the *Invincible* design by twenty-five feet, the amidships turrets, even with their new longer 12-inch guns, could be spaced so that the cross-deck fire became a possibility over a wide arc. The ships, with their already very high freeboard, also offered an admirable target, as the gunlayers of the *von der Tann* discovered at Jutland, when they sent the *Indefatigable* to the bottom after fifteen minutes' firing.

(Opposite, top and bottom) "An exceedingly tough antagonist in battle," Oscar Parkes has written. S.M.S. *von der Tann*, Germany's first battle cruiser, in 1911. One reason why she survived her fearful battering at Jutland was the extent of her armor belt, seen here below the stern 24-pounders. Her wing turrets offered a wide angle of cross-deck fire (44). *Richard Perkins*

What was altogether indefensible was the continuation of the *Invincibles'* inadequate protection.

The next round was opened by Germany in the spring of 1909, only two months after the *Indefatigable* was laid down at Devonport. The *Moltke* initiated a new genre of German warship design which was maintained right up to the *Tirpitz* and *Bismarck* of the 1940's, and which combined the internal and external strength, and the armament, of a battleship with the speed of the fastest battle cruiser. This was achieved by the use of the lightest materials where they would not jeopardize the strength of the structure (the *von der Tann* had begun this tradition by using small-tube boilers); the most advanced and efficient propelling machinery; and ingenious internal defense against

Starboard 12-inch wing turret and guns of H.M.A.S. *Australia*. She hunted the *Scharnhorst* and *Gneisenau* in the Pacific in 1914 (17). *Richard Perkins*

Battle cruiser *Moltke:* An increase in length of 32 feet, and in displacement of 3,600 tons, gave Germany's second battle cruiser an extra pair of 11-inch guns and enhanced protection all round. With her turbines developing 85,782 horsepower, she steamed 28.4 knots on trials (45). *Imperial War Museum*

the shell that penetrated the outer armor, and the mine and torpedo that attacked from below the surface. A note in a contemporary *Fighting Ships* hinted at the effort that was made to cut weight, and incidentally reduce fire risk to a minimum: "All cupboards, shelves, etc. are of light sheet iron, the only wood being the tables and chairs. There are no pictures, armchairs, settees or sofas in the wardroom. There are no ventilators on deck other than the erections around the fore funnel. . . ." Such austerity was not to be found in British battle cruisers, as Filson Young discovered when he visited Beatty's quarters in the *Lion* in *wartime*, and found that "the chintz, the fine engravings, the old furniture, enlivened by flowers and books, looked very homely and charming in the heart of this steel citadel." *

Like the *Indefatigable* the *Moltke* showed an increase in length over her predecessor, but in the German ship this was utilized to add an additional superimposed turret aft. The beam was also up to 96¾ feet, compared with the *Indefatigable*'s 80 feet. This was because the British built their ships to fit their docks, and under Fisher's arithmetical obsession it was more important to have new ships than new docks. The Germans spent money on new docks as well as Kiel Canal locks, and built wide-beamed Dreadnoughts

* *Ibid.*

with additional bulkheading and cleverly placed coal bunkers amidships to "cushion" torpedo and shell explosion. German Dreadnoughts shrugged off single torpedo hits. A contrasting table of statistics between these two 1909 contemporaries reveals some of the reasons why the First Generation German ships demonstrated marked superiority over the British in combat. They fought second last and last in the line at the opening of the battle-cruiser action at Jutland, before the *von der Tann* blew up the *Indefatigable*. The *Moltke* received less damage than any of the German battle cruisers (she was always a lucky ship), and Hipper transferred his flag to her when the *Lützow* began to go down:

	Indefatigable	*Moltke*
Displacement	18,500 tons	22,640 tons
Length and beam	555 × 80 ft.	610 × 96¾ ft.
Armament	8 12-inch	10 11-inch
	16 4-inch	12 5.9-inch
		10 4.1-inch
Protection	Belt 4–6 inches	Belt 5–11 inches
	11 feet deep	15 feet deep
	Turrets 7 inches	Turrets 8 inches
Machinery	Turbines 44,000 h.p.	Turbines 52,000 h.p.
	25 knots	25 knots
	(trials 26.7 knots)	(trials 28.4 knots)
Cost	$7,737,500	$11,000,000 approx.

One serious handicap to the *Moltke*'s very low freeboard was that at far below her very high maximum speed her forecastle was almost continuously awash in even a choppy sea. Her sister ship *Goeben* had the longest and most colorful career of any Dreadnought. With the light cruiser *Breslau* she was in the Mediterranean in 1914, and after a series of fortunate and skillful evasions, succeeded in escaping from a combined Anglo-French force that included a number of battleships and armored cruisers, and was headed by the three British battle cruisers *Indefatigable, Inflexible,* and *Indomitable*. She entered the Dardanelles on August 10, 1914. For the next four years she shelled and was shelled, operated against and fled from the Russian Dreadnoughts in the Black Sea, was bombed (the first capital ship to be subjected to air attack), and struck five mines. All this time she operated under the Turkish flag; and at the end of the war, while her sister ship was surrendered and was scuttled at Scapa, Turkey was allowed to retain the renamed *Yavuz Sultan Selim*. The French refitted her in the 1920's, and she was again modernized in 1938. She survived in the Turkish Navy until a few years ago, trim and spruce as ever, the pride of the service; and by a wide margin the longest-lived Dreadnought.

A somewhat enlarged version of the *Moltke* class, the *Seydlitz,* was included in the German program for 1910 and was completed within a year of the outbreak of war. Apart from the *Lützow,* which went down, she

Momentous artillery: the guns of the battle cruiser
Goeben (45). *Imperial War Museum*

suffered more hits from heavy shells at Jutland than any other Dreadnought,
the total being estimated at twenty-four. She was flooded to the middle
deck forward, torpedoed, and lost all her forebridge personnel. Two of her
turrets were burned out entirely, and at one stage or another all her main
armament was rendered useless. It was scarcely surprising that she was con-
fidently reported by the British to have been sunk. At intervals, in the smoke
and haze and half-light that prevailed during the later stages of the combat,
great tongues of flame could be seen rising from her and illuminating the
hazy sky with a ruddy glow. She was not the most heavily protected German
battle cruiser at Jutland, but the ability of all these ships to survive the
explosive power of British 12-inch, 13.5-inch, and 15-inch shells, and their
unsurpassed buoyancy, is underlined by H. W. Wilson's account of her last
hours of fighting and her safe return:

About 5 P.M. there was so much water in the ship forward that the bows were
almost flush with the sea and the vessel herself heeled over slowly to starboard. She
was badly hit by a big shell forward, on the port side, which made a huge hole,

Jutland survivor: after suffering some two dozen
heavy shell hits, and a torpedo, *Seydlitz* miraculously
crawled home to the Jade (46). *Imperial War
Museum*

and once more the water poured in. At 7.30 she sustained two bad hits, one on her
fourth turret and the other on her bridge, which killed all the officers and men
there and wounded several of the officers in the conning tower. Owing to the
damage by shells and the amount of blood in the conning tower the charts by
which the ship was being worked were rendered useless and illegible. The
reserve charts were in a compartment which was flooded and could not be
reached; the gyro compass broke down. Because of these troubles the ship ran
ashore at 1.40 A.M. of June 1, east of the North Buoy at Horn Reef. She was
able, however, to get off with the pull of her screws which were in deep water.

At 4.40 her draught had increased to 43 feet and the bulkheads threatened to
give way. Bucket gangs had to be employed to keep vital compartments from
being flooded. Though piloted by the *Pillau* and by German light craft, she ran
aground a second time near Horn Reef at 8 A.M. of June 1. She was got off
once more after considerable delay, but at 1.30 P.M. her position became critical.
She had to go astern to save her bulkheads and the sea and wind had risen suddenly.
An attempt by the *Pillau* to tow her off failed. Not till June 2 with the aid of

two salvage pump steamers did she reach the secure shelter of the Jade, after being for hours at the mercy of the British Fleet—if it had only closed Horn Reef.*

The final stage of German First World War battle-cruiser development was represented by the *Derfflinger*, *Lützow*, and *Hindenburg*, laid down in 1912 and 1913, the last of which was completed too late for Jutland. In these 26,000-ton vessels, German naval architects at last eschewed the beam turret, and their eight 12-inch 50-caliber guns were all on the center line, in the manner of the American *Michigan*. For 26-knot battle cruisers (over 28 knots when this was required), the actual weight of armor plate was considerably higher than in all but the latest British battleships, and their underwater protection even more comprehensive and elaborate than their predecessors'. The *Derfflinger* suffered 157 killed, and took almost as much punishment as the *Seydlitz* at Jutland; and with the *Hindenburg* went down finally under more humiliating circumstances than the *Lützow* in Scapa Flow.

So far in the battle-cruiser race Britain was winning hands down in numbers, but in the quality of the material Germany retained a handsome lead. The German naval authorities were not aware of the extent of the superiority of their force, and suffered a good deal of criticism for being one step behind in gun caliber—11-inch against 12-inch in the battle cruisers, 12-inch against 13.5-inch, then 15-inch, in the battleships. There was little popular disquiet in Britain; indeed, the public were in their usual state of euphoria. Writers in the technical journals, however, still expressed dismay at the dearth of armor, and at this class of vessel generally. A number of British naval architects were among these critics. They knew that the Board's policy in restricting the displacement of the first six battle cruisers was dangerous. High speed, they knew, demands size—if guns and armor plate are to be

* *Battleships in Action*, Vol. II, by H. W. Wilson (1926).

Captive *Hindenburg:* the last of the First World War battle cruisers at Scapa Flow in 1919. She went down a few weeks later. Behind her is the *Derfflinger* (see page 152) (47). *Imperial War Museum*

In its time the most formidable battle cruiser in the
world, the British-built *Kongo* as she appeared in her
early days before a searchlight tower was added between
her first and second funnels. The Imperial Japanese Navy
was the last to discard torpedo nets (54). *U.S. Navy*

carried on any sort of a scale. Vast boiler and engine rooms demand length.
Length demands more armor. Armor again raises tonnage. The trouble was
that very high speed—and that meant well over the 25 knots of the *Moltke*—
upset all the accepted compromise balance in heavy-warship design; and the
cries of those who demanded a halt in the tonnage race sounded hollow
indeed in 1911–1912.

The proof of all this was manifested in 1911 in a remarkable vessel of
Japanese overall conception, and British design and construction. In order to
acquire the benefit of the latest developments in British warship construction,
the Japanese Navy Department decided to build abroad the first of a new
class of vessel, although all the most recent Japanese capital ships had been
built in home yards. The *Kongo* was as far in advance of its time, and as
relatively greater in size, as the 1905 semi-Dreadnoughts *Aki* and *Satsuma*.
Her designer, Sir George Thurston, took the only possible step of going
to 27,500 tons; and on this tonnage packed an armament heavier than that

of any other battle cruiser until 1920; protection on a par with the *von der Tann*; and a margin of speed of some 2 knots above the German ship. The details of the *Kongo* caused a sensation. Her 14-inch guns jumped a stage in the caliber competition, even beyond that of the vaunted British 13.5. Compared with the most recently completed British battle cruisers, she showed a wide margin of superiority in both primary and secondary armament, in the disposition of the main battery, and in speed and protection. As we shall see, she was to have almost as checkered and eventful a life as the *Goeben*. Her three sisters, *Hi-ei*, *Haruna*, and *Kirishima* (the hundredth Dreadnought to be launched), were all built in Japanese yards, and provided together a most powerful and swift wing to the Japanese battle fleet for the next thirty years.

The construction of the *Kongo* by Vickers put the British Board of Admiralty in a most awkward position. If a small, new, and distant power could specify and pay for and build *in Britain* a battle cruiser combining the virtues of speed, strength, and hitting power, then there could be no excuse for continuing with smaller, cheaper, and obviously inferior warships like the

Haruna in her intermediate guise in 1931 before rebuild
(54). *U.S. Navy*

Hi-ei as a training ship in the early 1930's. Note absence
of armor and "Y" turret, removed under naval-treaty
terms. But they were soon in place again, and by 1939 she
had been rebuilt as the most formidable of all the *Kongo*s.
She was also the first to be sunk (54). *U.S. Navy*

Invincible. Nor was the position made easier by the fact that the Board had
recently invested rather over £6,000,000 ($30,000,000) in three more battle
cruisers, whose specifications had been widely heralded and publicized. They
were to be the last word in battle cruisers: 13.5-inch guns, and a tonnage
surpassing by more than four thousand tons the great super-Dreadnoughts
already under construction. The *Kongo*, however, was to be even bigger, her
guns even more powerful.

These three new British battle cruisers were the *Lion, Princess Royal,*
and *Queen Mary.* They represented a welcome if belated improvement in
every respect over the basic design of the *Invincible* family. For the first time
Sir Philip Watts recognized that if an "armored cruiser" was to carry a main
armament almost on a par with that of a battleship, together with a much
superior speed, a satisfactory and suitably protected basic design could be
obtained only by greatly raising the displacement. The first three of the four
"big cats" leaped forward to over 26,000 tons, and the main protective belt
was deeper and longer and about 50 percent thicker than that of the earlier
six battle cruisers. However, over many of their vital parts the plate was only

97

The big cats: *Lion* (below) and *Queen Mary* (above),
the biggest and swiftest British battle cruisers in August,
1914. *Lion*, Beatty's flagship, fought at Heligoland Bight,
and was severely damaged at Dogger Bank and Jutland.
The *Queen Mary* blew up at Jutland, the largest British
ship sunk in this action (18). *Imperial War Museum* and
Richard Perkins

H.M.S. *Tiger:* the biggest and fastest ship at Jutland. As
originally completed in 1914, many thought her the
noblest warship afloat; but here her lines have already
been marred by a mainmast, aircraft flying-off platforms,
and enlarged searchlight structure abaft the third
funnel (19). *Imperial War Museum*

six or four inches, and this was pierced at over 14,000 yards by German 11-inch or 12-inch shells. The general scale of protection, as Parkes has
written, "was very much on the second class scale and unworthy of 26,000-
ton ships"; * it was certainly far below that of the German *Derfflinger*,
which sank the *Queen Mary* with one salvo at Jutland.

Considerable improvements, influenced by the evidence of what the
Japanese could do—and British designers, too, when they were given their
head—were effected in the fourth ship of the class, laid down a year later,
in June, 1912. So many alterations were made that the *Tiger* was classed on
her own. Displacement was again, inevitably, increased, so that the Japanese
could boast the largest capital ship in the world for only a year. Little greater

* *British Battleships*, by Parkes.

Six-inch secondaries: amidships detail of the *Tiger* in
1928, at the end of her life (19). *Richard Perkins*

weight was allotted to armor, but this was more judiciously used; the power
of her turbines was also increased, and at her ultimate speed of 29 knots
they were developing over 100,000 h.p.; and finally, her four center-line twin
13.5-inch turrets were arranged to give a much wider bearing to the third
pair of guns, a handicap which had been much criticized in the *Lion*s. In

fact, superfiring was at last permitted in the Royal Navy, because the lower turret was sufficiently distant to remain undisturbed. Her appearance was much more satisfactory, especially in her early rig, before a stump mast was fitted just forward of the third of her evenly spaced, stately funnels. At her time, she was considered by many to be the most majestic and satisfactory-looking Battle Cruiser afloat. She was unquestionably the best battle cruiser in the Grand Fleet. She was rushed through her last stages of construction, joined Beatty in November, 1914, was too "green" to be of much use at the Dogger Bank, acquitted herself gallantly at Jutland where she survived twenty-one heavy shell hits and suffered sixty-one casualties.

One other very important point about the *Tiger:* she was the first British Dreadnought to mount a secondary armament of 6-inch guns. This was seen by many critics of the whole Dreadnought policy as something of a *volte-face.* From the time when the *Dreadnought*'s armament was first announced in 1905, the inferiority of the secondary battery of British capital ships had been attacked, with little apparent effect. *Dreadnought* herself carried only 12-pounders, scattered all over her, even on the turret tops, to deal with torpedo attack. This was a typical piece of Fisher extremism, and in subsequent classes, both of battleships and battle cruisers, the gun had been replaced by the new quick-firing 4-inch with its 100 percent heavier shell. Still, a lot of people remained dissatisfied. The less-perceptive critics thought that battles might still be fought at close range, particularly in the misty North Sea, and that "the hail of fire" from smaller guns would still count in future combats. There were others who thought more deeply about the problem of secondary armament, and recognized the threat of the ever-increasing range of the torpedo and the ever-increasing size of the torpedo-boat destroyer. By 1911 German destroyers, at some 650 tons, were four times larger than the torpedo boats she was completing at the turn of the century, and they were approaching 1,000 tons. Twelve-pounders, or even 4-inch guns, would be of little avail against a determined mass attack by destroyers of this size; and to deal with them with the slow-firing, slow-to-train main armament would be like "trying to destroy a couple of alien anarchists with 13.5 or 14-inch guns," as one Member of the Institute of Naval Architects put it; and continued: "The Japanese and Germans have long since seen the folly of putting in these little 4-inch guns, and, though our officers tell us they are sufficient to repel torpedo attacks, I do not believe that is so. We want our 6-inch guns back. . . ." * Mr. Hills could, in fact, have put the case more strongly. The Americans had begun their Dreadnought building with 3-inch, and then gone straight to 5-inch; the French had jumped straight to 5.5-inch; the Italians had built four ships with 4.7's, then increased to 6-inch; and the Japanese and the Germans had never installed any caliber smaller than 5.9 inches in their Dreadnoughts.

* Arnold Hills at the Spring Meeting of the I.N.A., 1911.

With the *Tiger* it appeared that the Board of Admiralty had at last faced reality; and certainly all subsequent British battleships were to carry a 6-inch or 5.25-inch secondary armament. But the *Tiger* for all her life remained as the only British battle cruiser capable of dealing with the largest destroyers at a useful range. When Fisher came back to the Admiralty in 1914, he saw to it that future battle cruisers reverted to a lighter secondary battery.

These new Fisher ships must be considered later, as a postscript to the real battle-cruiser period. This lasted from 1906, with the laying of the *Invincible*'s keel, to July, 1913, when the *Hindenburg* began life at Wilhelmshaven. No one knew it then, but the race was over; the score: Great Britain, 10; Germany, 7; Japan, 4; with America a notable, and wise, abstainer. From this time on, the shape, and meaning, of the type lost its definition. No longer was it to be "a Dreadnought that sacrifices gunpower and armor for the sake of great speed"—although German sacrifices from the beginning had been minimal. Where wise counsels prevailed, speed was to be gained only by ever-greater size, and there was to be no sacrifice for it. There were only to be fast big battleships, and slower smaller battleships. More great battle cruisers, some of such a size that the *Tiger* would have looked puny beside them, were to be laid down; some were even completed, and strange men-of-war they were. . . . But the real battle cruiser died at Jutland, with four of her kind and three of her armored-cruiser predecessors.

The battle cruiser was a curious, anomalous ship. No one quite knew what it was for, least of all Hipper and Beatty. It may have been mistakenly conceived; but it was the very embodiment of grandeur, pace, and power, and so caught men's imaginations that the name was never lost, however the ships' functions and design were changed. The battle cruiser spanned the whole Dreadnought era. The first was begun five days before the *Dreadnought* was launched; the last, the U.S.S. *Guam*, was not laid down until two months after Pearl Harbor. Throughout the period, thirty in all were built. Almost every one saw strenuous action, in the North Sea, the Mediterranean, the South and North Atlantic, the Indian Ocean, the China Sea, and the Pacific. Thirteen were sunk in combat, making a rate of destruction of rather more than 43 percent, or four times the rate of battleship destruction. Not a bad record for a deviate.

CHAPTER 5

Greater-Than-Ever Guns

In the last months of 1912 a new class of battleship was laid down in the United States at Quincy, Massachusetts, and Camden, New Jersey, which was to have a most profound and lasting influence on capital-ship design all over the world. The ships were the *Oklahoma* and *Nevada*, America's first Second Generation Dreadnoughts. They can be considered as the genesis of a family of ten more American battleships, and the family tree of every "Third Generation" capital ship can be traced back to them.

Since the earliest days of the ironclad in the 1860's, a number of theoretical wars had raged between various principles of design and degrees of compromise, between the value of the offensive and defensive, between various forms of propulsion (sail had fought bitterly to the end), between different types of gun. In very few cases was a conclusion reached, because there were very few battles. Deductions had to be drawn from the most tenuous evidence, on maneuvers, and even from accidents. For example, the ram was dropped only when it became disastrously evident that it was a greater threat to friends in peace than it was likely to be to enemies in war. Even from the few battles fought, the lessons were confused, contradictory, and mostly erroneous. The misguided belief about the deadly "hail of fire" has already been mentioned. Another so-called lesson from the Russo-Japanese War was that, after all, the torpedo was no real threat. But during the first fifty years of life of the armored ship of the line, the most violent theoretical hostilities of all had raged between the gun and armor. In the 1870's and 1880's especially, increases in the strength and resistance of armor plate, in the power of the high-explosive shell, and variations in the importance attached to speed, protection, and hitting power, all brought about fundamental changes in the shape and fighting capacity of the battleship, and in the degree of emphasis designers gave to guns and armor. At one stage in the guns versus armor contest the caliber of the primary weapons rose to 15-inch and 16-inch, and finally to 17.7-inch, a caliber to be exceeded later only by British and Japanese ordnance. To meet the threat of these giant shells, the weight and thickness of armor plate rose accordingly. The power of resistance of armor plate was also constantly increased. On some ships in the 1870's, the weight of armor began to account for a third of the total displacement, and the thickness went up to over 20 inches. Everything was sacrificed to a few big guns in impenetrable citadels; in others the armor was spread out here and there over the most vital parts in order that greater speed, and the ability to evade other battleships, could be obtained. These two grotesque and frightful extremes in men-of-war were very early prototypes of the Dreadnought battleship and battle cruiser of forty years later.

Battleships of the 1870's mounting the heaviest possible guns behind the thickest possible armor plate over vital areas were referred to as "all-or-nothing" ships. If you were hit where it mattered, it did not matter; if you were hit where it did not matter, then that did not matter either. That was

First 14-inch-gunned American: Rear-Admiral Hugh
Rodman's flagship *New York* in Scottish waters. The
New York, with the *Wyoming*, *Florida*, and *Delaware*,
later joined by the *Texas*, formed the Grand Fleet's
Sixth Battle Squadron (27). *Imperial War Museum*

the theory. Later, theorists thought that after all it might matter if the
stem, rudder, and propellers were riddled through and through and that the
ship might even sink. Therefore design principles went back again to the
earlier compromise arrangement of a bit of armor here and there where it
was especially important. This prevailed until 1912. In that year the design
staff of the American Bureau of Construction persuaded the Department
of the Navy of the benefits to be gained by returning again to "all-or-

nothing" principles. The *Oklahoma* and *Nevada* were therefore equipped with a single deep 13½-inch belt extending over the machinery, magazines, turret bases, conning tower, and funnel base; a thinner belt of some 8 inches over the propeller shafts, and so on, up to 18 inches on the turrets; and 3 inches on the deck. The secondary battery and large areas of the hull and upper works remained entirely unprotected. All battleships of all nations built after the First World War imitated this arrangement.

This was not the only formidable feature of the *Oklahoma* and *Nevada*. The 45-caliber 14-inch gun, first installed in the *New York* and *Texas*, was a fine piece of ordnance. In these new ships it was most economically installed in two triple turrets (the first in an American battleship) and two superfiring twin turrets, offering a broadside superior to all but the 15-inch-gunned British and German ships. However, when it became known that the latest class of Japanese battleship, laid down before either the *Oklahoma* or *Nevada*, showed a superiority of broadside amounting to 20 percent, steps were taken in 1913 to increase the gunpower yet again, with a corresponding rise in displacement, for the first time in the United States Navy to over the 30,000-ton mark. The Pacific battleship race, that was soon to dominate the naval scene and was stimulated into momentum by the North Sea contest, was already well under way. The *Pennsylvania* and *Arizona*, carrying twelve 14-inch, were built rapidly, and represented, according to *Fighting Ships* (1919), "one of the most successful, if not the most successful, of all Dreadnought designs up to the present time." The similar *New Mexico*, *Idaho*, and *Mississippi* of the 1914 program were followed by the *California* and *Tennessee;* and in 1916 authorization was given to yet another group, this time

Contempories and allies: H.M.S. *Marlborough* (right) and U.S.S. *New York*, both launched in 1912, and both carrying almost identical armament, at Scapa Flow at the end of the First World War (10) (27). *Imperial War Museum*

The United States Navy's first triple turret. Cleaning guns on the *Oklahoma*. She was also the last American Dreadnought to mount 14-inch main armament in a twin turret (28). *U.S. Navy*

Oklahoma and *Nevada* (opposite), the most formidable battleships in the world when completed in the month Jutland was fought. Besides being the first single-funnel American Dreadnoughts, they instituted the principle of "all-or-nothing" armored protection, which was later followed by every navy until the demise of the Dreadnought. *Nevada* is next seen in 1935, after her refit and reconstruction eight years earlier when vast tripods replaced lattice masts, funnel was moved aft, and secondary battery raised from its vulnerable position on the main deck to the forecastle deck. Finally, the same ship is seen transformed yet again for service in the new air age, with her old secondary armament replaced by sixteen paired 5-inch augmented by a multitude of light antiaircraft guns. *Oklahoma* succumbed at Pearl Harbor; *Nevada* survived her serious injuries (28). All *U.S. Navy*

The *Pennsylvania* sails into New York for the 1934
Fleet Review. The theoretical conflict between the big
gun and the airplane is symbolized in this seaplane
photograph of the rebuilt Dreadnought with four aircraft
on her two catapults (29). *U.S. Navy*

armed with eight 16-inch guns in four twin turrets. The last of these was
not completed until the end of 1923, a date that marks the end of the Second
Generation American Dreadnought. Their influence was fundamental; the
twelve vessels produced were not surpassed anywhere until the Third Generation Dreadnoughts of the 1930's and 1940's.

The characteristics of the American Second Generation ships were the
greatest acceptable artillery power mounted on a platform protected, "where
it mattered," by armor plate up to 18 inches thick on the turrets and 16 inches
on the deep belt. These two qualities were obtained at a sacrifice of speed,
contrary to contemporary Japanese practice, the revolutionary *Queen Elizabeth*s of the Royal Navy (about four knots faster), and the robust German
battle cruisers. To deal with the guns first. The twelve 14-inch of the *Pennsylvania, Arizona, New Mexico, Idaho, Mississippi, California,* and *Tennes-*

see offered a broadside weight of 16,800 pounds, compared with the German *Baden*'s 13,200 pounds and the *Queen Elizabeth*'s 15,360 pounds. The turrets in the American ships were roomy and well arranged. In the earlier ships the guns in the triple turrets could be fired together as one piece; in the later ships they were mounted in separate sleeves. Their rate of fire was higher than that of British and even of German heavy ordnance. Three rounds a minute were attainable. "To the foresight and good judgement of the men responsible for our battleships we owe the fact that . . . our gunners will be able to fire from 20 percent to 40 percent more projectiles in a given time than the enemy," reported *Current Literature* as early as July, 1911.

Experimental work on the 45-caliber 16-inch weapon was completed in 1917, just before the first of the *Maryland*s was laid down. The decision to go over to the 16-inch gun had been reached only after prolonged and fierce argument in the Navy Department. It was accepted that the 14-inch shell could pierce anything the 16-inch could pierce up to the gun's maximum range. On the other hand, the muzzle energy of the 16-inch was 100,000 foot-tons, compared with 70,000 of the 14-inch, and the range of the 16-inch at 30 degrees' elevation was some 33,000 yards, or almost 50 percent greater than that of the smaller gun, although this was improved by higher elevation and by the 50-caliber 14-inch in later ships. And of course the 16-inch shell

Destroyed by Japanese naval aircraft at Pearl Harbor in 1941, the *Arizona* here proudly flies the flag of President Herbert Hoover (29). *U.S. Navy*

U.S.S. *Idaho*, still with lattice masts and only rudimentary
aircraft protection, sails from Pearl Harbor. She was
modified before the Japanese attack, but she and her
sisters were absent on December 7, 1941 (30).
U.S. Navy

A year after her completion, the *New Mexico* is taken
through Pedro Miguel Lock, Panama Canal, in 1919.
Main-deck 5-inch casemates are already plated over as a
result of earlier experience (30). *U.S. Navy*

U.S.S. *California* as originally completed. For the first
time in an American Dreadnought, the main deck is clear
of all gunports, and her hull presents a clean line
from stem to stern (31). *U.S. Navy*

U.S.S. *California* after her first mild reconstruction (31).
U.S. Navy

Except for the Japanese *Nagato*, the *Marylands* were first
in the world with the 16-inch gun. This is *Colorado* as
she was completed; and (below) as modernized for war
in the Pacific. Note Japanese shellholes above waterline,
suffered during bombardment of Tinian, July, 1944
(32). *U.S. Navy*

Eight of *Yamashiro*'s 45-caliber 14-inch guns,
seen looking forward from the after superstructure. Note
coal on deck, and state of launch. This photograph was
taken in 1921, six years after her completion (50).
U.S. Navy

was much heavier at 2,100 pounds. However, in 1917 rumors of a British
18-inch, German 17-inch, and Japanese 16-inch were rife, and these settled
the matter. All future American battleships were armed with 16-inch guns.

The 5-inch topedo-defense weapons were mounted mainly in unprotected
casemates on the upper and main decks, the lower ones being removed later
when their limited value was recognized.

The rise in the standard displacement of these twelve vessels from 27,500
tons to over 32,000 tons was accounted for mainly by the improvements in
internal defense and in deck protection. The dangers from plunging fire and
internal explosion (as at Jutland), from submarine attack (the most fearful
preoccupation of fleet commanders in the First World War), and the future
threat of the aerial bomb, were all being increasingly recognized from 1916
to 1920, the years when the last five of these ships were laid down. All twelve
Second Generation battleships were turbine-driven, with oil-fired boilers.
All but the first four were fitted with a unique form of turboelectric drive,

Yamashiro, Fuso (50), and *Kongo* (54) in Tokyo Bay,
about 1936. Simple tripods have been built round with
Oriental skyscrapers, surmounted by 30-foot range
finder. The first two went down in Leyte Gulf.
U.S. Navy

which was highly successful and was developed to a more sophisticated
level later.

Second Generation Dreadnought construction was marked by two main
trends of fundamental importance. The first was the elimination of the lead
in material gained by Germany over Great Britain, which will be dealt with
later in this chapter. The second was the consistency and conservatism of
American policy compared with the daring experimental trend in Japan.
The United States Navy Department, having once found the secret of the
best possible compromise formula in the *Oklahoma* and *Nevada*, stuck to it
for ten years. In Japan the restless, pioneering, experimental spirit prevailed,
to dominate the policy of the Imperial Admiralty.

The First Generation *Kongo* battle cruisers were unquestioned successes.
Following the general decline in the status of the battle cruiser in the years

Ise after first refit in 1930 (above); and *Hiuga* in 1940 as
rebuilt with single funnel and pole mainmast. Three
Type-95 seaplanes and catapult at stern (51). *U.S. Navy,
Imperial War Museum*

immediately before the First World War, Japan next laid down in 1912 and
1913 a pair of most formidable battleships, *Fuso* and *Yamashiro*, carrying
the same number of 14-inch guns as the contemporary American *Pennsylvania* and *Arizona*, but in six center-line turrets. Armor protection on these
first Japanese Second Generation ships was on a slightly less extensive scale
than their American counterparts, but defense against the mine and torpedo
and aerial bomb, for which the Japanese always had the highest regard, was
quite as elaborate. In accordance with one consistent aspect of Japanese policy
from the time of the Russo-Japanese War to the extinction of the fleet in
1944–1945, the speed of these ships, though below that of the British *Queen
Elizabeth*s, was some three knots higher than that of the American battleships of the Second Generation. Their successors, the *Ise* and *Hiuga*, differed

from them mainly by the introduction of superfiring guns amidships. *Fighting Ships* wrote of them:

These ships are an improved and slightly faster *Fuso* type. It is unofficially reported that they are strongly protected against aerial attack by three specially thick protective decks over vital parts of the hull. Special attention is reported to have been paid to the rapid replenishment of fuel, stores, ammunition etc. Usual protection against mine and torpedo explosions by minute subdivision wing bulkheads over machinery and magazine spaces.

The *ne plus ultra* of the Second Generation were the mighty *Nagato* and *Mutsu*, designed just before Jutland and laid down during the last stages of the First World War. Reports reaching Washington of Japanese experiments with a gun even larger than the German and British 15-inch, which brought about the decision to arm the *Maryland*s with 16-inch weapons, were confirmed when details of these two latest Japanese super-Dreadnoughts became publicly known. They can be regarded as the First World War equivalents of the *Yamato* and *Musashi*, and when the *Nagato* was completed in 1920, at the height of American anxiety about the position in the Pacific, she was the only 16-inch-gunned battleship in the world and was exceeded in size only by the British *Hood*. The two ships had a most imposing and intimidating appearance, and looked the very epitome of brute strength and defiance at their maximum speed of 23 knots.

Nagato as completed, the first 16-inch-gunned battleship in the world. Heat, smoke, and fumes affecting bridge personnel caused cowl to be fitted to forefunnel soon after, and she was rarely seen in this simple guise (52).

There were a number of reasons for the general superiority of the German First Generation Dreadnoughts over the British in the crucial years of battleship competition from 1906 to 1912. First of all, German designers were at a great advantage. Their ships were intended for operation mainly in the Baltic and North Seas. Only a minimum provision therefore had to be made for their use as gun platforms in, say, Atlantic or Pacific rollers, while British ships had to remain stable in all locations, circumstances, and conditions. As mentioned earlier, the localized nature of likely German fighting activities also made it possible to economize on the crews' living quarters. If Jutland had been fought in heavy seas, close to the Equator, fifteen hundred miles from the nearest port (conditions which the British battle fleet had to be prepared to meet), the outcome might have been very different.

To the advantage of the German naval architect were a number of less tangible factors. First was the knowledge that the force he was creating was *attacking* the prestige and assumed omnipotence of an arrogant naval power intent on holding maritime initiative; this added zest to his work. Then, he was not encumbered by technical conservatism, and worse, the restraining influence of a hierarchy service weighed down with the burden of tradition. (Paradoxically, this accounted for Fisher's intolerance, and extremism, in itself to be a handicap to British designers.) In Germany small-tube boilers, which contributed so much to the strength and working efficiency of their Dreadnoughts, were accepted with delight by engineer staff. Parsons' efforts to have them accepted in later British battleships were fruitless, even though his words should have been treated as those of a prophet.

British optical-instrument manufacturers had stereoscopic range finders for the Admiralty if the Board had shown interest; and they were making range finders up to thirty feet between lenses for foreign navies when the Board was content with nine feet. British ordnance experts, besides being first with 13.5-inch and 15-inch guns, devised the triple turret, hailed as a great advance in the Russian and Italian ships for which they provided them; but the British Board would not consider them until the 1920's. The service was still mainly without director firing in the Grand Fleet in 1914, still without really effective mines or shells or range finders, or even secure anchorages. Not until 1912 was there even a Naval War Staff to decide and unify policy. "They did not want a special class of officer professing to be more brainy than the rest," wrote Churchill, who was chiefly instrumental in its formation, after a great struggle. At least another year passed before anyone could be trained for staff work. The brains were there, like the technical ability, but neither was given a lead until just before the war broke out, and then only reluctantly—for cleverness was middle class or Bohemian, and engines were for the lower orders.

The criticism of First Generation British Dreadnoughts for their frailty was justified. But the emphasis on speed and gunpower at the expense of protection was only partly caused by an underestimation of the power of the torpedo and mine; it was mainly a calculated policy rooted in Fisher's aggressive spirit. That maritime strategy, when war came, should be dominated on both sides by anxiety and caution was quite beyond his understanding, brilliant prophet though he was in so many spheres; and he never became reconciled to this reality, even though he was an avid advocate of the submarine that was the prime cause of the defensive spirit.

Fortunately for the Royal Navy, after the accession of Arthur "Tug" Wilson to the office of First Sea Lord in January, 1910, other counsels prevailed at the Board, and greater emphasis on protection was to be found in Dreadnought designs worked out over the next two years. The *Orions* of 1909, the first of the super-Dreadnoughts, with their ten center-line 13.5-inch guns, were followed by two similar classes in 1911 and 1912, each of four ships: *King George V, Centurion, Ajax, Audacious*; and *Iron Duke, Benbow, Emperor of India,* and *Marlborough.* The latter class was identifiable from the earlier by having their twin tall funnels of similar thickness, and carrying for the first time a secondary upper-deck battery of 6-inch guns. The *Iron Duke*s showed a number of other minor improvements, but the protection of both was on a similar and, as was to be proved, still inadequate scale. The *Audacious* went down after striking one mine early in the war;

King George V in her final form in 1920. Light pole foremast (the first fitted to a British Dreadnought) has given way to a heavy tripod to accommodate larger bridges and director tower; range clock on after superstructure; bearing dial on "Y" turret; and a pair of antiaircraft guns at the extreme stern (7). *Richard Perkins*

Amidships detail, *Marlborough*. She and her sisters
carried a tripod foremast from the beginning in order to
accommodate weight of director control gear. This
photograph was taken at Falmouth, 1930, shortly before
she went to the breakers (10). *Richard Perkins*

the *Marlborough* had later to haul out of line and limp home from Jutland
after a single torpedo hit.

With his last design as D.N.C., however, Watts at one stroke wiped
out the lead German designers had gained over the previous six years, and
produced the greatest all-round class of battleship ever possessed by the
Royal Navy. They were also the first of Britain's Second Generation Dread-

Jellicoe's flagship, H.M.S. *Iron Duke*, in 1914, with original rig. The only British Dreadnought to serve through two world wars, although German bombs incapacitated her at the beginning of the second and she remained grounded at Scapa Flow (10). *Richard Perkins*

Iron Duke as a gunnery training ship, with "Y" turret removed. Main-deck 6-inch embrasure was plated over soon after construction when it was found the gun could not be worked so close to the water; forward 6-inch were not much better, and impossible to train in any sort of sea (10). *Richard Perkins*

The three phases in the life of the "old lady," H.M.S.
Warspite: (*a*) in balanced and graceful twin-funnel form
in the First World War; (*b*) as reconstructed 1924–1926
with trunked funnels, remodeled bridgework, and
torpedo bulge; (*c*) as entirely rebuilt, 1934–1937, at a
cost of £3,000,000 ($15,000,000), with aircraft hangar
and cranes, tower superstructure, armored deck, new
engines, and greatly increased antiaircraft defense (11).
(*a*) and (*c*) *Imperial War Museum;* (*b*) *Richard Perkins*

noughts. The five ships of the *Queen Elizabeth* class of 1912–1913 represented
almost as great an advance over their immediate predecessors as had the
Dreadnought over the *King Edward VII*'s. The 15-inch gun, the first ever
to be fitted to a battleship, and which fired a shell of 1,920 pounds 35,000
yards, was only part of the story. The real secret of the *Queen Elizabeth*s
was to be found in their *balance* of qualities combined with successful innovation. The 15-inch gun, eight of them offering a broadside weight of
15,360 pounds against the *König's* 10,000 pounds, told its tale at Jutland

Queen Elizabeth at Scapa Flow in 1918, as Admiral Beatty's flagship. She had already fought the Turks and Germans. She was to fight the Germans again and, later, the Italians and Japanese too (11). *Imperial War Museum*

Queen Elizabeth digs in her nose (11). *Imperial War Museum*

Fueling: coaling, 1914 . . .

oiling, 1944. *Imperial War Museum, U.S. Navy*

with its record of damage, especially against Hipper's ships at a range that his could not match. So superior was its weight of shell and hitting power that the midships turret could be sacrificed to greater boiler space; the horsepower doubling that of the *Iron Duke*s: 75,000 instead of 29,000. In spite of a rise in displacement from 25,000 to 27,500, the speed of these new ships had shot up to an unprecedented 25 knots, a pace that was to prove its worth, time and again, in many combats in many oceans in two world wars. But, above all, the quality of the *Queen Elizabeth*s lay in their protection, adequate for the first time. The actual weight of armor was not significantly greater than in the *Iron Duke*s, but it was much more judiciously placed. The main belt was an inch thicker, and considerably deeper; the deck thicker amidships where it mattered, thinner forward and aft; the torpedo bulkheads much longer and thicker. The *Warspite* took a fearful hammering at Jutland from a great part of the main battle fleet, but remained a fighting unit to the end. The *Queen Elizabeth*s were full of new ideas, most obvious and most publicized being their oil-fired boilers, the first in any Dreadnought, and an advantage the Germans dared not follow because of the uncertainty of their oil supplies. Coaling was a prolonged, wasteful, and backbreaking task; and oil fuel at once offered greater economy, efficiency, and range.

Within a month of the laying down of the last of the *Queen Elizabeth*s the first of five more 15-inch-gunned battleships was laid down by Britain in order to drive home to Germany the futility of attempting to keep up with Britannia. The *Revenge* class of 1913–1914 (*Revenge, Ramillies, Resolution, Royal Oak,* and *Royal Sovereign,* or the "R's") were the last battleships to be built by Britain until after the war. They were slightly more robust, and considerably slower versions of the *Queen Elizabeth*s, carrying

Stately as a lion, enduring as the empire . . . The "R"s fought at Jutland, and saved many a convoy from annihilation in the Second World War. This is *Resolution* (12).

Full helm: *Royal Oak* on exercises, First World War
(12). *Imperial War Museum*

the same all-center-line armament of eight 15-inch guns, and a secondary
main-deck battery of 6-inch guns. Because of their slower speed (in a moment
of panic about oil, coal was at first specified, but Fisher stopped all that
when he returned to power), they were always rated below the earlier
vessels, and they were not treated to the expensive and elaborate reconstruction enjoyed by the *Queen Elizabeth*s; but they did sterling service in both
wars, in the Second mainly on convoy duties against German surface ships,
and on shore bombardment.

At the time when British ordnance factories were carrying out first experiments with the 15-inch, part of the vast resources of Krupps was being
devoted to the development of a gun of similar caliber that would wipe
out the caliber advantage held by the British since the *Dreadnought*. The
Krupp 15-inch gun, first fitted in the *Baden* and *Bayern*—Germany's only
Second Generation Dreadnoughts, and her last full-size battleships until
the *Tirpitz* and *Bismarck* of the Second World War—had its origins in a

Baden (above) and *Bayern*, first and only German
Second Generation Dreadnoughts, and last battleships to
join the High Seas Fleet. They have British-type tripod

decision reached by the German Admiralty on January 6, 1912. Krupps
was carrying out test firing about two years later, the new weapon hurling
an armor-piercing shell weighing 1,653 pounds, with a muzzle velocity of
about 2,300 feet per second, a distance of 22,200 yards at an elevation of
sixteen degrees—the maximum given to all German heavy ordnance at this
time. With an experienced, well-coordinated crew, the gun could be fired
at a rate of just over two rounds per minute. In range, penetrating power,
and weight of shell the German weapon was inferior to the British, in contrast
with the evident superiority of the German 12-inch gun. Neither the *Baden*
nor *Bayern* was ready for Jutland. The 15-inch fitted to the *Tirpitz* and
Bismarck was a very different and very much more formidable piece. The
British 15-inch was little modified, however, and continued in service use
longer than any other heavy ordnance, from 1914 to 1960.

foremast and the same main armament as *Queen Elizabeth*s and "R"s, with 22-pounder antiaircraft guns by the second funnel (41). *Imperial War Museum*

Both the German "biggest-ever" gun, and the platform on which to mount it, were conceived at the same time as the British. British expenditure, and superior shipbuilding resources, resulted in more than a dozen 15-inch-gunned ships joining the fleet before the Germans received their first, and only, two. The *Baden* and *Bayern* were good, worthy ships, as solidly constructed as their predecessors, and they would have been tough adversaries. But the margin of German superiority over the British had disappeared to nothing long before they were ready; and in ship-to-ship combat with one of the "R's," only good luck and a superior crew could have caused a conclusion. Their coal-firing and slow speed made them notably inferior to the *Queen Elizabeth*s.

On August 4, 1914, the great Anglo-German Dreadnought race, as a spectacle, was over. New Dreadnoughts would join the fleets; others would be laid down. But this was how the world saw the finish before the cloak of security fell over the shipyards, and the gray strip of sea between Britain and Germany:

GREAT BRITAIN	GERMANY
Dreadnought	Nassau
	Westfalen
Bellerophon	Posen
Téméraire	Rheinland
Superb	(all twelve 11-inch guns)
St. Vincent	Helgoland
Collingwood	Thüringen
Vanguard	Ostfriesland
	Oldenburg
Neptune	(all twelve 12-inch guns)
Colossus	
Hercules	Kaiser
(all ten 12-inch guns)	Friedrich der Grosse
	Kaiserin
Orion	Prinzregent Luitpold
Conqueror	König Albert
Thunderer	
Monarch	König *
	Markgraf *
King George V	Grosser Kurfürst *
Centurion	Kronprinz
Ajax	(all ten 12-inch guns)
Audacious	
Iron Duke	BATTLE CRUISERS
Emperor of India *	
Benbow *	von der Tann
Marlborough	(eight 11-inch)
(all ten 13.5-inch guns)	Moltke
	Goeben
BATTLE CRUISERS	Seydlitz
	(all ten 11-inch)
Invincible	
Inflexible	Derfflinger *
Indomitable	(eight 12-inch)
Indefatigable	
New Zealand	
Australia	
(all eight 12-inch guns)	
Lion	
Princess Royal	
Queen Mary	
Tiger *	
(all eight 13.5-inch guns)	

* Indicates completed before the end of 1914.

Two further Dreadnought battleships, mounting 12-inch and 13.5-inch guns, and ordered by foreign governments from British yards, were taken over and added to the Royal Navy in 1914. Both sides included a number of pre-Dreadnoughts in their first-line fleets. One German and four British battle cruisers were stationed outside home waters.

CHAPTER 6

The Dreadnought
at War

But timorous mortals start and shrink
To cross the narrow sea,
And linger shivering on the brink,
And fear to launch away.

—Isaac Watts

So this is the Dreadnought in 1914 on the eve of its greatest opportunity and testing time: in size greater than ever before, its guns more powerful and numerous than ever before, armor plating thicker than ever, more complex subdivision and compartmentation and damage control in case of a hit. Surely, it would seem, here was the magnificent supreme arbiter of the seas, manned by skilled crews hot for combat. Instead, the North Sea, for so long viewed as the future arena for furious hostilities between massed leviathans, quickly emptied of all but scurrying flotillas, the occasional light cruiser or mine-layer zigzagging at high speed, the sudden white trail of periscope or torpedo; while the battle fleets searched restlessly and distantly for a place of safety or lay peacefully at anchor, secure behind nets and booms and minefields. Everywhere there was a sense of disappointment and anticlimax. Only a handful of visionaries had recognized this state of affairs as the inevitable consequence of the nature of the Dreadnought herself. She was a victim of the gospel of fear that had been preached about her for so long.

Since *La Gloire* and the *Warrior* of the 1860's, science had brought about a fundamental change in the nature of the fighting vessel. From the moment the first iron sheathing was fitted to the hull of the ship of the line, considerations of defense had more and more dominated the policies of those who designed, manned, and formed the strategy of the fleet. With every increase in the power of the high-explosive shell, with the coming of the automatic torpedo, the mine, the torpedo boat, the submarine, and the size and cost of the ship itself, its preservation overcame all other considerations. And then the all-big-gun ship arrived, seemingly the epitome of aggression and defiance.

But never was there a more pathetic misnomer than *Dreadnought*. With her coming, the battleship's ability to intimidate reached an unprecedented level. Her appearance was deliberately contrived to instill fear in the enemy, from her broad underwater snout—intended to simulate the long-discarded ram—to her low, fine-pointed stern. Guns became bigger, longer, more frightful in their power. Figures of shells' penetrating power at ten miles were bandied about, the effects of lyddite and shrapnel widely proclaimed. But fear is a double-edged weapon, and evidence of precautions was all about those who served in the Dreadnought fleets: everywhere the hardened-steel armor plate, the bulkheads and flooding controls, the dozen or more smaller

The meaning of maritime power, 1914–1918: The Grand Fleet sails . . .

guns to fight off the torpedo boats, the great steel torpedo-protection nets that were swung out all round the ship when she was at anchor.

The 15-inch shell, the mine, the torpedo boat, the destroyer, the new long-range submarine—against these fearful threats the precious super-Dreadnought had to be defended at all costs, with profound effects on strategy and tactics. This emphasis on *defense* over so many years, becoming stronger as the gospel of fear was preached ever more loudly by both sides, also had a fundamental effect on the spirit of the men and their commanders, from the captain of a destroyer (now no longer purely a vessel of attack but also a *defender* of the battle fleet against enemy flotillas) to the commander in chief himself. In the days of sail and solid shot nobody thought of defending themselves or their ships. You attacked, and sometimes—but rarely—fled. But you did not defend.

At some stage in its life, usually just after it was built and by a politician anxious to justify to the taxpayer its cost, each Dreadnought was described as "unsinkable." It was a part of the Dreadnought jargon. Unsinkable? Who ever ascribed this negative quality to Nelson's *Victory* or John Paul Jones's *Ranger?* Certainly not those who sailed and fought in them. They did not give the matter a passing thought. They had nought to dread—or if they had, there was nothing much they could do about it. They were interested only in killing and sinking. They were innocent, simple warriors, not the victims of propaganda machines that ground out reassurance and defiance so loudly that everyone from Ingenohl and Jellicoe to Ordinary Seaman Jones and Schmidt, with the best intentions in the world, could think only of preservation—ship preservation, self-preservation.

Both sides wanted to sink the enemy. Victory at sea was aspired to as keenly as it was in the Napoleonic and Dutch wars. But science had wrought

... the High Seas Fleet surrenders. *Imperial War Museum*

such weapons of destruction that the delicate balance, and the means to achieve this victory, could be destroyed in seconds with a few well-aimed salvos or torpedoes. No one could forget the lucky—or accurate—shot that had killed Admiral Witthoft and his flagship's helmsman, or the mines that in one day had reduced Japan's battle fleet by a third. Both supreme commanders were selected for their steadiness, were tightly controlled through new means of communication by their Admiralties, and were never allowed to forget the fearful burden of responsibility they carried.

There were other reasons for caution, on both sides. The Germans had for long been deeply conscious of three handicaps: first of all their weak geographical position in which they could so easily be "locked in" to the Baltic and their own coastline by a superior blockading force; second, the tradition of invincibility of the British fleet, which seemed to be confirmed by the apparent German inferiority in material and undoubted inferiority in numbers; and, third, their accepted secondary role to the army, which was much larger, got far more money and attention, and was still buoyed up by the triumphs of 1870. The German Navy was without tradition.

A further very strong psychological handicap had been written in almost as a clause in the Navy's constitution long before it ever became a powerful force. ". . . it is not absolutely necessary that the German battle fleet should be as strong as the greatest naval power," ran one sentence in the explanatory Memorandum to the 1900 Navy Act; and later, "But even if it should succeed in meeting us with considerable superiority of strength, the defeat of a strong German fleet would so substantially weaken the enemy that, in spite of victory . . ." Thus was a sort of Pyrrhic principle established more than fourteen years before hostilities were opened. It is scarcely surprising that, in the words of Tirpitz, ". . . many of our senior officers . . . were

Fear of mines . . . *Queen Elizabeth* swings out paravanes
. . . and effect of mines . . . *Bayern* in drydock.
Imperial War Museum

too modest in their judgements of themselves and of our young navy." *
These same senior officers, and many junior officers and men, too, had their
self-confidence further undermined by the sharp losses and defeats the High
Seas Fleet suffered at the Heligoland Bight and Dogger Bank actions: after
which their timorous commander in chief was sacked for being too bold.

If there was no element of defeatism written into British policy, un-Nelson-
ian caution was evident in a momentous strategical decision reached in 1912, and
a tactical decision reached shortly after the war began. The first of these
was the replacement of a policy of close blockade (with the battle fleet
hovering offshore as in the Napoleonic campaigns) with an "observational
blockade" enforced by light craft or armed merchantmen in the center of
the North Sea, while the Dreadnoughts enforced invisible pressure more
distantly still, and beyond the threat of the torpedo boat and submarine. The
second decision was contained in Jellicoe's historic letter to the Board dated
October 30, 1914, in which he stated that it was his resolve to engage the
enemy only in the northern part of the North Sea close to British bases. As it
happened, the Grand Fleet soon discovered that the range of German submarines was much greater than was thought possible, that even distant
Scapa Flow was not safe against them. While defenses were being prepared,
Jellicoe had to withdraw even farther to Irish bases, and doing so lost the
Audacious, an exceedingly valuable super-Dreadnought, when it struck a
mine. This blow, added to torpedo losses in the North Sea (including three
armored cruisers in one day from one submarine), all helped to bring about
an infection of periscope-and-mine fever that the Grand Fleet never threw
off for the rest of the war.

In the first months of the war a policy of cautious defense was more
forgivable in the British than in the German fleet, which, had it only recognized its superiority in material and training, might have achieved decisive
victory in a classic gunnery duel. All Ingenohl needed was a fair measure
of luck, which has always played such a large part in naval warfare. At one
stage, when four battle cruisers (including the *Australia*) were pursuing von
Spee, the Germans possessed in the North Sea an actual superiority in this
class of Dreadnought; and in January, 1915, allowing for British vessels
refitting or not yet worked up, Jellicoe's superiority in battleships was down
to one. But the High Seas Fleet was never again to find itself on such favorable
terms. Over the next months the benefits of the huge building programs of
1911 and 1912 were felt, until at Jutland the ratio was 28:16 in battleships
and 9:5 in battle cruisers in favor of the British.

Before glancing at the activities of the Dreadnought in the First World
War, it is worth summarizing briefly the development of the torpedo that
was the main cause of the defensive role the battle fleets adopted in the

* *My Memoirs.*

First World War, and the main cause of any doubts about the supremacy of the battleship as the supreme naval weapon.

From the first years of the Whitehead torpedo in the 1870's this weapon caught the imaginations of many people, and engaged the interest of admiralties everywhere. Here, it seemed, might be the "leveler," a cheap, easily constructed instrument of destruction that could render the big gun and its expensive and complicated platform obsolete. The smallest navies bought them, and acquired their carriers, the torpedo boat. But the torpedo's range and efficiency remained limited, and as late as the Russo-Japanese War it could reasonably be argued that its use was limited to narrow and coastal waters against a careless enemy. Nevertheless, battleships were fitted with special underwater protection and numerous quick-firing guns to ward off the torpedo boat. Nets weighing hundreds of tons were hung out when the big ships were at anchor, and even sometimes when they were at sea. The torpedo's new carrier, the submersible, was again too slow, unreliable, and limited in range to cause grave anxieties, and experience in the Far East war seemed to support the big-ship advocates. Only a few radical theorists thought that the torpedo was likely to do more than mildly restrict the role of the battle fleet.

But from 1905 torpedo development was much more rapid. In the same month that the *Dreadnought* was launched, a report was given wide publicity that "from America comes word of a new engine of warfare, which, it is claimed, will further the interests of international peace—by being more destructive than the Whitehead torpedo. It is known as the Bliss-Leavitt turbine torpedo, and the authorities of the United States Navy think so well of it that they have decided to adopt it." * The Bliss-Leavitt was claimed to travel eight to ten knots faster than the current American torpedo, have twice the range, carry a charge of 132 pounds of wet guncotton, and be propelled by a 130-h.p. turbine engine. At the same time British torpedoes were increasing in size from 18-inch to 21-inch, and by the Hardcastle-Elswick heater, which eliminated cold from the compressed air, and ran its trials at the same time as the *Dreadnought*, were given a speed of 45 knots over short ranges, and a maximum range of 7,000 yards. The German 19.7-inch Schwartzkopf was equally powerful, and a great deal more reliable.

The doubts were still not widespread, and while the torpedo was accepted as a highly potent weapon the main trend of policy everywhere was "to keep the battleship away from it"—in distant bases, and at sea screened by flotillas of protecting destroyers. But there was also a good deal of confused thinking. The Germans believed in the mine; and so did the Russians, who had always been good at making them. Except for a handful of enthusiasts, neither the Germans nor the British, nor the Americans for that matter, had much confidence in the submarine except as a defensive vessel

* *Illustrated London News*, February 24, 1906.

or for local offensive operation. This is what Hovgaard had to say in *Fighting Ships* in 1910: "Mines have their field of use near ports, at the estuaries of rivers, and in narrow sounds and water . . . but they cannot greatly influence the operations of battleships in the open sea." Then again, "It is difficult to see how torpedo boats can, in general, have any prospect of successful attack even in night time against battleships in intact condition, properly prepared and properly protected by destroyers and cruisers." Yet only two years later, in the same annual, this highly influential authority was writing, "The improvements which have been effected in torpedoes both with regard to their speed, their charge, and their range of action have rendered this means of attack more and more dangerous, and still more so if one also takes into consideration the improvements that have been effected in the means of launching them whether from destroyers, torpedo boats, or submarines." It was, Hovgaard emphasized, absolutely necessary to employ "some thousands of tons of the displacement of a vessel worth some three millions sterling to guarantee it against the attacks of an arm of the value of some £500 sterling launched from a vessel costing hardly 50 thousand." And yet "the greater number of experts in warship architecture resolutely shut their eyes to a serious examination of the danger of underwater attack."

It was easy enough to discount the extremist fringe who sometimes were given a hearing and loudly proclaimed that the Dreadnought was finished. These advocates existed in all the great naval nations, and were not listened to very seriously. It was more difficult to disregard some of the wiser old admirals, progressive theorists, men like Hovgaard, magazines like the *Scientific American*, which kept a remarkably level head throughout all the Dreadnought's vicissitudes right down to the Second World War. In July, 1913, there appeared in that magazine a leader that combined a just and balanced judgment of the situation, and a prophetic glimpse into the future. "At the present stage of the development of naval warfare," it ran, "the battleship is supreme, or to speak more conservatively, it is believed to be supreme. . . . Now, although the general proposition is that a naval war can only be won by the destroyer of the enemy's battle fleet is undoubtedly correct, it is not equally certain that battleships can only be destroyed by battleships. So great has been the development of the newer means of attack, notably by the aeroplane and the dirigible, that the question arises as to whether the final outcome of a naval campaign lies so completely with the battle fleet as it is commonly believed." There was the well-understood menace of the destroyer. The submarine was "safe, seaworthy, accurate and capable of thorough control. And now comes Rear-Admiral Fiske with his bold proposal to substitute the 50 mph aeroplane for the 15 knot submarine. . . ."

But of course it was not in the nature of things to consider seriously even reducing the status of the battle fleet, especially at this late date. It was in no one's interests, certainly not in the vested interests of officers, politicians, or armament combines. The Dreadnought was to suffer again and again the attacks of the theorists, right up to its final demise. But it was secure enough in August, 1914, from the theorists and the enemy's artillery. Who could have believed that in four and a half years of the most frightful war the world had known not one Dreadnought battleship was to be sunk by the guns of another?

German maritime policy was based on the piecemeal reduction of British Dreadnought superiority by torpedo, mine, and gun action when favorable (that is, overwhelming in gunpower) circumstances occurred or could be arranged. Minefields were laid at once, and were both destructive and restricting. U-boats were dispatched far out into the North Sea, and to the surprise of the Germans as well as the British, did a lot of material and morale damage. Attempts were made to attack British light naval detachments with superior forces; but after the Heligoland Bight debacle, in which British battle cruisers intervened and created havoc among the German light forces, greater caution was ordered by the Kaiser. Other German naval forces gained, and held for most of the war, control of the Baltic, and caused great worry in distant oceans by sinking British merchantmen. It was all very courteously conducted. Officers gave up their berths to rescued enemy prisoners. U-boat and surface raider captains asked everyone to get off before they opened fire, and usually made sure those in the open boats knew where to go and had plenty of food and water. Good manners prevailed until unrestricted U-boat warfare developed later.

Cruisers in distant parts were hard to round up, and diverted, as they have always done, a quite disproportionate number of more powerful vessels in their pursuit. Stupidity at the British Admiralty caused a rather foolish admiral, driven on by old-fashioned notions of courage and self-immolation, to take a weak force of cruisers against Count von Spee's highly efficient and self-confident cruiser squadron. He met them at dusk off Chile. It was cold and windy, and his two ships were outlined against the setting sun. Von Spee's gunners, the best in a service with a very high standard, carried out some deadly target practice. The result was a nasty blow to British pride. By then Fisher had taken over at the Admiralty, and enjoyed himself hugely by sending off at great speed, and at considerable risk, two of his favorite battle cruisers to the South Atlantic. The day after their arrival in the Falkland Islands, by an extraordinary piece of good fortune, was the time von Spee had rashly decided to raid Port Stanley. He turned tail and fled. The *Invincible* and *Inflexible* finished coaling, got up steam, and began to pursue two distant flecks of smoke on the horizon. The sky was clear and there was plenty of time. It might have been a set-piece demonstration, laid on by Fisher, to convince his critics of the merits of the battle cruiser. The German ships could not escape; their guns were inadequate. Two of the best armored cruisers in the German Navy were slowly reduced, at long range, to riddled wrecks. Two more cruisers were also dealt with, and a third escaped.

Nearer home the German Navy suffered further defeat. Taking advantage of the distance of enemy Dreadnought bases, hit-and-run shelling raids against British east-coast towns had been authorized. They caused dismay and outrage, and strong countermeasures were demanded. These would have been more difficult to accomplish if the Germans had not been so free with their use of wireless, and the Russian Navy had not discovered the German code in a sunk German cruiser, and passed it over to the British Admiralty. It proved useful for years, and in part accounted for the greatly superior British intelligence. Beatty was given detailed particulars of a German east-coast raid to take place on the night of January 23–24, intercepted Hipper's battle cruisers, and chased them. The first Dreadnought engagement followed, with the *Lion, Tiger, Princess Royal, New Zealand,* and *Indomitable* opening fire at extreme range and at high speed at the *Seydlitz, Derfflinger,* and *Moltke,* the armored cruiser *Blücher,* a stop-gap reinforcement for Hipper, holding on as best she could at the rear. Smoke, the threat of mine-dropping and of torpedo attack, confusion over signals, and serious damage to Beatty's *Lion* all hampered the pursuit, and the only German casualty was the *Blücher,* which Hipper wisely left to its fate. The tremendous punishment inflicted on the *Blücher* before she finally succumbed confirmed what had been observed at the Falkland Islands: the sturdy construction and efficient buoyancy and damage control even of the German pre-Dreadnought ships. The rapidity and accuracy and speed of the German gunners in getting onto the target, which had been witnessed in earlier engagements, was also confirmed, particularly by those in the *Lion* and *Tiger.* Lessons from the engagement were taken to heart by both sides, but especially by the Germans, who fitted precautions to prevent the passing of flash from a hit on the turret to the magazine, and improved range finders. Beatty was furious that he had not sunk more than one ship, but a photograph of the *Blücher* going down, with her crew scrambling down her side, greatly cheered British newspaper readers.

There was not another big-ship engagement for fifteen months. The Germans expected an all-out attack by the British battle fleet, and had no intention of carrying one out themselves.

The British blockade operated from the first day of the war. The Grand Fleet might be without a suitable base (a further price of Fisher's arithmetical obsession), and be in a highly nervous condition far from the scene of possible action, but it was—and remained for the entire war—the concealed source of strength which made the blockade of Germany operable. Very few German merchantmen got through, except from Scandinavia. Those on the high seas which escaped ran for neutral ports. The blockade did not have much effect at first. Germany imported little or no food. But she had also made the mistake of failing to stockpile raw materials, and she later took so many men from the land that she no longer produced enough food

for her own needs. The blockade was referred to as "throttling." It did not
cause great difficulty at first, but it did later. Some neutrals, especially the
Americans, were upset because they could no longer export to Germany.
Trade with Britain remained, for the present, almost uninterrupted.

Once Scapa Flow had been made secure against submarine attack, the
main body of the Grand Fleet (the battle cruisers were normally anchored
farther south) remained there for most of the war. Individual battleships
went away to refit; other new ones arrived; there were "sweeps" from time
to time between the North Sea minefields; and gunnery practice was oc-
casionally indulged in. Otherwise, apart from the daily routine on board
ship and periodical leave, boredom in this barren, dull, godforsaken strip
of water was the main enemy. The British expected an all-out attack by the
German battle fleet, and had no opportunity of carrying one out themselves.

The two main battle fleets saw each other only once during the war, for
no more than a few scattered minutes between banks of mist, and smoke
from dozens of funnels and from burning wrecks. They fired mainly without
effect. Neither commander in chief was anxious to engage the other closely,
nor to fight to a finish. Fear dominated that anonymous stretch of gray water
off the Danish coast: not just the fear of all men at all battles at all times in
history. Above the ordinary fear of fifty thousand men, few of whom would
have withdrawn from the opportunities that combat seemed at last to be
offering them, was the fear of the leaders. These men—Jellicoe and Scheer,
Beatty and Hipper, Sturdee and Schmidt, Burney and Engelhardt, and all
the other admirals and ships' commanders too—had been incurably infected
during all their responsible careers by the cult of caution.

Behind every calculation, every decision, every signal, every turn of the
helm, was the deeply held conviction that the disaster of defeat must always
be greater than the rewards of victory. The belief that governed all the
tactical moves at this one confused melee was that the individual Dreadnought, the squadron, the fleet must be preserved, even at the cost of victory
over the foe. The material that the scientist had provided for the warrior
was so complex and precious that its loss could not be entertained. If Jellicoe
had suffered overwhelming defeat, nothing could have saved the Allies. As
Churchill confirmed, he was "the one man who could have lost the war in
an afternoon." And no one has doubted that if the High Seas Fleet had been
annihilated, defeat would have come to the Central Powers much earlier,
possibly in 1916. But an inconclusive result suited everyone. Both sides could,
and did, claim victory. There was a measure of disappointment, but very little

Fast North Sea sweep in 1918: "W"-class destroyer is
flanked by battle cruisers *Glorious* and *Courageous*.
Imperial War Museum

loss of prestige. A few thousand lives were lost, a few ships lost, new confidence in the big gun was established with its mass firing, the *status quo* was reestablished, and the Germans returned to the Jade and the British to Scapa Flow to sit out the rest of the war.

Briefly, for Jutland has been written about so often that it must be described either exhaustively or in outline, this is what happened:

Through the spring of 1916 a number of plans had been propounded by the naval leaders of both sides to bring the other to battle. Both sides badly needed a victory, and only at sea did this look possible. The hope was to destroy at the lowest possible cost the largest possible number of heavy units of the enemy. This, it was believed, could be achieved only by an overwhelming superiority in strength. The Germans therefore hoped to trap a detachment of the British main battle force as the first step towards equalizing strength. This was a reversion to the policy followed at the outbreak of the war and which had not been exercised since the Kaiser had replaced Ingenohl with Pohl, an even more cautious commander. The need for an offensive demonstration had become necessary in order to break the demoralizing monotony of life in port; and in order to justify the fleet's existence and by a rousing victory lift spirits depressed by the fearful casualties and the deadlock of Verdun. It was also necessary to devise some occupation for the U-boats. These had been withdrawn from their warfare against merchant ships after strong protests from America.

Vice Admiral Reinhold Scheer, the new and much more belligerent German commander in chief, devised two plans to cut off and destroy Beatty's battle-cruiser force during May, 1916. The first was to bombard Sunderland with battle cruisers and entice Beatty through a U-boat screen and onto the main force of the High Seas Fleet, which would complete the destruction done by the U-boats' torpedoes. The second was to demonstrate off the Danish and Norwegian coasts, attacking any British shipping seen, with the same intention of luring Beatty to his annihilation. In both cases the battle cruisers were to be the bait as well as the first target of German destruction, in a gun duel. These roles were far from what Fisher had had in mind when he pushed through the design of the *Invincible* eleven years earlier.

Admiral Sir John Jellicoe had similar plans in mind. He intended to send a battle squadron into the Skagerrak and light cruisers as far as the Kattegat in the hope of drawing Scheer out of the Heligoland Bight and into a trap laid by the full strength of the more powerful Grand Fleet.

Thus in the early summer of 1916, caution was not going to be thrown to the winds. Inferior forces from both sides were to be "lured" into "traps." The big gun might be fired, if it survived the torpedoes, but only when the odds were overwhelming. But the sense of anticipation of momentous events at sea rose throughout both fleets. In April the east-coast town of Lowestoft was bombarded by Hipper's battle cruisers. Early in May the Grand Fleet put to sea in support of a bombing raid on the Schleswig coast which, it was hoped, might draw Scheer out of his lair.

Scheer decided at the last moment that weather conditions favored the second of his two plans. At 2:00 A.M. on May 31st, Hipper left the Jade and steamed north along the swept passages through the minefields parallel with the Danish coast. He was followed later, and at a distance of about fifty miles, by Scheer with the battleships. Hipper had five battle cruisers, the *Lützow*, his flagship; *Derfflinger, Seydlitz, Moltke,* and *von der Tann.* Scheer had two squadrons of eight Dreadnoughts each, the first squadron composed of the four *Nassaus* and four *Helgolands*; the second of the four *Königs*, and four out of the five *Kaisers*, the *König Albert* being under refit. The *Friedrich der Grosse* was Scheer's flagship. He was also prevailed upon, by their eager admiral, to take with him six pre-Dreadnoughts. These should have been nothing but a liability but in fact were quite useful.

The British Admiralty knew that something was afoot on the morning of May 30th before Hipper and Scheer sailed, for the Germans were as free as ever with their wireless. Beatty and Jellicoe were therefore warned in the afternoon of likely activity. Beatty sailed from the Firth of Forth soon after 6:00 P.M. His orders were similar to Hipper's: to draw the other onto the guns of the main fleet following some way behind. He was to sail east toward the coast of Jutland until 2:00 P.M. on the following day when, if he had not sighted the enemy, he was to fall back on Jellicoe's main battle fleet which he would accompany through the following night toward the Skagerrak. Beatty had with him two battle-cruiser squadrons, the first consisting of the *Lion* (flag), *Princess Royal*, *Queen Mary*, and *Tiger*, and the second made up of the older ships *New Zealand* and *Indefatigable;* and the four immensely powerful and new fast battleships *Barham*, *Valiant*, *Warspite*, and *Malaya* under Rear Admiral Hugh Evan-Thomas. Jellicoe began to leave Scapa Flow at 9:30 P.M. and steamed southeast toward the rendezvous with Beatty on the following afternoon. He had with him sixteen battleships and three of the oldest battle cruisers, *Invincible*, *Indomitable*, and *Inflexible*. Eight more battleships of the second battle squadron sailed from Cromarty to join him.

When dawn broke over the North Sea on May 31st, fifty-eight Dreadnought battleships and battle cruisers were steaming north or east toward the greatest naval collision of arms between surface ships of modern times. Thirty-seven were British, twenty-one were German. The British thought the Germans were out. The Germans did not know the British were out. The intelligence situation was changed to the disadvantage of the British the next morning when the Admiralty overheard a signal from the Jade suggesting that Scheer was still in port after all. From this time almost until they met, neither fleet knew that the other was at sea. The newfangled means of scouting were a complete failure. Submarines, seaplanes and airships all failed. And the messages from the British Admiralty only muddled things more.

At 2:00 P.M. on May 31st, Beatty was approaching his turning point. Jellicoe was about seventy miles away to the northwest. Hipper was some fifty miles east of Beatty, steering north for the Norwegian coast, and the same distance north of Scheer. Visual contact was made just seven minutes later. The advance British scouting cruiser *Galatea* sighted suspicious vessels to the east. At 2:10 P.M. she signaled to Beatty: "Two-funnelled ship has stopped steamer bearing ESE (100 degrees). Am closing." The steamer was the small Danish freighter N.J. *Fjord*, the tiny catalyst of Jutland. Beatty had already turned northwest for his rendezvous with Jellicoe. At 2:30 P.M. he doubled back on his tracks when the *Galatea* confirmed that the enemy was in sight. His signal was not seen by Evan-Thomas, and the four fast battleships therefore got left ten miles behind. Beatty's suspicion that German heavy units were in the vicinity was confirmed when the *Galatea* reported a large amount of smoke to the northeast.

First information of contact between British and German light forces was received by Hipper from the light cruiser *Elbing* at 2:27 P.M. Scheer picked up the message, too, just as Jellicoe heard the *Galatea*'s report. Hipper at once turned toward the reported contact and increased speed. He had only a faint suspicion that British heavy units were about: he was really after the British light cruisers. During the hour from the first visual contact between the two light forces and the opening of fire by the big guns, British scouting proved greatly superior to the German.

Beatty sighted Hipper's battle cruisers at 3:30 P.M. He was in an excellent position. He possessed a superior force, even without Evan-Thomas's fast battleships, which had still not caught up. He could cut off the German retreat at will. Hipper at once turned away southeast toward Scheer at best speed, as if running for home. Beatty formed up on a parallel line. Visibility was unreliable; the sun was behind Beatty, and this was an advantage to the Germans. The phase of the battle that followed, in which Hipper continued to draw Beatty onto Scheer, is called the Run to the South. Fire was opened by both sides at 3:48 P.M., at a range of about 16,000 yards. A further signaling error caused *Derfflinger*'s gunlayers to be undisturbed by British fire for ten minutes. This gave them a great advantage, as their view was uninterrupted by splash. The *Lion* and *Tiger* were soon hit; so was the *Derfflinger* at 3:58 P.M. At 4:03 P.M. Beatty's oldest ship, the *Indefatigable*, was badly hit by the *von der Tann's* 11-inch shells, and her magazines blew up. Equality of numbers was therefore reached within fifteen minutes. The rate of fire on both sides was increased, and the secondary batteries came into action as the range closed. The *Derfflinger*'s gunnery officer "described how the shells burst with a terrific roar as they struck the water, raising colossal pillars of livid green water, which rose higher than the masts, and hung in the air for five or ten seconds before they crashed down in clouds of spray." * The *Lion* was saved from a fatal magazine explosion similar to the *Indefatigable*'s by a mortally wounded Royal Marines officer. At this stage the German fire was more accurate than the British.

A few minutes after the first British casualty, Evan-Thomas saw the German ships. The *Queen Elizabeth*s (she herself was away refitting) had proved the usefulness of their high speed by catching up nearly three miles on the battle cruisers. When their 15-inch guns opened fire at a range of 19,000 yards, dispatching high-explosive projectiles of twice the weight of any the Germans had, it was like a triumphant fanfare to the great work of Cuniberti, Watts, and Fisher. What was more, it was brilliant shooting, better than anything the battle cruisers had accomplished, and though the mist and smoke of battle gave them only fleeting glimpses of Hipper's force, the *von der Tann*, the last in the German line, was soon hit and took in 600 tons of water.

In spite of his early success against a superior force, Hipper had opened the range, and firing between the battle cruisers had momentarily ceased. At 4:12 P.M. fire was reopened, fiercely and resolutely. Beatty had largely cleared himself of the destroyers that were supposed to protect him from

* *Naval Operations*, III, by Sir Julian Corbett (1923).

Savagely mauled by guns of every caliber, the *Derfflinger*
limped into Wilhelmshaven in this condition. *Imperial
War Museum*

submarine attack but had only succeeded in obscuring his aim with their
smoke. In spite of this, Hipper continued to demonstrate his superior
gunnery. His own flagship took a salvo from the *Lion*, then hit Beatty's
flagship more seriously, causing a great fire. The *Derfflinger* thought she was
destroyed or crippled, and shifted fire to the *Queen Mary*, which was already
suffering from the *Seydlitz*, with fatal results. At about 4:26 P.M. she was
hit four or five times in quick succession by 12-inch shells. There may have
been more. It was the same story as before. Her magazine went up, and the
ship was split asunder while traveling at 25 knots. Flame and smoke towered
above as her torn hull drove into the sea. The *Tiger* and *Princess Royal*
passed close by the wreck to port and starboard, suffering a rain of appalling
debris.

Hipper with his more robust battle cruisers and his superior gunnery had altered the odds from six to five against him to five to four in his favor. But the fast battleships of Evan-Thomas were by now causing him grave anxiety and his gunners to lose their steadiness. The 15-inch shells were plunging all about his force. And Beatty, his battered antagonist, far from retreating, was closing the range by turning forty-five degrees toward him. At this point of the gunnery duel Hipper resorted to the torpedo, and sent in his destroyers, or torpedo boats as he still called them. The British destroyers charged at the same time, and the little boats met in headlong combat amid a maelstrom of fire from the big ships and from each other. Some succeeded in launching torpedoes, and both Beatty and Hipper turned away and out of gun range. Two German destroyers were sunk, and the *Seydlitz* was hit by a torpedo. She was saved from serious injury by her torpedo bulkhead.

While this was happening, the British light scouting cruiser *Southampton* had obtained important news. From her bridge, "stretching interminably to the south, the German Battle Fleet could be dimly made out, coming up at 15 knots. It steered first northwest and then west, to strike the British and get upon their line of retreat. . . ."* She signaled to Beatty: "Urgent. Priority. Have sighted enemy's battle fleet. . . ." On the open bridge of the battered *Lion*, Beatty realized that Hipper had been trying to draw him into a trap and that it was now his turn to lure on the enemy to destruction. His surviving battle cruisers turned at once toward the north, just as the High Seas Fleet came into view, and he sent a signal to Jellicoe with the news.

Now Jellicoe knew that the whole German fleet was at sea, in close proximity, and steering toward him. He also knew his own strength was overwhelming. Scheer thought he was at last about to cut off and annihilate a large (but not too large) detachment of the Grand Fleet. He thought that his own strength was overwhelming. Both commanders in chief were delighted with the situation, and increased speed, closing the distance between each other at a greater rate than at any time since they had left port during the night before.

The second phase of the battle is called the Run to the North. For most of the time Beatty remained out of range of the German heavy guns, but Evan-Thomas, again slow to turn, came within range not only of Hipper but of the leading and most powerful German battleships. His ships were hit, some of them badly, but their heavy armor prevented serious damage and all their 15-inch guns remained in action and caused savage damage to the enemy until the range became too great at about 5:30 P.M. At this time Beatty began a slow turn starboard toward the northeast. He had calculated that it was the moment to cut across Hipper's van, prevent him from sighting Jellicoe, and distract him with long-range gunfire from an advantageous position. He was magnificently successful. Hipper's gun crews were tired from firing without effect at Evan-Thomas's ships, and were at first out-

* *Battleships in Action*, II.

ranged by Beatty's 13.5-inch guns. When the distance between the lines shortened, they found themselves dazzled by the lower sun. The *Lützow, Derfflinger,* and *Seydlitz* were all hit, and Beatty's fire was this time so accurate and fast that Hipper was forced to turn away and fall back on Scheer's battleships coming up astern. Funnel smoke, the fires from two unfortunate British armored cruisers, and shortening visibility prevented Hipper or Scheer from sighting Jellicoe and Jellicoe from sighting the High Seas Fleet, whose course and bearing were not reported with sufficient accuracy.

The next and most important phase of the action lasted between about 6:25 and 6:35 P.M. During this time Rear Admiral H. A. L. Hood, leading Jellicoe's three advance battle cruisers, which had been ordered forward to support Beatty and had already wrecked three of the German scouting cruisers, came into contact with the head of Hipper's line. In a brief gun duel at 9,000 yards the *Derfflinger* was hit many times but struck back at Hood's flagship *Invincible* and blew her into two halves: "Flames shot up . . . masts and funnels collapsed and beneath a huge column of smoke the mother of all battle cruisers split in two, her bow and stern standing up out of the water as she rested on the sea bed, like gravestones to her thousand and twenty-six dead." * At the same time Jellicoe completed his deployment and sighted Scheer. His twenty-four battleships had been steaming at 20 knots in six line-abreast columns of four ships. He now had them in a single line, with Evan-Thomas's squadron joining on at the rear and Beatty linking up with the van: thirty-four Dreadnoughts in all in a great shallow arc. Jellicoe had deployed to port, bringing the Grand Fleet's battleships on an approximately easterly course, with the intention of crossing Scheer's "T" in the classic manner. It appeared that the trap had snapped shut and that the total annihilation of the High Seas Fleet was imminent. At 6:30 fire was opened on the head of the German line at a range of between 11,000 and 12,000 yards.

In the mist- and smoke-laden confusion, amid burning vessels, the continuous thunder and flash and whine and splash of shells, both commanders in chief were becoming aware of the real facts of the situation. Jellicoe now appreciated that an unprecedented and long-awaited opportunity had been presented to him. Scheer was suddenly made aware of the urgent and appalling predicament that faced him. Instead of cutting off and destroying eight of the enemy's heavy units, he had been drawn into a most perilous and long-dreaded situation, in which his entire force was faced by the greatly superior strength of the Grand Fleet's heavy guns.

This crucial moment of mutual recognition was followed by two decisions, one positive and one negative. They both once again reflect the policy of defensive caution propagated by the Dreadnought battleship among all those concerned with her design and operation in war. It was more

* *British Battleships,* by Parkes.

important that she should remain afloat than sink the enemy. The risk level in combat was so high that only under circumstances so extraordinary that they were unlikely ever to arise could a conclusion be reached. First Scheer escaped from the trap by carrying out an evolution that had been much practiced because it was important for the High Seas Fleet to be good at escaping. It was the *Gefechtskehrtwendung*, or battle turnaway together. To reverse course in succession would have brought every ship through a turning point at which they could have been destroyed at leisure by the guns of the whole Grand Fleet. It was successfully carried out under the most difficult circumstances, and in less than five minutes the whole High Seas Fleet, including the battle cruisers, had disappeared into the evening haze and behind the smoke screen laid by its destroyers.

Jellicoe had an advantage in fleet speed over Scheer of at least four knots, a huge advantage in numbers and gunpower. The light might be failing, yet there were still three hours before darkness fell in this northern latitude in summer. But he dared not chase the enemy. He had fixed, in writing, in his famous October, 1914, letter, and in the minds of all his subordinates, what might happen in pursuing an enemy that had turned away. The Grand Fleet might lose half its ships, for "if the enemy were to turn away from an advancing fleet, I should assume the intention was to lead us over mines and submarines, and should decline to be so drawn." Thus had the underwater weapon as early as October, 1914, almost certainly doomed for the duration of the war any chance of a decisive fleet action. The High Seas Fleet would obviously not voluntarily fight against heavy odds. It would therefore try to run away. And pursuit was ruled out in case mines were dropped and torpedoes fired. Instead, some five minutes later, Jellicoe began to take the whole vast fleet on a southeasterly course in the hope of eventually cutting off the High Seas Fleet from its bases. At the same time he asked Admiral Sir Cecil Burney, leading the First Battle Squadron, if he could see any enemy battleships. Burney, not surprisingly, answered "No." The battle between the fleets—if battle it could be called after a few minutes of sporadic firing—appeared to be over.

But Scheer then did an interesting thing. He doubled back again on his tracks toward the northeast. He said later that he wanted "to deal the enemy a second blow." This seems extraordinarily unlikely, as he had, fifteen minutes earlier, only just managed to escape disaster. It is much more likely that he wanted to get behind the Grand Fleet, perhaps do some damage to its rear, then escape home behind Jellicoe close to the Danish coast. If forced to action again, he would have the advantage of being east of the enemy and almost invisible in the twilight. But if he remained to the west the light would be against him and he would almost certainly be seen again on the 250-mile journey back to the Jade. But the Grand Fleet was not as far south as Scheer had expected. Soon after 7:00 P.M. he found himself driving straight toward it again and being fired on by Jellicoe's rearmost units. All the others soon joined in, and the most tremendous if brief gunnery duel in naval history began. The range was from about 9,000 to 12,000 yards —and everything favored Jellicoe.

Scheer reacted promptly and coolly to correct this second misfortune. He sent in his destroyers and battle cruisers: "Charge the enemy. Ram. Ships denoted are to attack without regard to consequences." Hipper's ships were already in a sorry condition. The *Lützow* was sinking, and the *Derfflinger*'s captain was in temporary command. All were again subjected to the fiercest fire from almost every British battleship; while to Scheer the Grand Fleet "was nothing but a long vista of formidable shapes half seen in the increasing gloom," and "for the second time he found himself enveloped in a flaming arc of gun flashes." * The death ride of the battle cruisers, as it has popularly been called, was halted by a barrage of high-explosive shell. Every ship was raked by shells of small and large caliber and almost every turret was put out of action. But the fire they brought upon themselves enabled Scheer to carry out a second *Gefechtskehrtwendung* in some semblance of order. His destroyers ensured his second escape. Their smoke screen again obscured the turn; the few torpedoes they were able to dispatch at extreme range once again obliged the whole Grand Fleet to turn away. The shattered German battle cruisers followed as best they could at the rear. Scheer had escaped a second time.

Once again, and in spite of a plea from Beatty, Jellicoe made no serious attempt to pursue the enemy. By 7:30 P.M. the light was very poor. Darkness was not long away, and the Grand Fleet did not fight at night because it was too risky. An hour later, as the two fleets continued on roughly parallel southerly courses with Scheer still to the west, contact was again briefly made between some of the heavy ships, and for the third time Scheer turned away, the pre-Dreadnoughts doing sterling service with their covering fire.

It was all over now for the main fleets. There was a lot of fierce fighting during the night between the light craft, and ships were sunk, including the German pre-Dreadnought battleship *Pommern* by a torpedo. Deeply disappointed, the Grand Fleet returned home. The Germans were in a more cheerful frame of mind. They had escaped and had inflicted some severe damage on the Grand Fleet.

Many interpretations can be made of the events of May 31, 1916. All sorts of claims were made at the time, and many more since. The facts on the material are clear. These were some of the most important. There was something wrong with British shells, and the battle cruisers were not thoroughly enough protected, especially against the flash of cordite to the magazines. British armor plate was as good as German, but on most of the ships it was not thick enough. The buoyancy and damage control of the

* *Naval Operations*, III.

Battered German battle cruiser after Jutland:
Wilhelmshaven dockyard in the first days of June, 1916,
with *Seydlitz* in foreground. Note in particular the hull
damage forward, absence of guns and roof from "A"
turret, and shellhole through bridge, which killed all
those inside. She had about 5,000 tons of water in her.
Imperial War Museum

German ships was much better than the British. High speed was useful, but
not at the expense of protection. The bigger the gun, as most people expected,
the better the result.

In combat skill the Germans were more consistent than the British.
British scouting, signaling, gunnery, and handling was either very good or
weak. The German standard rarely fell below a high level. Everybody be-
haved very bravely. The greatest British failure was in the misuse of their
material. Weakly protected battle cruisers should never have indulged in a
sustained gunnery duel, especially when there were four vastly more powerful fast battleships available in the same scouting force. Armored cruisers
should never have been there at all. Destroyers obscured the enemy. The
much-vaunted 13.5- and 15-inch guns, with their superior range, were

157

not used at maximum distance when the enemy could not have replied. The whole fleet was turned away from the threat of a few torpedoes.

The British suffered worse casualties than in any previous naval battle, and more than twice as many as the Germans. But the material losses were not so heavy as at first appeared. Because of the very rapid development of the Dreadnought-type ship, the *Invincible* and *Indefatigable* were already outdated. The *Queen Mary* was a more modern battle cruiser, but she was much less valuable to the British than was the brand-new *Lützow* to the Germans. The German loss of four light cruisers out of the eleven present was also much more serious to the Germans than the destruction of the three obsolete British armored cruisers, *Black Prince*, *Defence*, and *Warrior*, however regrettable was the more serious loss of British lives. None of this affected future events: the British blockade continued as if nothing had happened. The proportionate losses were about equal. Neither side was victorious. The Dreadnought battleship itself was one victor. By its survival (not one was lost) it had appeared to justify both its mighty artillery and the diabolical ingenuity that had been expended on its defenses. The other victor was the Dreadnought's first enemy, the torpedo, which governed commanders' judgments, by its threat or its reality caused squadron engagements to be broken off, and whole fleets to flinch away in fear. It was the torpedo's finest hour. The big gun scarcely spoke again: the torpedo dominated the war at sea until the armistice, and determined future German naval policy. After the unbearable risks involved in surface action had been recognized, and seen as confirmation of the early lessons of the Dogger Bank and Heligoland Bight engagements, unrestricted and all-out submarine warfare was again resorted

The end of the High Seas Fleet. The German battle cruiser *Derfflinger* scuttles herself at Scapa Flow.
Imperial War Museum

to. Shipyards engaged in battleship and battle-cruiser construction were turned over to building U-boats, and the best men from the High Seas Fleet were gradually drafted to the submarine branch as the new craft became available. The torpedo won Jutland. It nearly won the war for the Germans. But in the end it defeated them by drawing in the United States on the Allied side.

The Grand Fleet never fought again. New ships joined it to add to its strength. Beatty took over command and became just as cautious as Jellicoe had ever been. Some American battleships arrived to swell the vast concourse of Dreadnoughts at Scapa Flow and Rosyth. Inactivity in no way reduced the status of the Dreadnought. All the Allies were building them, the French, Italians, Russians, Americans, and Japanese, and of course the British.

By contrast, the German Dreadnought fleet was soon in a sorry state. The rise and fall of German naval power was astonishingly swift, and barely lasted the lifetime of a good battleship. In little more than a decade the German Dreadnought had challenged the Royal Navy in numbers and power, had failed to challenge it in combat, had been relegated to inactivity, then surrendered, and finally scuttled.

As the German High Seas Fleet settled into the mud of Scapa Flow, and most of the Grand Fleet went to the scrapyards, it appeared for a moment that the Dreadnought, and the naval competition it seemed to breed, was dead. On the contrary. With the shifting of the axis of maritime power from European to Far Eastern waters, naval history merely entered a new era. The shipyards at Yokosuka and Newport News, Kure and New York, were all filled to capacity, engaged on a super-super-Dreadnought program the like of which Britain and Germany had never experienced.

DREADNOUGHT LOSSES IN THE FIRST WORLD WAR

Great Britain	Audacious	mine
	Invincible	gunfire (Jutland)
	Indefatigable	gunfire (Jutland)
	Queen Mary	gunfire (Jutland)
	Vanguard	internal explosion
Russia	Imperatritsa Maria	internal explosion
	Catherine II	scuttled
Austria-Hungary	Szent Istvan	torpedo
	Viribus Unitis	limpet mine
Germany	Lützow	gunfire (Jutland)
Italy	Leonardo da Vinci *	internal explosion
Japan	Kawachi	internal explosion

* Although sabotage may have caused the loss of the *Leonardo da Vinci*, one conclusion that can be reached from this table is that the price of idleness was as high as that of gunnery action, all the internal explosions being caused, it was believed, by the deterioration of cordite charges.

CHAPTER 7

Dreadnought Survival and Renaissance

The pace of Dreadnought construction among the naval powers continued for much of the First World War. Some were abandoned when it was decided to divert the materials and labor to other armament manufacture. Others were abandoned when the end of the war appeared to be imminent; still more were scrapped, some at an advance stage of construction, under the terms of the Washington Treaty of 1921. The interim period in the life of the Dreadnought, covering the years before and after this treaty, are covered in this chapter. The aborted ships arouse a special feeling of melancholy nostalgia. They were begun with such high hopes, were worked on for years with the skill and brains of many men, and were even sometimes launched amid the celebration and relief of that ceremony. All for nothing. On one day the riveters were at work in the great empty shell; the next their work was being heartlessly destroyed. But some of these interim Dreadnoughts were completed, and they were remarkable vessels. A few words must also be added about the "Dreadnoughts that never were" because they form an important part of the history of the ship, and strongly influenced future design.

Britain laid down no new battleships during the First World War. In 1914–1915 the 15-inch-gunned *Queen Elizabeth*s and the "R's" were augmenting the power of the Grand Fleet, and giving it the overwhelming superiority it enjoyed for the rest of the war. Besides, Britain was busily converting itself into a major military power. But there still remained a shortage of battle cruisers, and in the early months of the war they were evidently proving their worth. Nobody believed this more passionately than Fisher, now back in the Admiralty. The victory at the Falkland Islands, and Fisher's enduring preoccupation with an invasion of the German coast, caused the laying down of five battle cruisers between January and June, 1915. One pair of these were to have been further "R"-type battleships, but their design was changed at the last minute. The other three were referred to by Fisher as "large light cruisers" in order to get them through the Treasury, and they had strange and colorful histories.

Fisher's orders to the D.N.C. for the *Repulse* and *Renown* required the highest speed of any Dreadnought afloat and an armament of 15-inch guns. He was not very interested in how much armor they carried. What the Grand Fleet received as reinforcements twenty months later were two of the loveliest and certainly the fastest ships afloat. But after Jutland the Grand Fleet was less interested in speed, and much more interested in protection—which in the *Repulse* and *Renown* was less than that of the late *Queen Mary*. They were given rude names like White Elephants, and sent back for more protection, especially over their magazines. Both ships could do 32 knots in their early days, but the numerous reconstructions that punctuated their careers in war and peace (they were also nicknamed *Refit* and *Repair*) later reduced this by several knots. They were to have had eight 15-inch guns, but Fisher was in such a hurry that the last two pairs were not ready in time,

Battle cruiser *Renown* in 1918 (top), and as rebuilt for the Second World War—hangar, cranes, and cross-deck catapult replacing turret flying-off platforms; 4.5-inch high-angle guns replacing tripled 4-inch; composite superstructure replacing the piled bridgework around the early heavy tripod. There was new armor over her magazines, and she had new small-tube boilers to keep her speed at 29 knots (20). *Imperial War Museum*

so they went through life with a main armament of six 15-inch—another "first" for this class. Fisher also insisted on going back to small-caliber secondary armament. They were unique triple-mounted 4-inch. Another Fisher legacy, which lasted all their lives, was their high-speed maneuverability, which helped the *Repulse* in 1941 to evade attack after attack by Japanese torpedo planes, before she became the first capital ship to succumb to air power at sea.

But if the *Renown* and *Repulse* were unusual vessels and a breakaway from the line of the Dreadnought's development, their younger cousins *Furious*, *Glorious*, and *Courageous* can only be described as bizarre—or as the "outrageous" class, as they were popularly named. They were later officially classified as battle cruisers, but in fact Fisher's camouflage description was

Repulse was less drastically modified between the wars than *Renown*. This shows her amidships in 1939, with her new hangars and handling cranes (20). *Richard Perkins*

Elegant white elephant: the frail battle cruiser *Glorious*
at anchor. *Imperial War Museum*

more appropriate. *Courageous* and *Glorious* each mounted a pair of 15-inch
guns fore and aft, a secondary armament of eighteen 4-inch, again in triples,
and were as fast, and as long, as the *Renown* and *Repulse*. Their reduction in
displacement by some 8,000 tons was caused by their fewer heavy guns, and
their almost total absence of armor plate. This was shallow and of only two
or three inches on the belt, an inch or so on the decks, with serious consideration given only to the turrets and barbettes. The same general pattern
was followed with the *Furious*, and provision was made for the same main
armament. But instead a new weapon of unprecedented caliber was fitted,
one fore and one aft, each capable of firing a shell weighing 3,600 pounds.
(See page 201.) This size of gun and weight of shell were not equaled until

One of Fisher's "large light cruisers" open for
inspection by the press while still fitting out late in 1916.
H.M.S *Courageous* in the Tyne (21). *Imperial War
Museum*

the Japanese *Yamato* and *Musashi* went to sea a quarter-century later. Immediately after the *Furious* was completed, and before she was commissioned, the forward 18-inch was removed and a short flight deck substituted—for *seaplanes*. "A trolley-and-rail method of launching was employed, the seaplane resting on a trolley which ran down a slotted rail fixed to the deck. On reaching the end of the deck, the trolley was arrested by two arms fitted with shock absorbers." * Later the other gun was removed and both were mounted on monitors for shelling Belgium and then shipped out to Singapore

* *British Battleships*, by Parkes.

H.M.S. *Hood*: For twenty years she was the largest,
fastest, and most handsome warship in the world. Here
she is at 32 knots, her main battery trained to port
(22). The Times, *London*

for shelling the Japanese. During her long life she was, then, called a large
light cruiser, a battle cruiser, and an aircraft carrier; and in this last guise
she sported in turn a flight deck forward, a flight deck fore and aft, a clear
single flight deck when her funnels, bridgework, and mast were removed,
and finally, for her Second World War service (which she survived), she
was given a vestigial mast and bridge. *Courageous* and *Glorious* were also
converted to carriers in the 1920's, with the elimination of all their heavy
guns and the retention of an offset mast and funnel. What happened to *their*
guns is told on pages 211 and 212.

As they were first built, these five curious ships were the epitome of the
Fisher battle cruiser. It seemed only just, therefore, that four of them (the
Furious was absent) were engaged in the last big-gun action with units of
the High Seas Fleet on November 17, 1917. It was only a high-speed pursuit
between minefields, and nothing much happened. The *Glorious* had one
further distinction: she was the only battle cruiser which German battle
cruisers tried to sink in the First World War and succeeded in sinking in
the Second (*Hindenburg* and *Moltke;* then *Scharnhorst* and *Gneisenau*).

In 1915 three 15-inch-gunned battle cruisers were being built in Germany.
The British Board of Admiralty therefore decided to offset the threat of
these ships with something more formidable than Fisher's "large light cruisers."
Four huge super-battle cruisers were therefore designed, and the first, the
Hood, was laid down a few hours before Jutland was fought. The building
of her sisters *Howe, Anson,* and *Rodney* was halted later when Germany
gave up building Dreadnoughts altogether in favor of U-boats. The *Hood*,
like the *Vanguard* of a later generation, was completed for war, but not in

The inspiration of British maritime might between the wars: *Hood*'s 15-inch battery from the forecastle (22).
Richard Perkins

H.M.S. *Hood* at anchor in Torbay, 1931 (22). *Richard Perkins*

time for it. For some twenty years she was the largest, most beautiful, and most esteemed Dreadnought in the world. Few carried a heavier broadside, none were faster, none more graceful nor more formidable in appearance. Everywhere she was the cynosure of the maritime world. When she was sunk by a few shells from a German battleship, it seemed to many Britons that they had been deprived of a part of their naval heritage. As first designed she was to have had a main hull belt 33 percent thicker than that of the first battle cruisers; as she was completed, with the lessons of Jutland seemingly learned, it had grown to 12 inches, and was 9½ feet deep. Other protection was also on a scale with that of the *Queen Elizabeth*s, with special emphasis on the protection of the magazines. This was inadequate to meet the rigors of 1939 artillery, bomb, torpedo, and mine. But there had been no time to give her the planned modernization before its urgent need was catastrophically proved by the *Bismarck*'s more modern 15-inch guns.

In the midst of a huge scrapping program in 1921, Britain became aware that her naval situation was being threatened by two of her friends, America and Japan, the reason being that these uneasy late Allies were themselves disputing maritime supremacy in the Pacific. Within a few years their vast programs of super-super-Dreadnoughts must wrest from Britain the crown she had worn since Trafalgar. In the face of extraordinary cost, which she could not afford, opposition from militarists, who believed the day of the capital ship was finished, and political pressure from the Treasury, and also the common people (for after all the war to end wars had only just ended), authorization was given for the construction of four battle cruisers. On October 21, 1921, amid great controversy, the keel plates of the four most powerful fighting ships in British history were laid. They were intended to carry the names *Invincible, Indomitable, Inflexible,* and *Indefatigable,* were to be of 48,000 tons, and to carry an armament of nine tripled 16-inch guns, all forward of the funnels, and sixteen 6-inch as secondary armament in twin turrets. The protection was to be on the scale, and on the "all-or-nothing" principle, established by the American *Oklahoma;* speed about 32 knots. They were, in fact, to have been the 1921 equivalents of the 1911 *Queen Elizabeth*s: fast, well-protected, immensely strong, the perfect fast battleship rather than battle cruiser. Three and a half weeks later all work on them ceased, as a result of the Washington decisions. But by arguing at this conference that much of British capital-ship tonnage was out of date, and would have to be scrapped long before the "Battleship Holiday" prescribed by the conference had ended, the British delegate gained permission to build two battleships that would offset the advantage America and Japan had gained with their 16-inch-gunned *Maryland*s and *Mutsu*s. These ships, *Nelson* and *Rodney,* were scaled-down versions of the aborted new *Invincible*s, and were under construction a year after the battle cruisers were scrapped. In order to get down to the displacement limit of 35,000 tons, sacrifices had to be made, and these were mainly in the engine room, the horsepower being dropped

Nelson and *Rodney* anchored in Torbay, 1929 (13).
Richard Perkins

The last of the Second Generation: midships detail of
Nelson showing paired 6-inch secondary armament, and
two of her 4.7-inch high-angle guns (13). *Richard Perkins*

from 160,000 to 45,000, the speed from 32 knots to 23 knots. There were small reductions in secondary armament, but the main armament remained the same, and unique in British practice in being disposed all forward, to economize in armor plate over the magazines, the center of the three triple turrets being raised. Theoretically this disposition should have allowed the guns to be fired well abaft the beam, but in practice it was not possible, owing to blast damage to the bridgework and control towers. The most popular defense put forward for this arrangement, in the best Beatty tradition (he was First Sea Lord now), was that British ships did not run away and were therefore not interested in firing backward. Nevertheless, the restriction was a great handicap, and these two ships came in for much criticism because of their low speed and poor handling.

The last of the *Oklahoma* school in America were the three *Maryland*s, mounting 16-inch guns and with an immensely high resistance level with their 16-inch main belt on the waterline. The completion of these fine ships (earlier referred to on pages 110–111) spanned the Washington Conference, and the fourth of the class, *Washington*, although more than 80 percent complete, was used for target practice. These vessels, and their predecessors the *Tennessee* and *California*, were the first fruits of an unprecedented program of heavy-ship building in which the United States indulged, through uneasy peace, war and uneasy peace again, for some five years. Japanese naval rearmament, and the battleship race that inevitably followed, closely matched the German pattern. Fifteen years after the German Naval Act in 1900, Japan announced to the world a program of Dreadnought construction that could only presage some future attempt to undermine American influence and interests in Asia, from the Aleutians to the subcontinent of India. America replied with the *California*, *Tennessee*, and *Maryland*, laid down in 1916 and 1917, planned three more *Maryland*s, six *Indiana*-class battleships, and six *Constellation*-class battle cruisers. Future construction of 18-inch-gunned battleships and battle cruisers was also in an advanced planning stage before the lunacy was ended.

The success of the British battle-cruiser engagements at Heligoland Bight, Dogger Bank, and the Falklands, the German hit-and-run raids against the English coast, and the general activity of this class compared with the inactivity of the battleships, led to a reappraisal of the battle cruiser in America, where it had previously been a despised vessel. In February, 1916, the president of the Naval War College, in the course of testimony before the Senate Naval Committee, gave his opinion that the United States should build no more battleships until two divisions of eight battle cruisers had been added to the fleet. Until the first was laid down five years later, the nature of these ships was debated more hotly and more openly than that of any other class of Dreadnought. The first plans called for ten 14-inch guns in two triple and two superimposed twin turrets, a displacement of 34,800 tons, a speed of 35 knots—and seven funnels. After Jutland, the vulnerability of these ships was criticized, especially as half the boilers were to have been disposed above the main belt. Many other people did not want to have anything to do with them: the battleship was the only capital ship worth having—none had been sunk at Jutland. "I believe the battle cruiser is a mongrel," wrote a correspondent to the *Scientific American* five months after that battle. "There are only two real types, the fast scout and the floating fortress. The battle cruiser tries to combine both qualities, and as a result is neither. . . . Pile on that armour," he pleaded, "fourteen or fifteen inches thick."

The ships remained in abeyance until after the war and until attention could be again concentrated on the dangers in the East. Then in 1919 new designs were drafted. The merits of the biggest gun and the heaviest armor were taken into account; and, as always, the answer was found in greater displacement. The chiefs of the bureaus of Construction, Steam Engineering, and Ordnance, after an exploratory tour round the European yards and fleets, decided that something closer to a fast battleship of the *Derfflinger* type would best suit America's needs. The 1920 design for the *Constellation*s reflected this. The protection and internal strength were increased; the boilers above the belt were placed behind armor, and speed was lowered to about 30 knots with 180,000 h.p.; displacement was increased to 43,500 tons, and the armament increased to eight 16-inch in pairs, supported by sixteen 6-inch. The keel of the first was laid on January 29, 1921.

Four months earlier, as proof of continued American confidence in the battleship, and continuing anxiety about Japanese plans, the United States Navy had under construction no less than nine battleships mounting 16-inch guns, and one new one in commission. Of these, three were of the 32,500-ton *Maryland* class, and six more were "ultimate Dreadnoughts" of the same displacement as the *Constellation*s, with speed reduced to 23 knots, increased protection, and twelve 16-inch guns in triple mountings, as in the *California*. These had been authorized in 1917 and 1918, as the *Indiana*, *Massachusetts*, *Montana*, *North Carolina*, *Iowa*, and *South Dakota*.

All that should now be added is that, of these twelve monster battleships and battle cruisers, only two were commissioned by the United States Navy— as the 33,000-ton aircraft carriers *Lexington* and *Saratoga*. Finally, a historical note for extremist addicts: the largest Dreadnought ever seriously contemplated for any nation was a mythical vessel proposed as a result of an inquiry included in the 1916 Naval Appropriations Act. The only limitation was that it should be able to pass through the Panama Canal. It was to have been of 80,000 tons, with an overall length of 975 feet, a speed of 35 knots, and a main protective belt of 16 inches. Fifteen 18-inch guns were to have been mounted in five triple turrets.

Aborted American Dreadnoughts, or "The ships that never were."

The navy that came nearest to building the ultimate Dreadnought of these dimensions and power was the Japanese. Japanese naval architects had already produced some of the most radical, powerful, and effective Dreadnoughts, which denied in appearance and a multitude of radical features the old saw that the Japanese were a race of imitators. Not all their ships—and especially their heavy cruisers—were unqualified successes. And their piled superstructures may have had a frightening effect on the enemy, but they must also have terrified those who endured battle in them.

Japanese naval construction really got into its stride when the Russian war debts had been worked off, and the European naval powers were too busy to take much notice of what was happening. Besides a number of very fast destroyers and light cruisers, a Dreadnought program of vast dimensions was put in hand in 1915–1916. From the meager information that was given to the world, it could be calculated that within little more than a decade Japanese naval power would dominate the Pacific. But the

"IOWA"

wording of the famous Navy Laws was so obscure and circumlocutory that it was difficult to tell for a certainty what would be the result. Its basis rested on "the 8–8 standard"; or an establishment of at least eight battleships and the same number of battle cruisers all less than eight years old. As Japan already had ten Dreadnoughts in commission or under construction in 1915, and the sixteen new ships of the 8–8 standard would be by no means obsolete when they were replaced in the first line, then it could be argued that Japan would have the most powerful fleet in the world by 1928 unless something was done about it. One consolation was that the Japanese were unlikely to have either the money or the shipbuilding facilities to manage such a gigantic program; on the other hand, when American intelligence from time to time picked up crumbs of information on new construction, the details were frightening.

The United States Department of the Navy thought it was at least one step ahead of its rival with its 16-inch gun when it was testing it at Indian Head in 1917. But Japanese development of a gun of the same caliber was in step, and the *Mutsu* and *Nagato*, with their two-knot superiority over the four *Maryland*s, gave away little to the American ships in protection. What was more, the *Nagato* had joined the fleet by the end of 1920, and within a few months the Intelligence Department of the United States Navy had discovered the specifications of two improved and enlarged *Nagato*s (*Kaga* and *Tosa*, 39,900 tons, ten 16-inch) already under construction; four giant battle cruisers (*Amagi*, *Akagi*, *Atago*, and *Takao*, 43,500 tons, eight 16-inch), two of which had already been begun; and finally even larger super-battle-cruisers of 47,500 tons mounting eight 18-inch and sixteen 5.5-inch guns with a speed of 30 knots, which would be ready by 1927.

This news galvanized the State Department into activity and caused the convening of the Washington Conference, one of the shrewdest acts of modern American diplomacy. Under its terms, worked out amid heated controversy, there would be no more Dreadnought construction for ten years, ships would not be replaced until they were twenty years old, and when they were would be limited in displacement to 35,000 tons. Battle fleets were to be limited to the following tonnage: Britain, 580,450; the United States, 500,650; Japan, 301,320; France, 221,170; Italy, 182,000. All Dreadnoughts launched or on the stocks were to be scrapped, with the exception of three of the American *Maryland*s and the Japanese *Mutsu*, to compensate for which Britain was allowed to build the *Nelson* and the *Rodney*. No one was much pleased by the result except America. The Japanese thought they were being frustrated, the British demoted, the Italians and French insulted. But they signed.

The *Tosa* was in fact launched and used as a target ship, the results being of great value when they tired of the "holiday" and began designing the *Yamato* and *Musashi*. *Kaga* and *Akagi* were both finished as large aircraft carriers.

Most of the other naval powers had given up their uncompleted wartime Dreadnoughts long before this. The French *Normandie* class of five ships to mount twelve 13.4-inch guns in three quadruple mounts, with a speed of 25 knots, remained on the stocks for some eight years. Their guns were purloined by the army; some were bored out to 15.75 inches; others were reputedly captured by the Germans and used against the French. Only the last ship, the *Béarn*, ever took to the water, and she was finished as an aircraft carrier. The Italians began building in 1914 a foursome of super-Dreadnoughts based very closely on the *Queen Elizabeth*s, but the need for these never arose, as the guns of the Austro-Hungarian battle fleet were as muted as the German.

After finishing repairs to the High Seas Fleet by the end of October, 1916, big-ship construction almost ceased in Germany. The *Baden*'s 15-inch-gunned sister ships *Sachsen* and *Württemberg* were never completed; nor were any of the seven battle cruisers. As improved *Derfflinger*s, these would certainly have been formidable foes indeed. The first class of four, *Mackensen*, *Graf Spee*, *Prinz Eitel Friedrich*, and *Fürst Bismarck* were laid down in 1913, and would have closely resembled the *Derfflinger*s, but with 14-inch guns. The main armament was increased again to eight 15-inch, arranged as in the *Baden*s of which they were battle-cruiser equivalents, in the *Ersatz-Yorck*, *Ersatz-Gneisenau* and *Ersatz-Scharnhorst*, laid down in 1915.* Few were launched; and after 1916 no new German Dreadnought was to take to the water until 1931.

This interim period in the Dreadnought's life conveniently comes to an end with the 1920's. The decade had begun in a frenzy of competition, when rumor and counterrumor of greater and greater gargantuan designs had flooded the world's admiralties and navy departments, along with argument and counterargument about the battleship being doomed by the torpedo and high-explosive bomb. The torpedo plane was recognized as a serious weapon; General Billy Mitchell, General Giulio Douhet, General Hermann Göring, and Air Marshal Hugh Trenchard advocated the giant bomber as the supreme arbiter and supreme deterrent of the future. The Grand Fleet and the High Seas Fleet both died, and the Pacific replaced European waters as the area of the future struggle for maritime supremacy. But with the Washington Treaty safely signed, and with the rapid growth of technology and new and more sophisticated weapons, few people thought that there would ever again be battle fleet competition. But the last battleship race had not been run. The Dreadnought—still following the same Fisher-Cuniberti basic formula—was by no means dead. Twenty years after they had been broken up on the slips or sent to the scrapyards, ships as mighty in size and power as the stillborn *Takao*, *Constellation*, and *Invincible* were to join the world's fleets and take part in the greatest maritime struggle of all time.

---

* Replacements for earlier ships carrying these names (*Die Deutschen Kriegsschiffe 1815–1936*, by Erich Groner [1937]).

CHAPTER 8

Refits, Rebuilds— and Rearmament

The completion in August, 1927, of the British battleship *Rodney*, the second of Britain's "equalizers," following the Washington Conference, marked the last of the line of Second Generation Dreadnoughts, a family which had begun with the Japanese *Fuso*, the British *Queen Elizabeth*s, the American *Oklahoma*, and the German *Baden*. Almost 90 percent of the construction was never completed, these romantic but aborted "lost causes" including the American *Washington* and Japanese *Tosa*—sacrificed, as has been told, to friendly gunfire in the cause of better future batttleships—the German *Mackensen*, and the British battle cruisers. The navalists and naval authorities of the great powers might have been disturbed by the prospect of

The Battleship Holiday, 1934: Twelve years have passed since the Royal Navy has laid down a new Dreadnought, and another seven will pass before it commissions the first of the Third Generation ships. Meanwhile the total strength is fifteen ships. Three of them—*Barham, Rodney, Nelson*—anchored in Torbay. *Richard Perkins*

ten years of *status quo* in Dreadnought construction; but the Washington Treaty acted like a soothing balm on feverish Treasury officials in Washington, London, and Tokyo. It was not just the cost of the ships—although the cost of a Dreadnought had risen from £2,000,000 ($10,000,000) in 1910 to £3,000,000 ($15,000,000) in 1915 (*Queen Elizabeth*) and finally to £7,500,000 ($37,500,000) for the *Rodney*. There was the upkeep of each ship (around £500,000, or $2,500,000, a year), the cost of supporting and auxiliary craft (a "Washington Treaty" 10,000-ton cruiser cost more than the *Dreadnought*), of dockyards and bases and shore establishments of all kinds at home and overseas. The Japanese were most vehement in their criticism of the treaty, although they would have been the first bankrupts if the race with America had run its course.

A similar policy was pursued by all the naval powers during the Battleship Holiday from 1922 to the mid-thirties. Money was short. Old tonnage was scrapped, and the money saved was carefully spread over the surviving battle fleet on a modernization program. By 1931 most of the prewar tonnage had gone to the breakers, except those of the minor powers, who remained loyal to their Dreadnoughts until after the Second World War. The following table shows the state of the world's battle fleets in that year:

UNITED STATES

3	Marylands	32,000
2	Californias	32,000
3	New Mexicos	32,000
2	Pennsylvanias	32,000
2	Oklahomas	29,000
2	New Yorks	27,000
1	Arkansas	26,000
total 15		

GREAT BRITAIN

2	Nelsons	34,000
5	Royal Oaks	29,000
5	Queen Elizabeths	31,000
1	Hood *	42,000
2	Renowns *	32,000
total 15		

JAPAN

2	Nagatos	33,000
2	Ises	30,000
2	Fusos	29,000
4	Kongos *	29,000
total 10		

FRANCE

3	Lorraines	22,000
3	Courbets	22,000
total 6		

ITALY

2	Duilios	22,000
2	Cavours	22,000
total 4		

RUSSIA

4	Marats	23,000
total 4		

* Battle cruisers.

A large proportion of this tonnage had been designed twenty years earlier (there were still quite a number of useless pre-Dreadnoughts left because they were not affected by the Washington Treaty) when oil-burning was the exception, director control of the main armament was scarcely known, and both active and passive defense against the aerial bomb was not even considered. Many of the older ships had already undergone quite drastic refits after Jutland, and the Grand Fleet, besides the new battle cruisers and the United States division, had presented a different picture in 1918 from that of 1914. There were range clocks on the masts and deflection scales on the turrets (to indicate to other ships the range and bearing of the guns), director fire control and new searchlight platforms, paravane gear and external bulges against mines and torpedoes, kite-balloon winches, and aircraft flying-off platforms on the turrets (the Grand Fleet could fly fifty aircraft and thirty kite balloons for zeppelin destruction and spotting). Some of the secondary guns had been removed for arming merchantment against U-boats, but in many cases these had been replaced by small-caliber anti-aircraft guns. Less apparent modifications included the provision of flash-tight doors to the magazines, and the increase of vertical protection to decks, especially around the magazines and shell rooms, and to barbette crowns, for the twin dangers from plunging fire and from the aircraft bomb were becoming increasingly recognized.

The drastic modernization carried out to nearly all the world's Dreadnoughts between the wars followed the same pattern. The "bomb versus

U.S.S. *Arkansas* in 1943: Her appearance was first transformed in 1925–1927 when the mainmast was replaced by a small tripod, two funnels were reduced to one, and a catapult fitted, her displacement increasing by 3,000 tons. For service in Second World War, her fore superstructure was rebuilt again, and most of the secondary armament was replaced by multiple high-angle guns (26). *U.S. Navy*

With only her twelve massive 50-caliber 14-inch guns to
identify her from the Dreadnought that sailed out of
Newport News in 1917, U.S.S. *Mississippi* steams
through Pacific waters in the closing weeks of the war.
Her survival had depended on her massed batteries of
light antiaircraft artillery (30). *U.S. Navy*

battleship" controversy and the tests carried out by the United States, British,
and Japanese navies drew further attention to the new vulnerability of the
capital ship. The more the validity of the vessel was questioned, the greater
was the attention given to its defenses, especially to the torpedo from aircraft
and submarine, and the high-explosive bomb. Antiaircraft guns became more
numerous and efficient, the lighter two-pounder and machine gun being
mounted in multiples to provide a "hose" of fire against attackers. Decks
were further strengthened. Antitorpedo bulges were fitted to many ships
not already equipped with them. Most ships carried a catapult and two or
even three planes. Because all this added to the displacement and reduced
speed, in many cases entirely new machinery was fitted. Thirty million

Maryland and *West Virginia*, though once identical,
presented different faces to the Japanese in war. Both
were at Pearl Harbor, *Maryland*'s damage being less
severe than that suffered by *West Virginia*, which was
rebuilt to a silhouette similar to that of *Tennessee* (32).
U.S. Navy

dollars was spent on the three *New Mexico*s alone, and the appearance of
the American battle fleet was changed by the substitution of British-type
tripods for cage masts. The British *Queen Elizabeths* were transformed from
balanced and graceful two-funnel vessels to hideous hybrids with a single
trunked funnel; and then, some fifteen years later, most of them were rebuilt
again as stocky, single-funnel ships, aircraft, hangars, catapults, and a multitude of high-angle guns reflecting the new influence in sea warfare. The
Italian *Cavours* were rebuilt from stem to stern, acquired new guns, lost
their midships turret, and with new oil-fired boilers and turbines gained
five knots. The Japanese *Kongos* underwent two transformations. First they
were converted from coal to oil burners, and were given new horizontal

Gone are the fine twin funnels and lattice masts, and the
balanced delicacy of the *California* and *Tennessee*. Here
they are, fully equipped for new functions in the Pacific,
their massive superstructures studded with radar aerials
and multiple antiaircraft guns (31). *U.S. Navy*

Denied new battleships by the Washington Treaty, the United States Department of the Navy did what it could to modernize the existing battle fleet in the 1920's and 1930's. This is U.S.S. *Texas* after the replacement of lattice with tripod masts and the elimination of a funnel with the change to oil fuel. She was originally completed in 1913 as the first 14-inch gunned American Dreadnought, and served nobly in two World Wars (27). *U.S. Navy*

Queen Elizabeth in the Second World War, with new, higher-elevating 15-inch guns, a hangar for three planes, catapult and cranes, 4.5-inch dual-purpose secondary armament, multiple antiaircraft guns, and simplified superstructure (11). *Imperial War Museum*

No Dreadnoughts were more comprehensively rebuilt than Italian First Generation ships. Elimination of midships turret and upper- and main-deck secondary battery, new 12.6-inch guns, the stocky main superstructure and twin squat funnels close-placed amidships transformed their appearance. This is *Conte di Cavour* (60).

Japanese *Haruna* in 1934 after her final and most drastic rebuilding. As a "fast battleship" she was now four knots faster than when she had been built as a battle cruiser (54). *Imperial War Museum*

protection and funnels, losing several knots in the process; later, with new engines, they were able to steam faster than ever in spite of additional heavy batteries of antiaircraft armament. The *Ise* and *Hiuga* later suffered the most complete transformation of any Japanese capital ships by being converted, like the British *Furious* in 1917, to battleship-aircraft carriers, with the removal of the two aft 14-inch turrets and the substitution of a flight deck and hangars to accommodate twenty-two bombers. This was done after the catastrophic losses at Midway. *Fuso* and *Yamashiro* were also elaborately modified between the wars, sprouting the enormous pagoda-like piled forward superstructure—designed to give strength and vibrationless rigidity for directors, range finders, and searchlights—that marked all the rebuilt Japanese battleships. The already aggressive appearance of the *Mutsu* and *Nagato* was further increased when the fore funnel was swept back during their refit in 1924–1925, and again in 1934–1936 when it was removed at the same time as their machinery was replaced (speed up now to 26 knots); guns were given greater elevation; and bulges, a triple bottom, strengthened decks, and many more antiaircraft guns as well as aircraft were added.

Few Dreadnoughts escaped the metamorphosis. Brazil's *Minas Gerais*, the pride of the nation and, like her sister, always immaculate, was practically rebuilt from the hull shell over five years in the 1930's, and reappeared with a single stubby funnel and lean, purposeful lines. Argentina's *Rivadavia* and *Moreno* were less drastically rejuvenated in America. Like the Italian ships,

The hermaphrodites: The same sudden demand for air
cover in two World Wars caused the creation of these
strange hybrids. In 1917 *Furious* (above) was completed
with flying deck and hangar forward, replacing one of
the two 18-inch guns the battle cruiser was to have
carried. The enemy were German zeppelins. Twenty-six
years later, after Midway, the Japanese Navy stripped
battleships *Ise* (shown here) and *Hiuga* of two twin
14-inch turrets, and fitted hangar and flying deck aft.
The enemy were American dive and torpedo
bombers. Radar aerial tops fore superstructure;
main-deck secondary battery is stripped to save weight
(51). *Ise—Imperial War Museum; Furious—Richard
Perkins*

Fuso (above) and *Yamashiro*, after conversion in mid-thirties, now with single funnel, hair-raising superstructure, improved protection, and many more light and heavy antiaircraft guns (50). *Imperial War Museum*

Midships detail, *Mutsu*. When fore-funnel cowling proved inadequate, it was brought back like this in 1924. Below: in 1934–1936, she was extensively modernized, with her sister ship *Nagato*. This shows the work nearing completion in 1936, with new, massive torpedo bulge; secondary armament and fore funnel have been removed. "B" turret is still absent; it was being modified to permit greater elevation for 16-inch guns. She blew up by accident (52). *U.S. Navy, Imperial War Museum*

France's *Lorraine* lost a turret and found a catapult and three aircraft. And so it went on, right up to and during the early years of the Second World War. Some Dreadnoughts gained as much as 7,000 tons in displacement; many were modernized so completely that they became almost as useful in their wartime role as the new ships of the Third Generation still to be laid down or under construction.

At the height of the world slump in 1930, the great naval powers met again and decided that they could not afford new Dreadnoughts to replace their aging fleets, at least until 1937. Air-power advocates thought they had won a final victory; and a number of important people, who were later to regret their words, said that the Dreadnought must be obsolete, as no one could afford them. Even the construction of new cruisers and destroyers was limited. But the Italians and French were allowed to replace some of their oldest tonnage. By the time the delegates met again in 1935, the world was an uneasier place; and, as always before, the new anxieties brought hints of new Dreadnoughts, in spite of new doubts about their maritime supremacy. Germany had built three extremely clever "pocket battleships" (supposedly within the limits set down by the peace treaties); and there were hints of trouble in the Mediterranean and the Far East. America talked about new giant battleships in two years' time. Japan, with her powerful cruiser fleets, and conscious of her inability to match American resources, wanted Dreadnoughts to be banned altogether. Britain wanted small ones. Eventually a limit of 35,000 tons and 14 inches for the caliber of the main armament was agreed on: and no one was to lay a keel down until 1937. Japan and Italy refused to sign. The new battleship race was on, six * of the third and last generation of super-super-Dreadnoughts were under construction, and even before the conference met, the preliminary designs of the greatest battleships the world was ever to see were being discussed in Tokyo.

By 1937 fifteen new Dreadnought battleships and battle cruisers were under construction, their displacement varying from little over 30,000 to nearly 70,000 tons, and guns of every caliber from 11-inch to 18.1-inch were being built for them. Thousands of men, skilled in crafts and trades they

* Two German, two French, two Italian.

The United States Navy at peace: (*a*) Exercises in
calm . . . (*b*) and heavier seas (above, *Arizona*; below,

Delaware). Gunnery practice: (*c*) Main armament by
day . . . (*d*) and secondary 5-inch by night. *U.S. Navy*

had not practiced for so many years, and many more who were to learn from them, were recruited. Dozens of great plants, made idle or turned over to other uses after the war to end wars and the reconciliations of an already distant pacific era, were retooled for the manufacture of the multitudinous specialized components—from the most delicate optical and radio equipment to massive plates of hardened steel more than a foot thick. Sounds that had rung out on the Clyde, the Tyne, and the Mersey, the Jade, the Elbe, and the Weser during the most fevered years of pre-1914 Anglo-German rivalry were heard again. Shipbuilding, armament, and steel shares did especially well. The arithmetical calculations and permutations were indulged in once more: Germany had a head start—would the five new *King George V*'s be ready before Germany's next two to hold the balance? As usual, the Japanese situation was uncertain. But the Americans were, as ever, quite forthcoming. After a slow start, four really big ones were coming along nicely before war broke out in Europe. And of course, like all the others, they would be unsinkable. . . .

In this brief account of the Third Generation Dreadnoughts, German activities are best dealt with first, as her "pocket battleships" were miniature prototypes of later construction and were specifically intended for one of the four roles—commerce destroyer, commerce protector, instrument of bombardment, and antiaircraft-gun platform—which the Dreadnought was to fill during her final and most active years. By the 1930's and 1940's the term "battleship" became as great a misnomer as "Dreadnought." The ancient line of battle, from which the largest and most powerful class of fighting ship derived its name, had already been made invalid by the bomb and torpedo. It was as dead as the High Seas Fleet, which would never again sail out of the Jade in stately line-ahead. Germany had learned again the throttling capacity of a blockade and the mortal damage that could be inflicted on an enemy by destroying its merchant shipping. In March, 1934, Germany renounced the Versailles Treaty and began again to build U-boats, six years after she had laid down the first of her surface commerce raiders.

Bigger heavy cruisers than the *Deutschland* (later renamed *Lützow*), were built, though none with 11-inch guns. She qualifies as a battleship because of the strength of her construction, her combination of high speed and heavy broadside, and the ingenuity of her specification. Nor was she of 10,000 tons' displacement in accordance with treaty limits; she was nearer 12,000. Her armament of six 11-inch and eight 5.9-inch, combined with a speed of around 28 knots, was reminiscent of Cuniberti's *Vittorio Emanuele*s of 1901. With this gunpower she could fight off any 10,000-ton, 8-inch-gunned Washington Treaty heavy cruiser, and only three British battle cruisers could catch her. Although classified as a *Panzerschiffe* (or armored ship), her real purpose, and the fundamental change in German naval strategy, were seen in her great cruising range of 10,000 miles, and the better accommodation offered to her

Deutschland (later renamed *Lützow*) cruises off the
Spanish coast during the civil war. She was heavily
bombed by Republican aircraft (42). *U.S. Navy.*

crew. The British Admiralty recognized the frightful dangers if half a dozen
of these ships, refueled from time to time from carefully disposed oilers, were
to break lose into the Atlantic. Two more ships, *Admiral Graf Spee* and
Admiral Scheer, followed in 1931 and 1932. They carried the same armament,
were somewhat more heavily protected, and displaced over 12,000 tons, although this was not known until later. The three ships bristled with radical
innovations. To save weight, now more important than ever, the hull was elec-
trically welded, and incorporated the armor belt. All the interior detail work
was designed with lightness in mind, and the diesel engines (how Fisher would
have loved them!) had a very high power-to-weight ratio. They were also
exceedingly unreliable and gave trouble all their lives.*

With the abrogation of the Versailles Treaty, Hitler ordered two more
formidable big ships, and these much-debated battle cruisers, the *Scharnhorst*
and *Gneisenau* (their names commemorating two famous earlier commerce
raiders), were ready for the war in 1939. The 11-inch gun, with its high
muzzle velocity and rate of fire and 33,000-yard range, was retained, a second superimposed triple turret being added forward. With a speed of 32

---

* Several reports from Montevideo in 1939 stated that engine breakdown, unconnected
with her recent action, decided the *Graf Spee*'s fate.

Admiral Scheer, second of Germany's 12,000-ton
"pocket battleships," precursor of the Third Generation
Dreadnought. An era of more elaborate technology has
already destroyed the simplicity of the German warship
(42). *U.S. Navy*

knots and an alleged displacement of 26,000 tons, it appeared on paper that the
Renown and *Repulse* should be able to deal with them. Only later was it discovered that they displaced over 31,000 tons, that with their 13-inch main belt
and traditional German structural strength, they could take a tremendous
hammering. After being defeated in a fair fight with the *Duke of York* in December, 1943, the *Scharnhorst*, like the *Bismarck* and *Lützow* before her, had
to be sent to the bottom with torpedoes after gunfire had reduced her to a
hulk. The capacity of German Dreadnoughts to resist shellfire was not surpassed by those of any other navy. Both ships were the target for some 2,000
tons of R.A.F. bombs when they were at Brest, and were frequently torpedoed
and mined. After surviving all this, the wrecked *Gneisenau* was humiliatingly
sunk as a blockship in the last months of the war.

If the Second World War had not broken out four or five years earlier than the German Admiralty staff had been led to believe, Britain would have been faced with a fleet of twelve or thirteen modern commerce raiding battleships and battle cruisers. Britain, too, would have built up her battle fleet by then, but her margin of superiority over the German would have been made up from Second Generation ships. It was as well that Hitler invaded Poland in 1939 instead of 1944, and later canceled the 50,000-ton *Friedrich der Grosse* and *Gross Deutschland* with their eight 16-inch guns and 30-knot speed. As it was, the *Bismarck* engaged the attention of eight capital ships and sank the *Hood* before she herself went down, and her sister ship was for two and a half years a grave anxiety, and tied up British capital ships in home waters when they could have been out in the Pacific. *Tirpitz* and *Bismarck* were the last in the long, and always formidable, line of German Dreadnoughts, of which thirty-three in all were completed. They carried the same armament of eight 15-inch guns as the uncompleted First World War battle cruisers, and were enlarged and heavier-protected versions of these ships with a radius of action of over 8,000 miles.

The German Dreadnought fleet in the Second World War never reached half the numbers of the First World War, and its numerical ratio with the British fleet was always lower. But as in 1914–1918 the Royal Navy could not afford for a day to divert attention from it, at least until 1944. Only gross mismanagement and a policy of timidity and confusion on the German side, and alertness and skill by the British, combined with some good fortune, pre-

The *Gneisenau*, Germany's last battle cruiser to survive. For more than four years she and her sister *Scharnhorst* were thorns in the flesh of the Royal Navy. They were first fitted with a straight stem, but a cutaway bow replaced this in order deliberately to confuse her identity with *Hipper*-class cruisers and *Tirpitz* and *Bismarck* (48). *Imperial War Museum*

Biggest quarry: Eight Dreadnoughts and two carriers
sought the *Bismarck* in the greatest maritime hunt of all
time (43). *Imperial War Museum*

vented the seven Third Generation German Dreadnoughts from running amok among the North Atlantic convoys.

In the years between the wars Japan had developed the most powerful and efficient naval air arm in the world. In numbers and quality of aircraft and their carriers, she was ahead of America and far ahead of Britain. The limitations in capital-ship tonnage imposed on Japan by the Washington Treaty had caused Japan to develop her air arm in order to offset some of America's preponderance in battleship strength. Confidence in this new arm grew with

Tirpitz: For two and a half years she was the target of
every weapon as she lay camouflaged and at anchor in
Norway. It took a 12,000-pound bomb to capsize her at
last (43). *Imperial War Museum*

18-incher: 18-inch artillery was planned for a number of
British, American, and Japanese Dreadnoughts during
the First World War. Only the Royal Navy completed
and fitted them. This is the single 18-inch gun of the
Furious.

its efficiency. There remained many big-ship advocates, but even the most
conservative viewed the capital ship more as an instrument of deterrence and
prestige, and as the air arm's protector, than as a big-gun platform in its own
right.

The four Japanese *Yamato*s were originally intended to form a force of
invincible giant Dreadnoughts capable of facing and defeating in combat a
superior force of American 16-inch and 14-inch battleships. They were to
achieve this by indestructibility by ordnance or torpedo, very high speed, and
a main battery overwhelmingly superior to that possessed by any other battleship in the world. The British had built an 18-inch gun; both Japanese and
American ordnance experts had studied the possibilities in the early 1920's and
had designed ships with this caliber in mind. The Japanese Navy Department
continued development in the 1930's, and were confident that a successful gun
could be produced. Its theoretical advantages were enormous. Its penetrating
power would be all that Fisher had prophesied for it. At long range it would
pierce any armor in existence. The explosive power of several shells within a
ship must be catastrophic. Each weighed 3,200 pounds; the weight of broad-

The greatest of them all: the 68,000-ton battleship *Yamato* making 27 knots on her trials (53). *Imperial War Museum*

Admiral Yamamoto's future flagship *Yamato* fitting out
at Kure in 1941 (53). *U.S. Navy*

side of nine would be 28,800 pounds against the *Maryland*'s 16,800 pounds,
and the latest American Second Generations ships' 18,900 pounds. The weight
of their gunnery installations alone was nearly 12,000 tons, and the weight
of their armor was 2,000 tons more than the total displacement of the *Kawachi*,
herself the biggest Dreadnought of her time.

Every feature and statistic of the *Yamato*s was calculated to startle. They
were the most hyperbolic Dreadnoughts of them all. A special ship had to be
built to move their guns from the ordnance factory to their yards. Special

hangars had to be built for their boats in order to protect them from blast, and for the same reason all the light antiaircraft guns had to be behind shields. These high-angle guns at first numbered twelve 12.7-cm., twenty-four 25-mm., and four 13-mm., besides the tripled 6.1-inch dual-purpose guns in turrets. After the Battle of the Philippines in July, 1944, the *Yamato*s' light antiaircraft guns were increased to twenty-four 12.7-cm., one hundred and thirteen 25-mm. in triple and single mountings, and four 13-mm. This formidable battery of light high-angle artillery was exercised more often than the main battery.

There is no record that the *Yamato*s ever fired a full broadside, in practice or in anger. The effect of the simultaneous discharge of these nine pieces of ordnance must certainly have been shattering. Some hint of the impression on both the ship's crew and structure can be judged from this account of the firing of the single 18-inch gun of the *Furious:* "I think it had a range of something like thirty miles and I don't imagine it would ever have found the right target, but it certainly was very spectacular. You could see the projectile going away for ages and ages on firing. The recoil was tremendous. . . . Every time she fired it was like a snowstorm in my cabin, only instead of snowflakes sheared rivet-heads would come down from the deckhead and partition." *

The *Yamato*s were built under even more stringent security conditions than usual. A vast sisal rope curtain covered their slips, the area was entirely cleared of civilians when they were launched, and they were fitted out behind screens and under camouflage. The *Musashi* saw no important action during her two and a half years of service. She was sunk in the Sibuyan Sea during the Leyte Gulf carrier action by American torpedo- and bomb-carrying aircraft, suffering an estimated seventeen heavy bomb and twenty torpedo hits before going to the bottom. The *Yamato* survived for longer. She was completed a few weeks after Pearl Harbor. It has been told † that her last role was that of a massive maritime Kamikaze, when she was dispatched to Okinawa with enough fuel for only a one-way trip, in order to divert attention and offer the air Kamikazes a better chance against the American aircraft carriers. On April 7, 1945, she too proved the strength and formidable protection of her class when she survived seven heavy bomb hits and at least twelve torpedo strikes before blowing up (see page 230).

The third of the *Yamato*s was completed as the big aircraft carrier *Shinano;* the fourth was never laid down. Before leaving these greatest of all battleships, it is worth recording that there is some evidence that, like the *Dreadnought* herself, of which they were the final extension, the dimensions of the potential enemy's main strategic canal may well have conditioned their size. Just as a ship as vast as the *Dreadnought* in 1906 demanded the expensive

* *Early Bird,* by W. Geoffrey Moore (1963).
† *The Design and Construction of the Yamato and Musashi,* by Captain Kitaro Matsumoto and Commander Masatake Chihaya: *Proceeding of the United States Naval Institute,* October, 1953.

All the contrived "fierce-face" characteristics of earlier
French battleships had disappeared with her Third
Generation construction. This is *Dunkerque* in 1937. The
main armament is all forward in quadruple turrets (57).
Richard Perkins

and prolonged rebuilding of the Kiel Canal locks, so the Panama Canal would
have had to be widened to pass through American 18-inch-gunned ships as
mighty as the *Yamatos*.

By comparison with the monster Eastern pair, the other European Second
Generation Dreadnoughts were puny and their total combat experience very
slight. The French remained loyal to the quadruple turret with their *Strasbourg* and *Dunkerque*, scuttled by their own crews at Toulon in November,
1942; and again with the much larger 15-inch-gunned *Jean Bart*, *Richelieu*,
and *Clemenceau* laid down between 1935 and 1939. All three of these
last French Dreadnoughts were caught up in the tide of the German advance
in 1940, the *Clemenceau* being taken from her drydock uncompleted, and
the *Richelieu* and *Jean Bart* escaping, the latter in a very incomplete state.
The *Richelieu* was eventually completed in time to take part in the last of the
Pacific operations; the *Jean Bart*, left in a very battered condition, was not
ready for sea until 1949, and so became the last Dreadnought in the world to
be commissioned. She and her sister ship survive to this day, bizarre relics of
a style of maritime architecture that in the past had produced some of the
most unorthodox of all capital ships. The hull of the *Clemenceau* was broken
up in 1946.

A great deal more beauty and practical sense was evident in the Italian
answer to these strange French vessels with their armament all concentrated
forward in two turrets; although the history of the *Littorio* (later renamed
Italia), *Roma*, *Vittorio Veneto*, and *Impero* was, if anything, rather more un-

Completed at last after an eventful war in Europe,
Richelieu sails for the Far East (58). *U.S. Navy*

Jean Bart, after hazardous escape from France in an
uncompleted state, arrived at Casablanca in 1940. Some
of her guns and equipment were used to complete her
sister ship in time for the Japanese war. In 1949 she
became the last Dreadnought ever to be completed, and
survives to this day (58). *U.S. Navy*

Vittorio Veneto, of the Italian Third Generation, steams
to her surrender in September, 1943 (62). *Imperial
War Museum*

distinguished. The *Impero*, like the *Clemenceau*, was never completed; none
of the other three in more than three years of war took serious steps to challenge the hard-pressed British Mediterranean Fleet, even when the Germans
had given them command of the air. In September, 1943, they did their best
to surrender, along with other surviving Italian Dreadnoughts, but the *Roma*
was destroyed en route to Malta by a German radio-controlled bomb, and the
Italia was damaged on the same occasion. It is perhaps doubtful if these sole
Italian Third Generation representatives of the Dreadnought would have stood
up to the rigors of bombardment from the air as well as the *Richelieu*, the
British *Nelson* and *Rodney*, and the American battleships in the Pacific. But
with their nine tripled 15-inch guns, their lightweight construction, combined
with very high speed (31 knots was not beyond their powers), they met very
closely Italian needs in the Mediterranean; and were in the direct line of
descent from the remarkable products of Benedetto Brin and his pupil Vittorio
Cuniberti.

The first of Britain's Third Generation Dreadnoughts was not yet ready
in September, 1939, and the Royal Navy's battle fleet consisted of thirteen
Second Generation ships and the *Nelson* and *Rodney*. Another year passed
before the new *King George V* (the second of only two British Dread-

First of the British Third Generation: *King George V*
class, laid down in 1937. Superimposed turret forward
was also to have been a quadruple, but two 14-inch guns
were sacrificed to obtain better protection (14).
P. A. Reuter

noughts carrying the same name) joined the fleet. In spite of international tension, and the fleet's desperate need for new capital-ship tonnage to meet the new German fleet, it was not a simple business to reestablish the long-neglected and extremely complicated machinery necessary for the construction of the largest warships. The main bottleneck was in the ordnance factories. No big guns had been built since the *Nelsons'* 16-inch. In 1935 Britain, France, Russia, and America had agreed to limit the guns of their future battleships to 14 inches. When Japain failed to sign, and it became evident that her new ships would be armed with bigger guns, America took advantage of a let-out clause and settled on 16-inch artillery in time for her new ships. But the British mountings and guns had been advanced too far for a change to be made by 1937 when 16-inch and 45,000 tons were the only limitations. The British naval staff gave a spirited reply to the criticism of this choice of caliber, using similar arguments to those put forward by the German naval staff in the pre–First World War years. The *King George V*'s, it was pointed out, would carry as many as twelve, and they would have a great range and a higher rate of fire than any 16-inch gun. Unfortunately, the number had to be reduced to ten to provide suitable magazine protection within

209

The greatest British Dreadnought: *Vanguard*
incorporated the latest and most comprehensive
antiaircraft defenses, could steam 30 knots, and was a fine
seaboat. But she missed the war. The eight 15-inch guns,
turrets, and mountings were once on the battle cruisers
Glorious and *Courageous* (15). *P. A. Reuter*

the agreed displacement of 35,000 tons. These were disposed in two quadruple
turrets, following the French practice, fore and aft, with another pair superimposed forward. In accordance with contemporary fashion, the secondary
battery of new 5.25's could be used against surface vessels and aircraft, and
was supported by a large number of light high-angle guns. There was a hangar
for four amphibians amidships, but when it was decided later in the war that
catapulted aircraft with all their fuel were a greater menace than an asset, it
was turned into a cinema. The total weight devoted to armor of the *King
George V, Prince of Wales, Howe, Anson,* and *Duke of York* was around
12,000 tons, and with deck armor of six inches and a belt of fourteen and
fifteen inches, was on a par with German contemporaries. The designed speed
of 27½ knots was well exceeded in service; and altogether they were most
successful ships, although they did not reach a state of full efficiency until
some time after their commissioning. The *Prince of Wales* was too new from

The last of the long line of British Dreadnoughts, *Vanguard* and one of the *King George V*'s laid up before going to the breakers (14 and 15). *P. A. Reuter*

the builders when she met the *Bismarck* and still had dockyard civilians on board. She later took five Japanese torpedoes before going down. Her sister ship *Duke of York* proved more than a match for the *Scharnhorst*, and all were kept a great deal busier than their Grand Fleet ancestors.

The first two ships of a new class of four 40,000-ton British battleships were abandoned on the stocks a year later. They were intended to meet the new German ships to follow the *Bismarck* and *Tirpitz*, and followed the same general lines laid down with *King George V*'s, their nine 16-inch guns being placed in three triple turrets to fire three aft and six forward. In spite of this serious cancellation and the rise in status of the aircraft carrier, the British battleship was not yet dead; and Fisher's trail was to endure from the genesis to the final extinction of the Dreadnought. Somebody pointed out that there were some old guns, turrets, and mountings from Fisher's "large light cruisers" lying about unwanted. The *Glorious* and *Courageous* had been stripped of these on their conversion to aircraft carriers, and it seemed a waste that they should not be used in wartime. Here, it seemed, was a way of getting a cheap battleship quickly—one that might be ready before the end of the war. So the design of the abandoned *Lion*s was modified to take these four 15-inch-gun turrets; some lessons from the *King George V*'s were taken into consideration, and the *Vanguard* was laid down shortly before Japan came into the war against Britain. Unfortunately, Fisher's guns but not his driving force went into the new odd ship with her twenty-five-year-old artillery, and by the time she was ready the war, and the age of the battleship, were over. This was a pity, as she was, from all reports, a fine ship, steady in any sea. Britain's biggest Dreadnought took the Queen, when she was Princess Elizabeth, to South Africa with the Royal Family, and served as flagship of the Reserve Fleet before being scrapped. The *Vanguard* had one other distinction: she was relatively the cheapest battleship ever built in a British yard.

The United States was by far the most prolific producer of Third Generation Dreadnoughts, commissioning in all a round dozen, all of which survived hectic careers, mainly in the Pacific. The same problems of construction arose here as in Britain. The Washington Treaty and the reluctance to reappraise the international scene in the 1930's together resulted in a rundown of the plant and the special skills demanded by heavy-warship construction. Fourteen years passed between the completion of the last of the *Maryland*s and the laying down late in 1937 of the *North Carolina*. The exact nature and artillery of this ship, and her sister the *Washington*, were the subject of much debate within the Department of the Navy, so that the United States was the last of the great powers to begin Third Generation construction. The success of the design was proved both statistically and in active service. On a displacement little more than the *Maryland*'s, the *Washington*'s incorporated a main armament of nine 16-inch against eight in the earlier ships (the guns were more powerful 50-caliber weapons), and a massive secondary and high-angle armament, ranging from 5-inch to .5-inch machine guns, that heralded a new numerical scale of antiaircraft protection, and ensured the success of these ships as aircraft-carrier escorts. Above all, the speed had gone up from 21 to some 28 knots. Superior machinery largely accounted for this rise in speed. But American naval architects were now up to all the weight-saving tricks, using extensive electric welding and structurally strong lightweight metals.

The *Washington*s made a striking departure from the traditional line of American Dreadnoughts. Gone now was the heavy piled-up effect with elaborate bridgework, heavy mainmast, and upper-deck casemate batteries of secondary armament. With their long, sweeping, unbroken flush deck, and their pronounced flare forward, they appeared much more graceful and fleet than their predecessors, their tall twin funnels adding a last touch to the overall balanced impression.

The sharp distinctions between all the three generations of American Dreadnoughts was also made clear when the *Washington*'s successors made their appearance. From the *South Carolina* of 1906 to the *New York* of 1911,

U.S.S. *Washington* passing through the Panama Canal
on October 11, 1945. *U.S. Navy*

U.S.S. *Indiana:* Here is the personification of the American Third Generation, with the effect of the big guns overwhelmed by more recent manifestations of the age of military technology: radar scanners and fire-control director equipment, 5-inch, 40-mm., 20-mm., and m.g. high-angle artillery wherever space can be found. She is on her way to attack Taroa airfield on Maloelap in the Marshalls (34). *U.S. Navy*

the formula had included paired 12-inch or 14-inch guns in up to six turrets, turbine or reciprocating engines offering a speed of around 20 knots, and "compromise" armor protection over most of the hull and vital parts varying from five to twelve inches in thickness. With the *Oklahoma* of 1912, the pattern of the Second Generation, which was to last a decade, was set: armor on the "all-or-nothing" principle, triple turrets when called for, the wider use of electric power, immense internal structural strength, all at the expense of speed. Finally came the *Washington*s, *South Dakota*s, and *Iowa*s, in which high speed and defense against the aerial bomb and torpedo were combined on a greater displacement with no loss of heavy firepower. The cost had risen some ten times, the displacement more than three times, the weight of broadside from 14,000 pounds to 18,000 pounds. Ten Dreadnoughts of the First Generation, twelve of the Second and ten of the Third were completed—plus two oddities.

The *South Dakota*s followed as closely the pattern of the *Washington*s as did the *Pennsylvania*s the *Oklahoma*s. The *South Dakota*, the *Alabama*, *Indiana*, and *Massachusetts* were laid down in the second half of 1939 or early in 1940, and, in a time of ever-growing anxiety and war, were built more speedily. Still nominally of 35,000 tons displacement, like the *Washington*s and the British *King George V*'s, their tonnage was increased before completion with the addition of more high-angle guns and increased protection against aerial attack. Speed was now up to a good 30 knots, freeboard was raised to diminish optical and artillery interference in high seas, and the two funnels of the *Washington*s were trunked into one squat smokestack.

American Dreadnought construction reached its zenith with the six *Iowa*s, the first of which was laid down as Hitler was sweeping across Europe in 1940. The *Kentucky* and *Illinois* were never completed, but the *Iowa*, *New Jersey*, *Missouri*, and *Wisconsin* all saw service against Japan, although mainly after the Japanese Dreadnought fleet had ceased to count. Again the same design pattern was followed. No change in the main battery was made, the increase of 10,000 tons in displacement and 200 feet in overall

U.S.S. *Alabama* on Russian convoy duties, April, 1943
(34). *U.S. Navy*

U.S.S. *Alabama* (opposite) takes to the water in February, 1942, and steams into Puget Sound during the closing months of the war (34). *U.S. Navy*

"Come into port greatly, or sail with God the seas . . ." —EMERSON.
The final word in American Dreadnoughts—U.S.S. *Iowa* (35). *U.S. Navy*

U.S.S. *Missouri* crushes her way through heavy seas on
her way back from Korean duty in 1951 (35). *U.S. Navy*

Duty accomplished: "Mighty Mo," Third Fleet Flagship,
sails from Pearl Harbor on September 29, 1945 (35).
U.S. Navy

length being accounted for by the additional machinery, and its protection,
which made them among the fastest battleships in the world.* This high
speed was necessary no longer for the purpose of outmaneuvering the enemy
and crossing the "T" in battle, but in order to keep up with the ultrafast
aircraft carriers soon to join the American fleet, for whose protection they
were to be chiefly responsible.

Like the British and German admiralties, the Department of the Navy
was authorized to lay down a quota of behemoths, none of which reached
the launching stage. There were to have been five ships in the 58,000-ton

* No figures are available, but probably only the Italian *Roma* class were faster.

Ordered in 1940, as enlarged 58,000-ton *Iowa*s with twelve
16-inch main armament, this is how the five *Montana*s
would have appeared. *U.S. Navy*

Montana class, including the *Ohio*, *Maine*, *New Hampshire*, and *Louisiana*,
further enlargements of the *Iowa*s and this time carrying twelve 16-inch,
and otherwise reminiscent of the aborted *Indiana* class of just twenty years
earlier.

It is convenient that the Dreadnought story can be rounded off in a
manner and style of which Jackie Fisher would have warmly approved.
It is also appropriate that it can be closed on the theme of the battle cruiser,
the Dreadnought principle in its most extreme form. The *Alaska* and *Guam*
were the last Dreadnoughts to be completed and to have fought—four more
ships, the *Hawaii*, *Philippines*, *Puerto Rico*, and *Samoa*, being abandoned.
They were officially defined as large cruisers, but were battle cruisers in
all their characteristics, with a maximum speed, unsurpassed by any other
Dreadnought, of some 36 knots, armor plate in the same ratio to the *Washington*'s as the *Invincible*'s had been to the *Iron Duke*'s, and nine quick-firing
12-inch guns—besides the usual huge battery of light and heavy high-angle
guns. It is true that these two ships were hybrids and that, in the words of
Fighting Ships, "it is a little difficult to find the precise *raison d'être* of these
overgrown cruisers." It is significant, however, that the fastest Dreadnoughts
were built in world wars and that even the Japanese and Russians learned
in their Far East 1904–1905 conflict the importance of speed in capital-ship
design. The *Hood*, *Renown*, and *Repulse*, the *Glorious* class, the *Ersatz-
Yorck* and her sisters, the aborted American *Constellation*s all were conceived in the heat of conflict. Just as the battle of the Falkland Islands and
Dogger Bank emphasized the need for ever greater speed to bring about
a conclusion, and resulted in the design of the fastest capital ships of their
time, so the *Bismarck* hunt, the successful evasion of the *Scharnhorst* and

Gneisenau, and the continued ability of the Italian fleet to avoid battle suggested the need for ever higher speed. And the *raison d'être* of the *Alaska*s was not entirely incomprehensible. Besides rumors of the construction of 17,000-ton cruisers armed with six 12-inch guns, the Japanese had built between the wars some extremely powerful heavy cruisers, which were faster and more heavily armed than the Washington Treaty American cruisers.

And so it came about that the world's greatest naval power, which had never before completed a battle cruiser, turned at last to this class of vessel after it had been discarded by every other navy. Certainly the role of these two ships was clearer than that of the First and Second Generation battle cruisers. Certainly they were never misused as they were in the First World War. And certainly, had Fisher been alive, he would have relished them and seen in their high speed, light protection, and rapid-firing guns the ultimate manifestation of everything he and Gard had dreamed of forty years earlier.

U.S.S. *Alaska:* An unexpected reversion to the swift, lightly armed and lightly plated principle of Dreadnought dating from the *Invincible* of 1906. There were to have been six in this class of 12-inch-gun battle cruiser, but only *Alaska* and *Guam* were completed (36). *U.S. Navy*

CHAPTER 9

The Second World War

When naval warfare was continued in European waters in September, 1939, it was possible to draw parallels with the situation in 1914. The British fleet was back in Scapa; the German fleet a threat. The blockade was reestablished. German U-boats were already at sea, puncturing Britain's trade arteries. Scouting forces, distantly supported by the heavy units, searched the gray horizons for a sign that the German Dreadnoughts might come out. A Shetland crofter gazing down at the tripods of Dreadnoughts—many the same ships he had seen anchored there twenty-one years before—could be forgiven for believing that time had stood still. Then, when the fleet hastily left after the sudden discovery that the base was insecure against the U-boat, the similarity with the late summer of 1914 was too close for comfort. The undersea weapons struck once more. The *Royal Oak* was sunk by torpedo, with fearful loss of life, just as the *Aboukir, Hogue,* and *Cressy* had gone down in 1914. The *Nelson* struck a mine off the coast, just as *Audacious* had done in October, 1914.

But a reconsideration of the activities of the much-reduced battle fleets soon revealed a striking contrast between the two wars, and the fundamental changes that had overtaken their function. In the First World War the mine and torpedo restricted the Dreadnought's activities and confined it for most of the time to protected anchorages, from which it influenced maritime conditions and events by its concealed and distant presence and its unexercised but latent power. Two decades after the passing of the Grand and High Seas fleets, the age-old principle of maritime strategy was unchanged. The control of the seas remained the final objective, for the purpose of providing and denying the free movement of trade and military needs. But the means of exercising this control was vested as well, and within its ever-increasing range and power, in the aircraft, from shore or carrier. Now the North Sea was disputed territory. Regardless of the great superiority of the British fleet, air power made it possible for Germany to invade and hold Norway, to dispatch surface raiders into the Atlantic, to lay mines rapidly in distant parts, to pass convoys across the North Sea, even to send heavy naval units up the English Channel. The Dreadnought was used by Germany for its new function of commerce raiding against the Atlantic trade lanes; by Britain as hunters of these raiders, as protectors against them, and as aircraft-carrier escorts.

The German Dreadnought commerce raiders, when loose, engaged the attention of a quite disproportionate number of British capital ships. The successful hunting down of a surface raider has always required a force of between five and ten times the raider's own strength. The modern construction, speed, strength, and long range of the German Dreadnought commerce raider were also strong factors acting to its advantage. Other factors worked to its disadvantage and caused it to be much less successful than it might have been. First was the timidity and confused thinking of the German High Command and naval staff. They never seemed able to make up their minds, and were always quarreling among themselves. The second was the searching range and striking power of British aircraft. And finally the absence of any base for refueling, recuperation, and repair. This brought about a state of acute anxiety to avoid even slight damage, which might slow them or restrict their range, laying them open to destruction by slower ships. This is just what happened to the *Bismarck*, and many convoys were saved when seen to be accompanied by a single slow and obsolete British Dreadnought. German Dreadnoughts again proved to be unsinkable by shellfire alone: both the *Bismarck* and the *Scharnhorst* had to be finished off with torpedoes.

In the early days of the Second World War in Europe, only smaller or lightly constructed warships succumbed to the bomber. Bombing attacks against British and German Dreadnoughts were ineffective. When the bomber was increased in size, range, and power it proved its destructiveness, and destroyed the *Tirpitz*, and two of the pocket battleships. The torpedo bomber showed itself as a more potent weapon, and even in comparatively crude form was able to cripple Italian Dreadnoughts in the Mediterranean.

Before command of the air was gained in the Mediterranean, the British Dreadnought proved her worth by escorting convoys, her big guns deterring interference by Italian battleships, her numerous antiaircraft guns helping to beat off bomber attacks against the aircraft carriers and merchantmen, her armor and structural strength resisting the power of the smaller high-explosive bomb. Later, when command of the air was gained, the Dreadnought took on a new and extremely useful task. British battleships, designed to fight in the line against the High Seas Fleet in the North Sea at a time when aircraft were considered only as unreliable reconnaissance machines, were used for shore bombardment in support of amphibious operations and landings on North African, Sicilian, Italian, and French coasts, against Italian industrial targets, German defense points and enemy bases. None was sunk by enemy gunfire or by air attack: one was sunk by U-boat, two more were crippled while in harbor.

Throughout nearly six years of maritime warfare in European waters and the Atlantic, the small force of British Dreadnoughts was always fully stretched and fully occupied on important duties. They may, indeed, have been made obsolete in tactical terms before the war began; or they may have been almost entirely occupied on functions for which they had never been designed. It could be argued, and was argued, that the wealth and materials expended on the five *King George V*'s would have been better used on swift armored aircraft carriers with fighters and bombers in their hangars as modern as those possessed by the R.A.F. But what mattered was that Britain, like all the European great naval powers, had again invested heavily in the Dreadnought, that it again strongly influenced events at sea throughout the war, and that Britain at least, as the perpetrator of the Dreadnought and the builder of more than any other power, employed them

Six of *Rodney*'s nine 16-inch guns at full forty degrees
of elevation, at which they could—and did—fire against
aircraft (13). The Times, *London*

busily right up to the end of hostilities. The variety and intensity of their
work can best be judged by briefly summarizing the war career of one of
them, H.M.S. *Rodney:*

September, 1939, at Scapa Flow with sister ship *Nelson*, three R-class battleships,
battle cruisers *Hood* and *Repulse*. Until the end of November was occupied on
patrol in North Sea, intercepting enemy shipping searching for German surface
raiders, including the *Gneisenau*, and escorting an important iron-ore convoy
from Norway. After Scapa was proved unsafe, operated from the Clyde and
Loch Ewe; suffered mechanical trouble, rejoined the fleet in the New Year,
returned to Scapa when base made secure. Struck by a heavy bomb, and armored
deck aft pierced, during Norwegian operations in April, 1940; fifteen casualties.
Covered evacuation of British forces from Norway. During period of most

intense commerce raiding, winter 1940–1941, with *Nelson* covered the Iceland-Faeroes passage. January, 1941, off to hunt the *Scharnhorst* and *Gneisenau* in North Atlantic and Arctic. Also covered convoys, picking up survivors from those mauled by German battle cruisers. Sighted enemy briefly and gave chase, but *Scharnhorst* and *Gneisenau* slipped into Brest. Covering another convoy when called away for the *Bismarck* hunt. Covered her possible line of retreat into Bay of Biscay, then ordered out when *Prince of Wales* and *Repulse* forced to seek fuel in Iceland. Joined *King George V*, and her third 16-inch salvo scored first hit on *Bismarck*. Given freedom to maneuver (unlike *Prince of Wales* earlier), escaped damage from *Bismarck*'s guns, then helped reduce her to a blazing hulk. Remarkable speed reported to have been achieved by tiring machinery during chase. With Force H (as flagship) September, 1941, and on hectic Malta convoy with *Nelson*, *Prince of Wales*, and carrier *Ark Royal*. In 1942, when threat of commerce raiding by *Tirpitz*, *Scheer*, *Gneisenau*, *Scharnhorst*, and heavy cruisers renewed, with Home Fleet again. Another Malta convoy in August, 1942: very heavy air attacks, during which her 16-inch guns were used at maximum elevation at range of nine miles. First shore bombardments during North African landings, and in following year (1943) with *Nelson*, *Warspite*, *Valiant*, and two carriers operated east of Sicily to protect invasion forces. September, 1943, supported Salerno landings, bombarded defenses at Reggio: beat off German torpedo-bomber attacks. Was present at surrender of Italian Fleet September 9th. Back to home waters for D-Day and with *Warspite*, *Ramillies*, and monitor bombarded German strongpoints. Later, in June, 1944, to German dismay, bombarded armored-vehicle concentration *seventeen miles* inland, with aid of air-spotter. Also bombarded German batteries on Alderney, before going north to escort Murmansk convoy still threatened by *Tirpitz*. Steamed 156,000 miles on war service.

While H.M.S. *Rodney* was undergoing a much-needed overhaul in the United States, the Dreadnought was suffering its greatest single blow at Pearl Harbor, where within a few minutes more of her kind were sunk or put out of action by the torpedo and aerial bomb than ever the high-explosive shell had accomplished. The event that led some three years later to the extinction of one of the world's most powerful battle fleets also set the pattern for the greatest maritime struggle of all time and reestablished the new role of the battleship in the Pacific as radically as it had been reestablished in European waters. Within three days at Hawaii and in the South China Sea four Dreadnoughts had been destroyed, five crippled or damaged by the bomb and torpedo—mainly the torpedo. Of these casualties the most significant were the *Repulse* and *Prince of Wales*, the first Dreadnoughts to be sunk by aircraft while *at sea*. These ships were in full operational condition, close to their base, but without air cover, the carrier that was ordered to accompany them having been damaged accidentally and delayed.

The Japanese Naval Staff had early recognized the most useful purpose for the Dreadnought in an amphibious Pacific war. Their functions were twofold, according to their speed. The very fast, very old, but entirely rebuilt *Kongo*s acted as escorts and artillery supports for the swift carrier wings that early ranged far, from Ceylon to Port Darwin, gaining maritime control wherever they sped. The slower Dreadnoughts were used as distant artillery support in the Pearl Harbor operation, when in Churchill's words "the mastery of the Pacific had passed into Japanese hands," and again at Coral Sea and Midway. The real significance of Pearl Harbor was not the temporary loss of the greater part of United States Dreadnought power but the escape of the precious and vulnerable carriers, the new capital ships, whose aircraft were, by the summer of 1942, regaining the initiative.

As the American carrier fleets grew, so the battleship strength was augmented by the arrival of new tonnage and those vessels that had escaped Pearl Harbor or had been repaired after the carnage. They performed similar duties to those of the Japanese Dreadnoughts, providing artillery support to the amphibious forces during the prolonged and deadly rolling back of Japanese strength, island by island, area by area, to the Solomons, the Marshall Islands, the Philippines, and at last to the mainland of Japan itself. Except for the first assault on the Solomons, every major amphibious operation was preceded by the thunder of the Dreadnoughts' guns, in every case saving American lives and easing their assault task. In the last phase the big-gun platform also caused great damage to industrial targets in Japan and elsewhere. At the same time the new fast ships worked with the carrier task forces in a curious role of mutual support, the carrier's fighters providing the big ships with air cover while they in turn provided the carriers with protection from enemy bombers with their massive and latterly almost invulnerable antiaircraft artillery defense.

As in the war against Germany and Italy, it was fruitless at the time to conjecture whether the Dreadnought had been made obsolete by the bomb, torpedo bomber, or submarine—at Taranto, Singapore or Pearl Harbor or Midway. There it was in all its sublime greatness and grandeur, the final manifestation of the work of Cuniberti, Fisher, and Gard, and all the subsequent naval architects of Britain and America, Italy and France and Japan, Russia and Germany. All that mattered was that, where command of the air helped to grant command of the ocean's surface, the battleship performed usefully; scarcely ever in the role for which it was once devised, but very often to good purpose. When command of the air was lost—as, say, at Pearl Harbor to the Japanese and at Leyte Gulf to the Americans—then the battleship succumbed.

In July, 1945, two of the last three surviving Japanese Dreadnoughts had been destroyed—only the *Nagato* survived. The first two were sunk at Guadalcanal, the *Hi-ei* on Friday, November 13, 1942, by the combined efforts of big guns and carrier- and land-based aircraft. Two days later another of the always hard-pressed *Kongo*s went down, the first Dreadnought battleship (her status had been changed between the wars) ever to be sunk by gunfire alone. Almost two years passed before Dreadnought again fought Dreadnought in the Pacific. Then in the frenzied air-to-air, air-to-sea, and

sea-to-sea contests about the Philippines, the *Fuso* and *Yamashiro* went down to American gunfire, and the mighty *Musashi* to a wildly brave and sustained attack by American carrier aircraft. The last of the *Kongo*s (the name ship was victim to a submarine's torpedoes) was pounded into a wreck in the Inland Sea in July, 1945; and on the same day other carrier aircraft put an end to the *Ise* and *Hiuga*, the worst day for the Japanese battleship since two had gone down to Russian mines in 1904. Yamamoto's *Yamato* was already at the bottom.

There was no longer any Japanese battle fleet. The force that had so painstakingly been built up from foreign construction at the beginning of the century, had been nursed into a formidable fighting force by Togo, had

Shore bombardment in the Pacific: The *Pennsylvania*
(opposite) shells Guam in July, 1944. . . . The *Alabama*
(above) fires a 16-inch salvo (29), (34) *U.S. Navy*

Mitsubishi nightmare: In the role of antiaircraft gun
platform, the defenses of U.S.S. *New York* (below) were
almost impenetrable, even by a kamikaze. Carriers
found comfort in the proximity of such formidable
batteries (27). *U.S. Navy*

The last moments of the greatest Dreadnought: The
Yamato blows up under a rain of bombs and torpedoes
from United States Navy planes. *U.S. Navy*

triumphed so splendidly at Tsushima, and grown to become one of the world's
greatest, had been as utterly annihilated as the Russian Baltic Fleet in 1905.
It was fitting that the Dreadnought should have taken a leading part in this
melancholy task.

To illustrate the range and variety of work accomplished by the American
"battlewagon," it is again convenient to follow by means of a much-condensed
log the activities of one of them. None can be more deserving of this small
recognition than the U.S.S. *Washington*, whose great guns were heard during
more than three years of war from the Hebrides to the New Hebrides:

Commissioned May 15, 1941, flagship Battleship Division Sixth Atlantic Fleet.
March, 1942, as flagship Task Force Thirty-nine to Scapa Flow, under opera-

tional control of British Home Fleet. April–May, 1942, with British units as cover for Murmansk convoys. Iceland, back to Scapa where inspected by King George VI, and further convoy cover operations before returning to New York, July 21, 1942. Left for Pacific on August 23rd, Tonga, September 14th; then to Solomons where escorted task forces and covered landings on Guadalcanal. November 13th, flying flag Rear Admiral Lee, formed Task Force Sixty-four with *South Dakota* and sailed to east of Savo Islands in search of enemy transports. Night of November 14th intercepted Japanese bombardment group with battleship *Kirishima* and four heavy and light cruisers, and after confused and damaging action between light escorting craft, with *South Dakota* engaged in gun duel, *Washington* scoring some nine 16-inch hits on *Kirishima*, leaving her wrecked and in flames. She was later scuttled. *South Dakota* received bad superficial damage, flagship unharmed. Until late April, 1943, continued to engage in carrier and task-force escort in Solomons campaign. Overhauled at Pearl Harbor in May–June; August to New Hebrides; November with Task Group 53.2 to Fiji, then with 50.1 to Gilbert Islands supporting carriers during air attacks and assault forces during Tarawa and Makin landings. Heavy air attacks November 27–28—no damage. Early December, 1943, formed Task Group 50.8, including most powerful single concentration of Dreadnoughts in any ocean: with *Washington, North Carolina, Indiana, Massachusetts, Alabama, South Dakota.* After carrier plane attack on Nauru, heavy 16-inch bombardment; followed by 5-inch. To Ellice Islands mid-January, 1944, covered air strikes on Taroa Islands and Kwajalein Atoll on January 29th and 30th, followed by bombardment. Collided with *Indiana* in dark on February 1st, and after temporary repairs, to Pearl Harbor, thence to Puget Sound for more permanent repairs. By mid-June, 1944, *Washington* back in action, again supporting air strikes and bombarding in the Marianas, covering the Marines' landing on Saipan on June 15th. Battle of the Philippine Sea began June 19th: with six other Dreadnoughts engaged in

Symbol of naval victory: U.S.S. *New Mexico* anchors in the shadow of Mount Fujiyama as the Pacific war closes. *U.S. Navy*

The birth and death of a great Dreadnought: 16-inch
guns are hoisted for fitting onto H.M.S. *Rodney* in 1926
as she completes her fitting out; and, severed by the
shipbreakers, are hoisted off again twenty-two years
later. The Times, *London; Messrs. Thomas Ward, Ltd.,
of Sheffield*

the famous "Marianas Turkey Shoot" against hundreds of Japanese land- and
carrier-based aircraft. Only *South Dakota* hit, not badly; and only 35 of 430
Japanese carrier planes left operational next day. From early September, 1944,
to mid-February, 1945, as unit of Fast Task Force 34.1 supported a long and
arduous succession of carrier strikes ranging from Okinawa to Saigon, Hong
Kong to Tokyo. Added her share of 16-inch shells in massive bombardment of
Iwo Jima on February 19–22—her last war assignment being bombardment of
Okinawa-Jima April 19, 1945. Returned to Pearl Harbor for last time in war,
thence to Puget Sound for much-needed overhaul, missing the surrender celebra-
tions.

Dreadnought Losses in the Second World War

FRANCE

Bretagne	Shellfire	Oran	July 3, 1940
Dunkerque	Scuttled	Toulon	November 27, 1942
Provence	Scuttled	Toulon	November 27, 1942
Strasbourg	Scuttled	Toulon	November 27, 1942
Courbet	Scuttled	Arromanches	June 6, 1944

GERMANY

Admiral Graf Spee	Scuttled	Montevideo	December 17, 1939
Bismarck	Shellfire and torpedoes	North Atlantic	May 27, 1941
Scharnhorst	Shellfire and torpedoes	North Cape	December 26, 1943
Tirpitz	Bomb	Tromsö Fjord	November 12, 1944
Gneisenau	Scuttled	Gdynia	March 28, 1945
Admiral Scheer	Bombs	Kiel	April 9-10, 1945
Lützow (ex-Deutschland)	Bombs	Swinemünde	April 16, 1945

GREAT BRITAIN

Royal Oak	U-boat torpedoes	Scapa Flow	October 14, 1939
Hood	Shellfire	Off Greenland	May 24, 1941
Barham	U-boat torpedoes	East Mediterranean	November 25, 1941
Prince of Wales	Aircraft torpedoes	South China Sea	December 10, 1941
Repulse	Aircraft torpedoes	South China Sea	December 10, 1941

ITALY

Conte di Cavour	Bombs	Trieste	February 20, 1945
Roma	Bomb	Strait of Bonafacio	September 9, 1943

JAPAN

Hi-ei	Shellfire, bombs	Guadalcanal	November 13, 1942
Kirishima	Shellfire	Guadalcanal	November 15, 1942
Mutsu	Internal explosion	Hiroshima Bay	June 8, 1943
Musashi	Aircraft torpedoes, bombs	Sibuyan Sea	October 24, 1944
Fuso	Shellfire	Leyte Gulf	October 25, 1944
Yamashiro	Shellfire	Leyte Gulf	October 25, 1944
Kongo	Submarine torpedo	Northwest Formosa	November 21, 1944
Yamato	Aircraft torpedoes and bombs	East China Sea	July 4, 1945
Hiuga	Aircraft torpedoes and bombs	Inland Sea area	July 24, 1945
Ise	Aircraft torpedoes and bombs	Inland Sea area	July 24, 1945
Haruna	Aircraft torpedoes and bombs	Inland Sea area	July 24, 1945

UNITED STATES

Arizona	Aircraft torpedoes and bombs	Pearl Harbor	December 7, 1941
Oklahoma	Aircraft torpedoes and bombs	Pearl Harbor	December 7, 1941

The last fighting Dreadnought. In 1967–8 the U.S.S.
New Jersey was reactivated for bombardment service off
Vietnam, where her 16-inch guns proved highly effective.
Here she is before completing her refit at Philadelphia
Navy Yard; the author is in the foreground. *U.S. Navy*

Dreadnought Specifications

The following tables give the chief characteristics of every class of all-big-gun capital ship completed since 1906. The figures have been taken from *Jane's Fighting Ships* and added to or amended from a number of other sources where, mainly for security reasons, there were inaccuracies on first publication. The figures given are for the ships *as completed*. Small variations in displacement and secondary armament between ships of the same class often occurred. In addition, every ship listed was subsequently modified or rebuilt to a greater or lesser degree, usually resulting in an increase in displacement (often due to additional protection, armament, aircraft launching equipment, and so on) varying from a few tons to as much as 10,000 tons. It has not been possible to record these variations, and in many cases no records exist. Nor has any attempt been made to specify antiaircraft armament fitted to later Dreadnoughts and added to earlier ships, as this varied widely from ship to ship and, under war conditions, sometimes from month to month.

The dates beneath each class record the month (when known) and year when the first was laid down and the last completed. The speed shown is the *designed* speed. There were variations between ships of the same class, and in most cases the designed speed could be exceeded, especially during a vessel's earlier years. Displacement given is Standard Displacement. The thickness of armor plate given is for the thickest part of the belt; as can frequently be seen from the silhouettes, this was often narrow, and often tapered above and below and forward and aft. The same applies to the turret armor plate; the sides and roof were frequently thinner than the turret face.

The numerals in parentheses at the head of each class correspond to those shown in the captions to the illustrations in the text.

The silhouettes are reproduced by kind permission from *Jane's Fighting Ships*, and remain the copyright of that invaluable annual. The date in parentheses records the year of issue from which they have been taken.

GREAT BRITAIN

BATTLESHIP (1)

Dreadnought
Oct., 1905–Oct., 1906

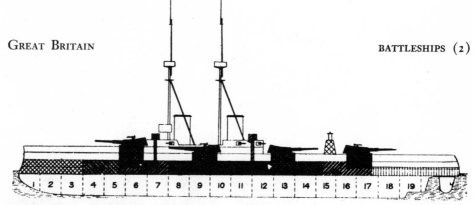

17,900 tons

21 knots

10 x 12 in. 27 x 12 pdr.
Belt 11 in. Turrets 11 in.

————————————————————————————— (1914)

GREAT BRITAIN

BATTLESHIPS (2)

Bellerophon
Superb
Téméraire
Dec., 1906–May, 1909

18,600 tons

20.75 knots

10 x 12 in. 16 x 4 in.
Belt 10 in. Turrets 11 in.

Fore and aft superstructures were elaborated during First World War.

————————————————————————————— (1914)

GREAT BRITAIN

BATTLESHIPS (3)

St. Vincent
Collingwood
Vanguard
Feb., 1907–April, 1910

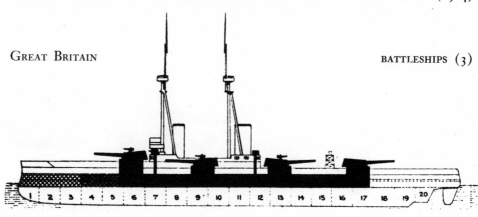

19,250 tons

21 knots

10 x 12 in. 20 x 4 in.
Belt 10 in. Turrets 11 in.

Unlike *Téméraire*s, fore funnel is thinner. In 1917, exposed 4-inch was removed or
added to built-up fore superstructure.

————————————————————————————— (1914)

237

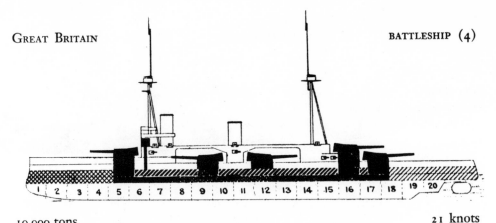

Neptune
Jan., 1909–Jan., 1911

19,900 tons   21 knots
10 x 12 in.   16 x 4 in.
Belt 10 in.   Turrets 11 in.

All secondary armament is in superstructures. Cruising turbines were used for economy.

——— (1914)

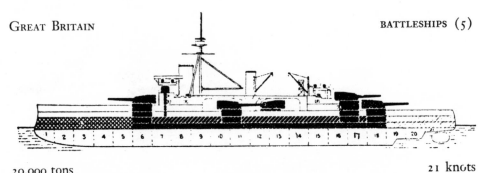

Colossus
Hercules
July, 1909–Aug., 1911

20,000 tons   21 knots
10 x 12 in.   16 x 4 in.
Belt 11 in.   Turrets 11 in.

——————————————————— (1919—but should show after flying boat deck removed)

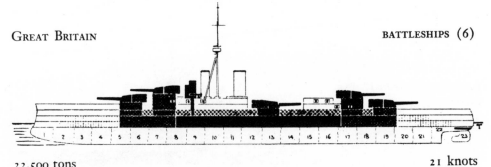

Orion
Thunderer
Monarch
Conqueror
Nov., 1909–Nov., 1912

22,500 tons   21 knots
10 x 13.5 in.   16 x 4 in.
Belt 12 in.   Turrets 11 in.

Conqueror made 23 knots on trials. First "super-Dreadnoughts." Director control equipment and turret runways later fitted—as in all British Dreadnoughts of this period.

——— (1919)

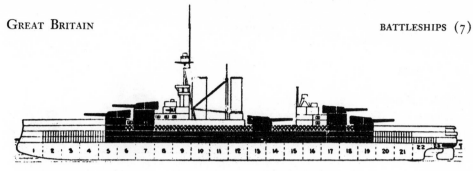

King George V
Audacious
Centurion
Ajax
Jan., 1911–Oct., 1913

23,000 tons   21 knots
10 x 13.5 in.   16 x 4 in.
Belt 12 in.   Turrets 11 in.

—————————————————————————— (1919)

GREAT BRITAIN   BATTLESHIP (8)

Erin (originally laid down
as Turkish *Reshadieh*)
Aug., 1911–July, 1914

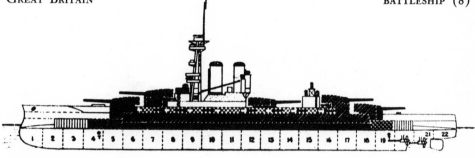

23,000 tons   21 knots
10 x 13.5 in.   16 x 6 in.
Belt 12 in.   Turrets 11 in.

Greater beam than contemporary British Dreadnoughts allowed heavier secondary battery on similar displacement.

—————————————————————————— (1919)

GREAT BRITAIN   BATTLESHIP (9)

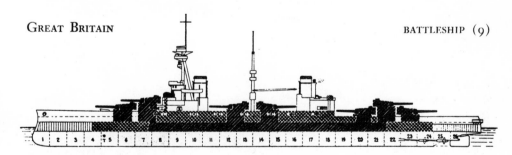

Agincourt
(ex-*Sultan Osman I*,
ex-*Rio de Janeiro*)
Sept., 1911–July, 1914

27,500 tons   22 knots
14 x 12 in.   20 x 6 in.   10 x 3 in.
Belt 9 in.   Turrets 12 in.

Ordered by Brazil, auctioned before completion in Britain, and bought by Turkey; taken over for the Royal Navy in 1914, served in Grand Fleet, fired ten full broadsides at Jutland, scrapped in 1922.

—————————————————— (1919–with flying boat bridges removed)

Iron Duke
Marlborough
Benbow
Emperor of India
(ex-*Delhi*)
Jan., 1912–Nov., 1914

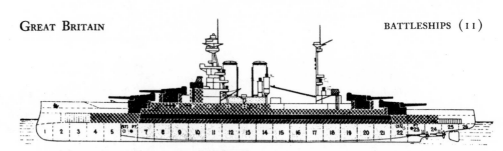

25,000 tons   21 knots
10 x 13.5 in.   12 x 6 in.
Belt 12 in.   Turrets 10 in.

Last of British First Generation and in Britain most highly regarded pre-First World War ships.

——————————————————————————————— (1919)

Queen Elizabeth
Warspite
Valiant
Barham
Malaya
Oct., 1912–Feb., 1916

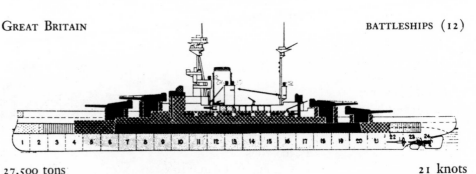

27,500 tons   25 knots
8 x 15 in.   12 x 6 in. (*Queen Elizabeth* 16 x 6 in.)
Belt 13 in.   Turrets 13 in.

Best British Dreadnoughts. Fastest battleships until 1930's. Fought in every theater and ocean. Funnels were trunked 1920's. *Barham* was refitted 1930–1933, *Malaya* 1934–1936; others were completely rebuilt 1934–1941.

——————————————————————————————— (1919)

Royal Sovereign
Royal Oak
Resolution
Ramillies
Revenge
Nov., 1913–Sept., 1917

27,500 tons   21 knots
8 x 15 in.   14 x 6 in.   2 x 3 in.
Belt 13 in.   Turrets 13 in.

Little modified during long life, though new antiaircraft guns, clinker screens, searchlights, etc., were added over years.

——————————————————————————————— (1919)

Nelson
Rodney
Dec., 1922–Aug., 1927

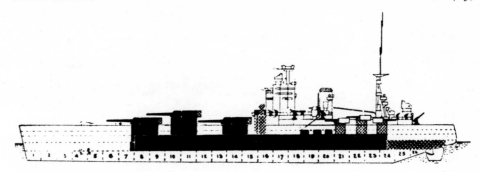

33,900 tons   23 knots
9 x 16 in.   12 x 6 in.   6 x 4.7 in. A.A.
Belt 14 in.   Turrets 16 in.

Scaled-down aborted 1920 *Invincible*s. First British Dreadnoughts with triple turrets; and, with four Third Generation French ships, these were the only Dreadnoughts to carry all main armament forward.

———————————————————————————————— (1931)

GREAT BRITAIN   BATTLESHIPS (14)

King George V
Duke of York
Prince of Wales
Anson
Howe
Jan., 1937–Aug., 1942

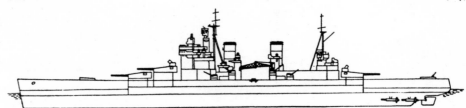

35,000 tons   28 knots
10 x 14 in.   16 x 5.25 in.
Belt 15 in.   Turrets 16 in.

Only British Dreadnoughts to mount quadruple turrets. New 14-inch fired two rounds a minute to 36,000 yards; 5.25-inch fired eighteen rounds a minute to 22,500 yards.

———————————————————————————————— (1951–1952)

GREAT BRITAIN   BATTLESHIP (15)

Vanguard
Oct., 1941–April, 1946

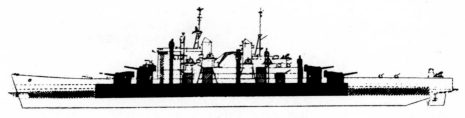

44,500 tons   30 knots
8 x 15 in.   16 x 5.25 in.
Belt 14 in.   Turrets 13 in.

———————————————————————————————— (1951–1952)

Invincible
Indomitable
Inflexible
Feb., 1906–Oct., 1908

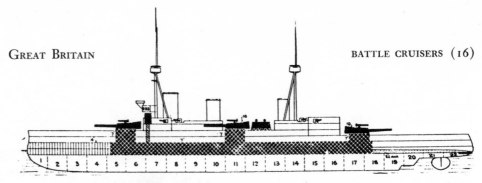

17,250 tons   25 knots
8 x 12 in.,   16 x 4 in.   1 x 3 in.
Belt 6 in. Turrets 7 in.

First-ever battle cruisers. Belt very narrow. New 4-inch fired 31-pound shell at twelve rounds a minute; were later given shields or placed in superstructure. Fore funnel lengthened 1910–1915. Made 28 knots in service.

——————————————————————————————— (1914)

Indefatigable
Australia
New Zealand
Feb., 1909–June, 1913

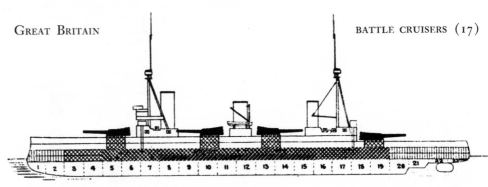

18,800 tons   25 knots
8 x 12 in.   16 x 4 in.
Belt 6 in. Turrets 7 in.

Enlarged *Invincible*s; and better sea boats. They were capable of 27 knots for short spells.

——————————————————————————————— (1914)

Lion
Princess Royal
Queen Mary
Nov., 1909–Sept., 1913

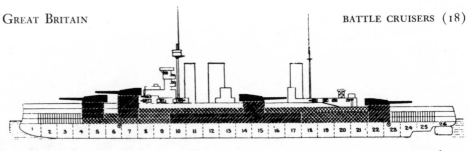

26,350 tons   26 knots
8 x 13.5 in.   16 x 4 in.
Belt 9 in. Turrets 9 in.

Fire control on foremast became untenable on trials, and mast was rebuilt forward of funnel as pole—later strutted. *Queen Mary* had round funnels, others oval.

——————————————————— (1914, after foremast was moved forward)

Tiger
June, 1912–Oct., 1914

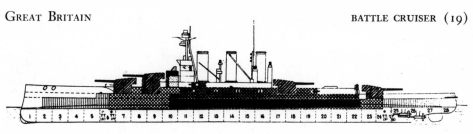

28,500 tons
8 x 13.5 in.   12 x 6 in.
Belt 9 in.   Turrets 9 in.

29 knots

Largest and fastest Dreadnought of her time. Only British battle cruiser with 6-inch secondary armament. Her protection was superior to that of *Lion*s.

——————————————————————————————————— (1919, with mainmast)

GREAT BRITAIN

BATTLE CRUISERS (20)

Renown
Repulse
Jan., 1915–Sept., 1916

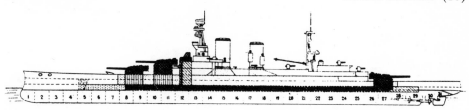

26,500 tons
6 x 15 in.   17 x 4 in.   2 x 3 in. A.A.
Belt 6 in.   Turrets 11 in.

30 knots

32 knots in service made them fastest in world at the time. Numerous refits, especially to *Renown*, were mainly concerned with adding to protection. Main belt was deepened and increased to 9 inches.

——————————————————————————————————— (1919)

GREAT BRITAIN

BATTLE CRUISERS (21)

Courageous
Glorious
May, 1915–Jan., 1917

18,600 tons
4 x 15 in.   18 x 4 in.
Belt 3 in.   Turrets 13 in.

31 knots

Lightest-armored Dreadnoughts. Made 33 knots in service. Converted to aircraft carriers. Sister ship *Furious* (two 18-inch) was completed as aircraft carrier with single 18-inch.

——————————————————————————————————— (1919)

GREAT BRITAIN — BATTLE CRUISER (22)

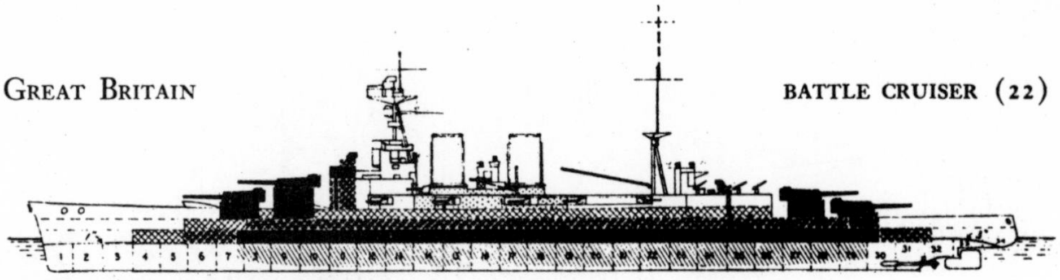

Hood
May, 1916–March, 1920

41,200 tons — 31 knots
8 x 15 in. 12 x 5.5 in. 4 x 4 in. A.A.
Belt 12 in. Turrets 15 in.

For more than half Dreadnought era, largest warship in the world. Last British battle cruiser. Her protection was still inadequate by German First World War standards.

(1919)

UNITED STATES — BATTLESHIPS (23)

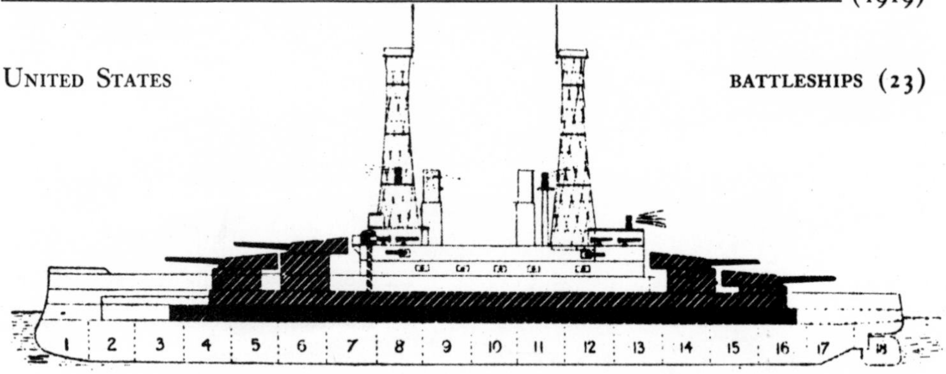

South Carolina
Michigan
Nov., 1906–Dec., 1909

16,000 tons — 18.5 knots
8 x 12 in., 22 x 3 in.
Belt 11 in. Turrets 12 in.

Designed and approved before *Dreadnought*–"may be considered as the first Dreadnoughts. . . ." (*Fighting Ships*). Only Spanish Dreadnoughts and "Pocket Battleships" were smaller. First with superimposed turrets; first with all-center-line main armament.

(1914)

UNITED STATES — BATTLESHIPS (24)

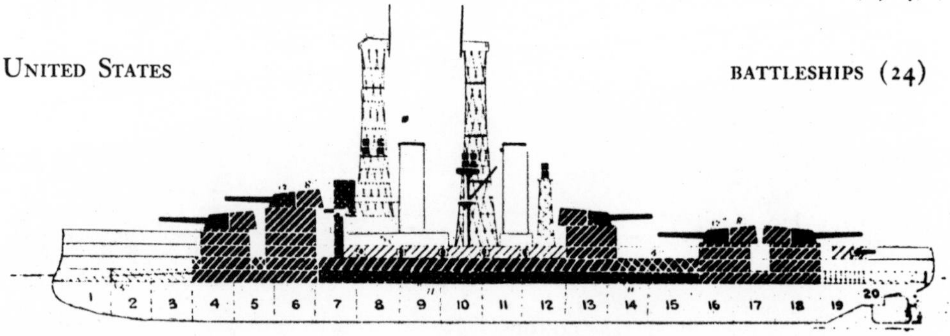

Delaware
North Dakota
Nov., 1907–April, 1910

20,000 tons — 21 knots
10 x 12 in. 14 x 5 in.
Belt 11 in. Turrets 12 in.

Turbines in *North Dakota*, which gave her about 4 knots better speed than *Michigan. Delaware* was completed in 26 months.

(1914)

Utah
Florida
March, 1909–Sept., 1911

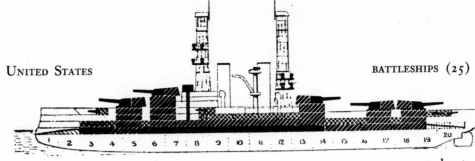

21,825 tons   20.75 knots
10 x 12 in.   16 x 5 in.
Belt 11 in.   Turrets 12 in.

New elaborate damage control and underwater protection. Foremost upper-deck 5-inch was removed during First World War.

——————————————————————— (1914)

Arkansas
Wyoming
Jan., 1910–Sept., 1912

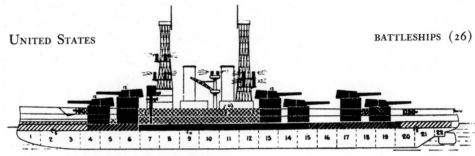

26,000 tons   20.5 knots
12 x 12 in.   21 x 5 in.
Belt 11 in.   Turrets 12 in.

Five main and upper-deck 5-inch removed during First World War. First (and only American) Dreadnoughts to mount six center-line turrets. *Arkansas* was fitted with massive light antiaircraft artillery for Second World War; *Wyoming* was used as gunnery training ship with three main turrets removed.

——————————————————————— (1914)

New York
Texas
April, 1911–April, 1914

27,000 tons   21 knots
10 x 14 in.   21 x 5 in.
Belt 12 in.   Turrets 14 in.

Early reports stated fifteen 12-inch in five triple turrets to be fitted. Because turbine builders would not meet Navy Dept. specifications, these reverted to reciprocating engines. Secondary armament was reduced in First World War. Tripods, new fire control, oil installation, eight 3-inch antiaircraft, catapult on "Q" turret all fitted in 1920's refit. Many light antiaircraft guns were fitted for Pacific war.

——————————————————————— (1914)

Oklahoma
Nevada
Oct., 1912–May, 1916

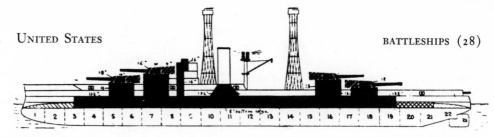

27,500 tons

20.5 knots

10 x 14 in.   21 x 5 in.
Belt 13½ in.   Turrets 18 in.

Reintroduced "all-or-nothing" armor-plate principle, first used by Nathaniel Barnaby some forty years earlier for Royal Navy battleships. Secondary armament reduced by nine guns during First World War, and moved from upper and main decks to forecastle during 1920's refit. *Oklahoma*, reciprocating engines. Tripods replaced lattice masts. *Oklahoma* capsized at Pearl Harbor and was later written off. *Nevada* was rebuilt when repaired.

——————————————————————— (1919—aft 5 in. removed)

Pennsylvania
Arizona
Oct., 1913–Oct., 1916

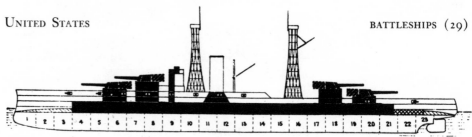

31,400 tons

21 knots

12 x 14 in.   22 x 5 in.
Belt 14 in.   Turrets 18 in.

Heavier main battery and heavier armor protection than *Nevada*s. Eight 5-inch guns removed soon after completion. Both radically refitted between wars. *Pennsylvania* served through Second World War, reequipping with salvaged 14-inch from *Oklahoma* and *Arizona* lost at Pearl Harbor.

——————————————————————— (1919—aft 5 in. removed)

New Mexico
Idaho
Mississippi
Jan., 1915–March, 1919

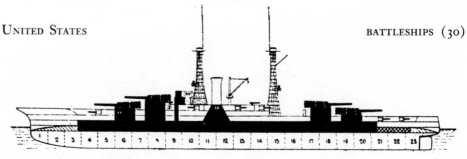

32,000 tons

21 knots

12 x 14 in.   14 x 5 in.
Belt 14 in.   Turrets 18 in.

Internal protection further enhanced. New 50-caliber 14-inch guns. Turbo-electric drive. Suffered customary refits in early 1930's and during Second World War, when they avoided Pearl Harbor attack.

——————————————————————— (1919—aft 5 in. removed)

California
Tennessee
Oct., 1916–Sept., 1921

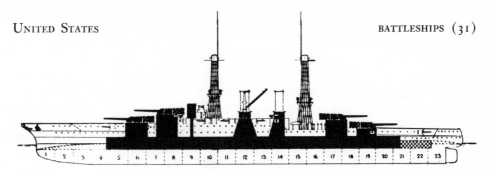

32,600 tons   21 knots
12 x 14 in.   12 x 5 in.
Belt 14 in.   Turrets 18 in.

Almost identical to *New Mexico*s. Both badly damaged at Pearl Harbor and rebuilt to entirely new silhouette.

——————————————————————————————— (1919–aft 5 in. removed)

Colorado
Maryland
West Virginia
April, 1917–Dec., 1923

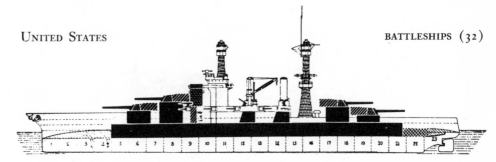

32,500 tons   21 knots
8 x 16 in.   12 x 5 in.
Belt 16 in.   Turrets 18 in.

16-inch-gunned versions of *California* and *New Mexico* classes. Retained lattice masts between wars, but *West Virginia,* badly damaged at Pearl Harbor, was rebuilt as *California.*

————————————————————— ————————————— (1931)

Washington
North Carolina
Oct., 1937–March, 1942

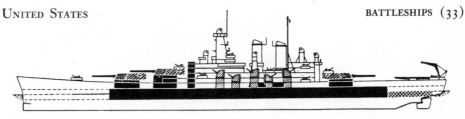

35,000 tons   28 knots
9 x 16 in.   20 x 5 in.
Belt 16 in.   Turrets 18 in.

Initiated a new formula and specification for America's last generation of Dreadnoughts, as the *Oklahoma*s had done twenty-five years earlier. These two ships, with *South Dakota*s and *Iowa*s, were more capable than any others of resisting air attack. Inferior sea-keeping characteristics corrected in successors.

——————————————————————————————————— (1944-1945)

Alabama
Massachusetts
Indiana
South Dakota
July, 1939–Nov., 1942

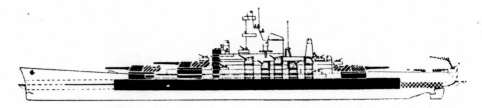

35,000 tons   28 knots
9 x 16 in.   20 x 5 in.
Belt 18 in.   Turrets 18 in.

Higher freeboard and 25 feet shorter overall than *Washington*s. Protection was even more substantial.

——————————————————————————————— (1944–1945)

Iowa
New Jersey
Missouri
Wisconsin
June, 1940–June, 1944

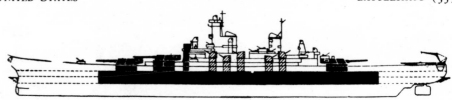

45,000 tons   33 knots
9 x 16 in.   20 x 5 in.
Belt 19 in.   Turrets 18 in. (?)

Most heavily protected Dreadnoughts ever built. *New Jersey* was last Dreadnought to fire its guns in anger, off Vietnam in 1968.

——————————————————————————————— (1944–1945)

Alaska
Guam
Dec., 1941–Sept., 1944

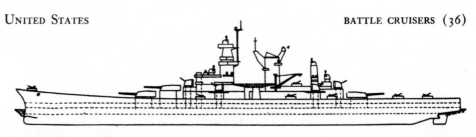

27,500 tons   33 knots
9 x 12 in.   12 x 5 in. A.A.
Belt 9 in.   Turrets (face) 12¾ in.

First and only American battle cruisers; and although German *Scharnhorst* and *Gneisenau* were officially classed as such, these ships were the first since British *Courageous* and *Glorious* to possess speed-armament-protection ratio as conceived by Admiral Fisher. Thin belt and light deck protection were compensated by highly elaborate internal compartmentation and damage control. *Guam* was last Dreadnought to be laid down and completed.

——————————————————————————————— (1944–1945)

Westfalen
Nassau
Posen
Rheinland
July, 1906–May, 1910

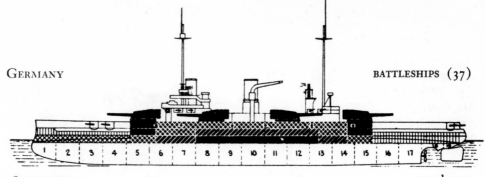

18,900 tons   19.5 knots

12 × 11 in.   12 × 5.9 in.   16 × 3.4 in.
Belt 11¾ in.   Turrets 11 in.

Very large number of guns on small displacement and short length caused discomfort and poor accommodation for crew; but ships were never intended to be lived in for long. Uneconomic disposition of main battery, but steady platforms. Elaborate underwater protection and damage control.

——————————————————————————————————————— (1914)

Thüringen
Helgoland
Ostfriesland
Oldenburg
Oct., 1908–July, 1912

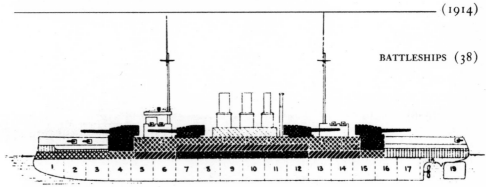

22,800 tons   20 knots

12 × 12 in.   14 × 5.9 in.   14 × 3.4 in.
Belt 11¾ in.   Turrets 12 in.

Similar merits and demerits as *Nassaus*, but less cramped. 12-inch shell weighed 980 pounds against 11-inch of 760 pounds. Like all First World War German Dreadnoughts, later fitted with about four 22-pounder antiaircraft guns.

——————————————————————————————————————— (1914)

Kaiser
Friedrich der Grosse
Kaiserin
Prinzregent Luitpold
König Albert
May, 1909–Nov., 1913

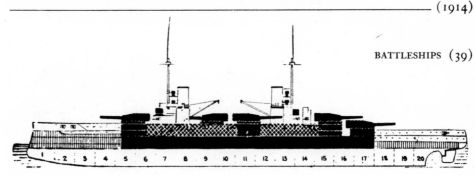

24,700 tons   20.5 knots

10 × 12 in.   14 × 5.9 in.   12 × 3.4 in.
Belt 13¾ in.   Turrets 12 in.

First German Dreadnoughts with superimposed turret; and echelon arrangement offered (in a crisis) 25 percent heavier broadside with two fewer 12-inch guns than in predecessors. *Kaiser* steamed 23.6 knots on trials.

——————————————————————————————————————— (1914)

König
Grosser Kurfürst
Markgraf
Kronprinz Wilhelm
May, 1911–July, 1915

GERMANY

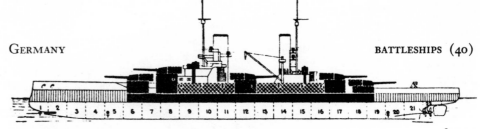

BATTLESHIPS (40)

25,390 tons 21 knots
10 x 12 in. 14 x 5.9 in. 10 x 3.4 in.
Belt 14 in. Turrets 14 in.

First German battleships with all-center-line main armament; last with 12-inch guns. Armor on a formidable scale, with belt over citadel never less than 10 inches.

——————————————————————— (1918)

Baden
Bayern
Feb., 1914–March, 1917

GERMANY

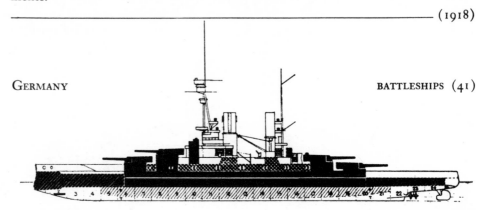

BATTLESHIPS (41)

28,000 tons 22.3 knots
8 x 15 in. 16 x 5.9 in. 2 x 5.9 in. A.A.
Belt 13¾ in. Turrets 13¾ in.

First 15-inch-gunned German Dreadnoughts, representing a new and less defensive tactical philosophy. Only Second Generation German Dreadnoughts; sister ships *Sachsen* and *Würtemberg* (with more emphasis on vertical defense) launched but uncompleted at end of war. Both were scuttled at Scapa Flow, but *Baden* in shallow water and was salvaged.

——————————————————————— (1919)

Deutschland
(later renamed *Lützow*)
Admiral Graf Spee
Admiral Scheer
Feb., 1929–Nov., 1934

GERMANY

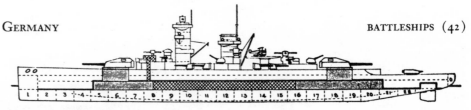

BATTLESHIPS (42)

12,100 tons 26 knots
(*Deutschland* 11,700 tons)
6 x 11 in. 8 x 5.9 in. 6 x 4.1 in. A.A.
Belt 4 in. (3 in *Deutschland*) Turrets 5½ in.

Prototypes for all Third Generation Dreadnoughts, with emphasis on weight economy where practical without weakening structural strength, suitable protection from bombs and torpedoes carried by aircraft, and speed of early battle cruisers. Diesel propulsion (experimented with before First World War); extensive electrical welding of hull; oil bunkers for radius of 10,000 miles. Diesels qualified success.

—— (1942—*Deutschland* had different fore superstructure and other variations.)

Bismarck
Tirpitz
1936–1941

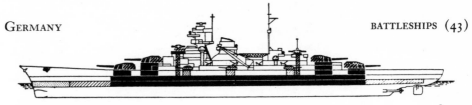

41,700 tons   30 knots
8 x 15 in.   12 x 5.9 in.
Belt 12.6 in. Turrets 14 in.

German principle of immense internal strength, first established with *Nassau*s thirty years earlier, exploited to full in these ships. Some 84 antiaircraft guns (though modest by later American and Japanese standards) formidable for early war years. Radius of action over 8,000 miles.

—— (1942)

von der Tann
March, 1908–April, 1910

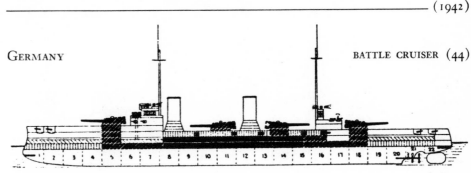

19,100 tons   26 knots
8 x 11 in.   10 x 5.9 in.   16 x 3.4 in.
Belt 9¾ in. Turrets 9 in.

First German battle cruiser, with greater ability to resist punishment than contemporary British battleships. Made 27.5 knots at Jutland. As with most of her contemporaries, majority of 3.4-inch 24-pounders were removed after Jutland, and were doubtless fitted to new U-boats.

—— (1914)

Moltke
Goeben
(later Turkish *Yavuz*)
April, 1909–May, 1913

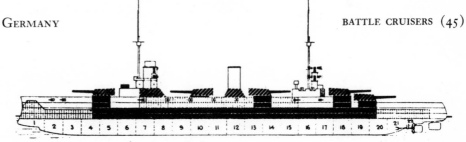

22,640 tons   27 knots
10 x 11 in.   12 x 5.9 in.   10 x 3.4 in.
Belt 11 in. Turrets 10 in.

Goeben only German capital ship in First World War to serve outside High Seas Fleet. Fought in Mediterranean, Dardanelles, and Black Sea under German and Turkish flags. First capital ship to be damaged by aerial bomb. Longest-lived Dreadnought. Fire-control and optical equipment destroyed by German crew at end of First World War. Rebuilt in French yard 1926–1930, refitted 1938. *Moltke* steamed 28.4 knots on trials.

—— (1914)

Seydlitz
Feb., 1911–May, 1913

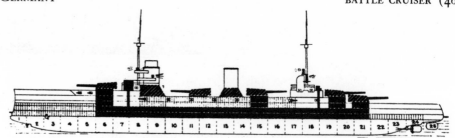

25,000 tons

26.5 knots

10 x 11 in.   12 x 5.9 in.   12 x 3.4 in.
Belt 11 in.   Turrets 10 in.

Enlarged *Moltke* class, with higher freeboard. Better sea boat than earlier German battle cruisers. Made 29 knots on trials.

——————————————————————————————— (1914)

Hindenburg
Derfflinger
Lützow
March, 1912–Oct., 1917

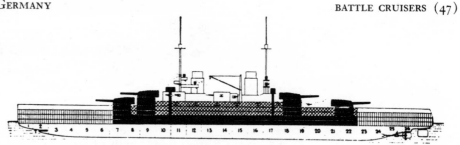

26,180 tons

26.5 knots

8 x 12 in.   14 x 5.9 in (12 in *Derfflinger*)   12 x 4.1 in.
Belt 12 in.   Turrets 11 in.

First flush-decked German battle cruisers. Capable of over 28 knots. Finest all-round ships to fight in First World War.

————————————————— (1918—minor variations between these ships)

Gneisenau
Scharnhorst
1934–Jan., 1939

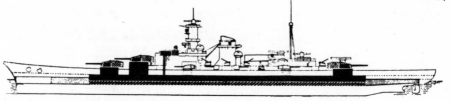

31,300 tons

32 knots

9 x 11 in.   12 x 5.9 in.   14 x 4.1 in.
Belt 13 in.   Turrets 13 in.

Stated displacement 26,000 tons. As in *Deutschland*s, 11-inch new Krupps model of greater efficiency than First World War model.

——————————————————————————————— (1942)

Settsu
Kawachi
Jan., 1900(?)–1912

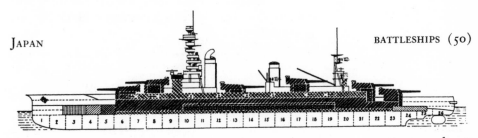

21,420 tons   20.5 knots
12 x 12 in.   10 x 6 in.   8 x 4.7 in.
Belt 12 in.   Turrets 11 in.

Kawachi blew up in an accident, July, 1918; *Settsu* scrapped under Washington Treaty.

——————————————————————————— (1914)

Fuso
Yamashiro
March, 1912–April, 1917

29,300 tons   22.5 knots
12 x 14 in.   16 x 6 in.
Belt 12 in.   Turrets 12 in.

Fore superstructure built up and other modifications in 1920's. Rebuilt 1933–1935 when fore funnel was removed, antiaircraft protection augmented, catapult fitted to "C" turret (to stern of *Yamashiro*), and fire control elaborated. Took little part in Pacific war until sunk in Leyte Gulf.

——————————————————————————— (1931)

Ise
Hiuga
May, 1915–April, 1918

29,900 tons   23.6 knots
12 x 14 in.   20 x 5.5 in.
Belt 12 in.   Turrets 12 in.

Modifications similar to those of *Fuso*s in 1920's, but more radically rebuilt 1936–1937 when re-engined (speed now 25.25 knots) and additional armor and antiaircraft protection increased displacement to 35,800 tons. In 1942–1943 converted to battleship-aircraft carriers with flight deck and hangar replacing "X" and "Y" turrets. Both wrecked and bottomed July 28, 1945; later salvaged and scrapped.

——————————————————— (1931—with elaborated fore superstructure)

Nagato
Mutsu
Aug., 1917–Oct., 1921

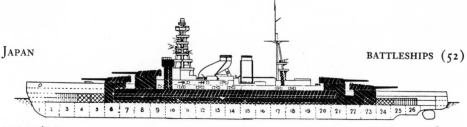

32,720 tons   23 knots
8 x 16 in.   20 x 5.5 in.
Belt 13 in.   Turrets 14 in.

First 16-inch-gunned Dreadnoughts; and only Japanese with this caliber main armament. Made over 26 knots on trials. Followed reconstruction pattern of other Japanese capital ships, with thorough refit in 1920's and rebuild in 1930's. Fore superstructure built up, fore funnel bent back, antiaircraft guns augmented, in first; re-engined circa 1936, with omission of fore funnel, fitting of catapult and multiple light antiaircraft guns, and raising of 16-inch guns' elevation to 43 degrees.

———————————————————————— (1931—with trunked fore funnel)

Yamato
Musashi
1937–Aug., 1942

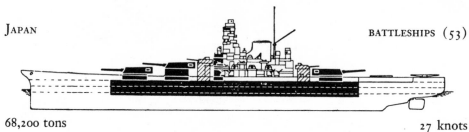

68,200 tons   27 knots
9 x 18 in.   12 x 5.1 in.
Belt 16½ in.   Turrets 18 in. (?)

Date of laying of keel of *Yamato* uncertain. *Musashi* March 29, 1938, completed August 5, 1942. Main armament caliber approximately 18.1 inches. Weight of 18-inch turret 2,774 tons. Full load displacement 72,809 tons. Deck plates about 8 inches, up to 22 inches on barbettes. Main belt extended over only 53.5 percent of waterline. 1,147 compartments. At one time carried 7 aircraft.

———————————————————— (1944–1945—this plan inaccurate in several features)

Kongo
Hi-ei
Haruna
Kirishima
Jan., 1911–April, 1915

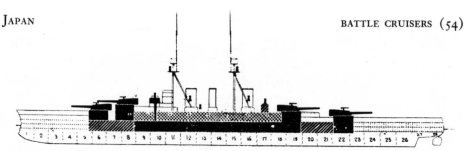

27,500 tons   27.5 knots
8 x 14 in.   16 x 6 in.
Belt 8 in.   Turrets 10 in.

British-built prototype *Kongo* differed slightly from others. Rebuilt 1928–1932 with additional armor and antiaircraft guns, added 3,000–3,500 tons to displacement and dropping speed to about 26 knots. All except *Kirishima* rebuilt again as "high speed battleships" 1937–1940 for fast carrier escort, with new engines and multiple antiaircraft armament: speed up to over 30 knots, displacement to about 37,000 tons. December, 1941, *Hi-ei* and *Kirishima* with Pearl Harbor force, *Kongo* and *Haruna* searching for *Prince of Wales* and *Repulse*.

———————————————————————————————— (1914)

Courbet
Jean Bart
Paris
France
Sept., 1910–Aug., 1914

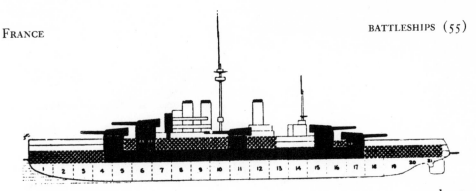

20 knots

23,467 tons
12 x 12 in.   22 x 5.5 in.
Belt 11¾ in.   Turrets 12½ in.

Rebuilt with tripod foremast and one and two funnels trunked in 1920's. Mainmast of *Paris* and *France* cut down to stump 1918–1919. *France* was lost in August, 1922.

——— (1914)

Bretagne
Lorraine
Provence
June, 1912–July, 1916

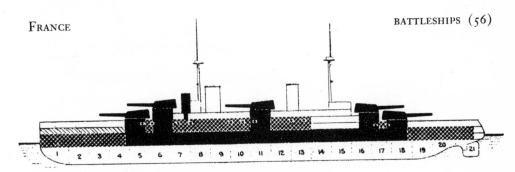

20.5 knots

23,189 tons
10 x 13.4 in.   22 x 5.5 in.
Belt 10¾ in.   Turrets 17 in.

Tripod foremast fitted and fore funnel raised in 1920's. Antiaircraft armament augmented and catapult fitted between wars, *Lorraine* losing "Q" turret.

——— (1919)

Dunkerque
Strasbourg
Dec., 1932–Dec., 1938

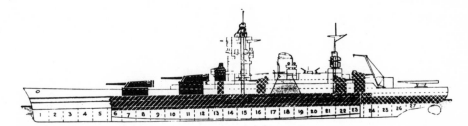

29.5 knots

26,500 tons
8 x 13 in.   16 x 5.1 in.
Belt 11 in.   Turrets 14 in.

Many features in common with British *Nelson*s. First quadruple-turreted ships to be completed. Hangar and catapult at stern.

——— (1942)

Richelieu
Jean Bart
Oct. 1935–Jan., 1949

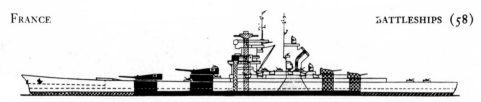

38,500 tons   **30 knots**
8 x 15 in.   9 x 6 in.
Belt 15¾ in.   Turrets 17 in.

32 knots on trials. Weight of armor 14,000 tons. Unique both in appearance
and in proportion of displacement devoted to protection. Only two non-American
surviving Dreadnoughts: *Richelieu*, Naval Reserve Officers' School, Brest; *Jean
Bart*, Gunnery School, Toulon (1964).

———————————————————— (1951–1952—*Richelieu* has different superstructure.)

ITALY   BATTLESHIP (59)

Dante Alighieri
June, 1909–Sept., 1912

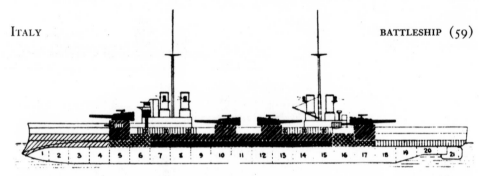

20,500 tons   **23 knots**
12 x 12 in.   20 x 4.7 in.   16 x 3 in.
Belt 9⅞ in.   Turrets 11 in.

Cuniberti conception and design. Guns and turrets of British Armstrong design.
First Dreadnought with triple turrets.

———————————————————————————————————— (1914)

ITALY   BATTLESHIPS (60)

Conte di Cavour
Giulio Cesare
Leonardo da Vinci
June, 1910–April, 1915

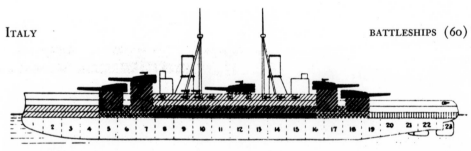

22,380 tons   **22 knots**
13 x 12 in.   18 x 4.7 in.   18 x 3 in.
Belt 9¾ in.   Turrets 9½ in.

Improved and enlarged *Dante Alighieri*. Gun disposition unique; midships triple
turret omitted when re-engined and refitted with ten 12.6-inch in 1930's. Appearance entirely changed after rebuild, with speed up to 27 knots and enhanced
protection. *Leonardo da Vinci* was destroyed by internal explosion August, 1916.

————————————————————————————————— (1914)

Caio Duilio
Andrea Doria
March, 1912–May, 1915

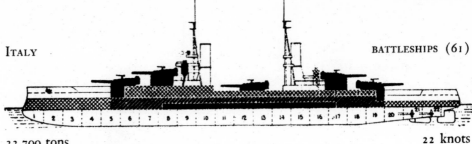

22,700 tons   22 knots
13 x 12 in.   16 x 6 in.   18 x 3 in.
Belt 9¾ in.   Turrets 9½ in.

Closely similar to *Cavours*, with heavier secondary battery. Rebuilt as *Cavours* in 1930's.

——————————————————————————————— (1914)

Roma
Littorio
(later renamed *Italia*)
Vittorio Veneto
Oct., 1934–May, 1940

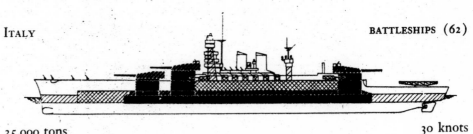

35,000 tons   30 knots
9 x 15 in.   12 x 6 in.
Belt 12 in.   Turrets 12 in.

The final expression of Italian heavy warship construction. Very high speed (around 35 knots readily obtainable) attained at expense of some protection compared with contemporaries. Secondary armament in triple turrets. Catapult at stern. *Roma* sunk while steaming to surrender, 1943. A fourth ship, *Impero*, launched but never completed.

——————————————————————————————— (1942)

Gangut
Poltava
Petropavlovsk
Sevastopol
June, 1909–Jan., 1915

23,370 tons   23 knots
12 x 12 in.   16 x 4.7 in.
Belt 8¾ in.   Turrets 12 in.

Based on designs prepared by Cuniberti, and closely follow Italian *Dante Alighieri*, with icebreaking bows. Fore funnel later raised and taken sharply back to avoid interference by fumes and smoke with controls in fore superstructure. Mildly refurbished between the wars. Revolution caused names to be changed respectively to *Oktyaberskaia Revolutia*, *Mikhail Frunze*, *Marat*, and *Parizkaia Kommuna*. All later reverted to original names, except *Mikhail Frunze*, which was scrapped before the others.

——————————————————————————————— (1918)

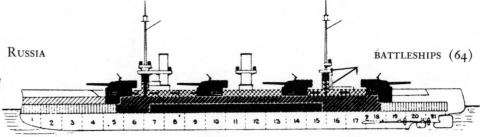

Imperator Aleksandr III
Imperatritsa Yekaterina II
Imperatritsa Maria
Nov., 1911–1917

22,400 tons   21 knots

12 x 12 in. 20 x 5.1 in.

Belt 12 in. Turrets 12 in.

Closely similar to Russian Baltic Dreadnoughts, but with second turret facing forward. *Imperator Nikolai II* reported as over 27,000 tons and some 45 feet longer overall. Various names obscure, but believed *Imperator Aleksandr III* renamed *Volia* (and survived war), *Imperator Nikolai II* renamed *Demokratiya* and/or *Svobodnaya Rossia*; *Imperatzia Maria* destroyed at Sevastopol in 1916, before revoluton.

——————————————————————————————— (1918)

AUSTRIA-HUNGARY   BATTLESHIPS (65)

Viribus Unitis
Tegetthof
Szent Istvan
Prinz Eugen
May, 1910–1915

20,000 tons   21 knots

12 x 12 in. 12 x 6 in.

Belt 11 in. Turrets 11 in.

Simplicity combined with economic big-gun disposition made these highly satisfactory ships.

——————————————————————————————— (1914)

SPAIN   BATTLESHIPS (66)

España
Alfonso XIII
Jaime I
Dec., 1909–1921

15,700 tons.   19.5 knots

8 x 12 in. 20 x 4 in.

Belt 8 in. Turrets 8 in.

Constructed at Ferrol, *Jaime I* being delayed by nondelivery of materials from Britain. *España* was wrecked in 1923; *Alfonso XIII* was renamed *España*.

——————————————————————————————— (1914)

Minas Gerais
São Paulo
1907–July, 1910

19,200 tons

21 knots

12 X 12 in.   22 X 4.7 in.
Belt 9 in.   Turrets 9 in.

Built in Britain, being first Dreadnoughts completed for minor naval power. Extensively refitted in U.S.A. from 1917 and in late 1930's.

———————— (1914)

Rivadavia
Moreno
May, 1910–March, 1915

27,720 tons

23 knots

12 X 12 in.   12 x 6 in.   16 x 4 in.
Belt 11 in.   Turrets 12 in.

Only foreign Dreadnoughts constructed in U.S.A., and only American-built battleships with wing turrets. Substantially refitted 1924–1925.

———————— (1914)

Almirante Latorre
Dec. 1911–Sept. 1915

28,000 tons

22.75 knots

10 X 14 in.   16 x 6 in.
Belt 9 in.   Turrets 10 in.

Building in Britain at outbreak of First World War, as *Valparaiso*. Taken over by the R.N. as *Canada*, when it was only 14-inch-gun ship at Jutland. Sister ship *Almirante Cochrane* converted to British aircraft carrier *Eagle*.

———————— (1919)

Index

Figures in italics refer to pages on which illustrations of subject appear.